SOUTHERN LITERATURE, COLD WAR CULTURE, AND THE MAKING OF MODERN AMERICA

SOUTHERN LITERATURE, COLD WAR CULTURE, AND THE MAKING OF MODERN AMERICA

★ ★ ★ ★ ★ ★

JORDAN J. DOMINY

University Press of Mississippi / Jackson

The University Press of Mississippi is the scholarly publishing agency of
the Mississippi Institutions of Higher Learning: Alcorn State University,
Delta State University, Jackson State University, Mississippi State University,
Mississippi University for Women, Mississippi Valley State University,
University of Mississippi, and University of Southern Mississippi.

www.upress.state.ms.us

The University Press of Mississippi is a member
of the Association of University Presses.

Copyright © 2020 by University Press of Mississippi
All rights reserved
Manufactured in the United States of America

First printing 2020

∞

Library of Congress Cataloging-in-Publication Data available

LCCN 2019030043

Hardback ISBN 978-1-4968-2640-4

Trade paperback ISBN 978-1-4968-2641-1

Epub single ISBN 978-1-4968-2642-8

Epub institutional ISBN 978-1-4968-2643-5

PDF single ISBN 978-1-4968-2644-2

PDF institutional ISBN 978-1-4968-2645-9

British Library Cataloging-in-Publication Data available

For Jessica, Oliver, and Henry

CONTENTS

Acknowledgments ix

Introduction Southern Culture, US Nationalism, Late Modernism, and the Cold War xi

PART I SOUTHERN CANONS AND THE VITAL CENTER

1 Reviewing the South: Competing Canons in *South Today* and the *Kenyon Review* 3

2 Southern Studies as Area Studies: Faulkner and Provincial Nationalism during the Cold War 29

3 American Canons, Southern Fiction, and the Institution of Literary Prizes 49

PART II THE RETURN TO POLITICS

4 Eudora Welty and the Problem of Crusading 75

5 Suburbs, Civil Rights, and Southern Identities 95

Epilogue White Working-Class Identity and US Nationalism in Twenty-First-Century
Popular Texts 123

Notes 139

Bibliography 143

Index 155

ACKNOWLEDGMENTS

This book is just as much the product of my labors as it is the product of the love and support I have received from family, friends, mentors, and colleagues. I owe much gratitude to Susan Hegeman, who provided the earliest feedback on this project; it certainly would not have gotten off the ground without her guidance. Phil Wegner, Marsha Bryant, and William Link also contributed feedback in the book's earliest forms, for which I am grateful. I thank many friends and colleagues who read one or more chapters; provided comments, criticism, or assistance; offered advice; or served as a sounding board for my ideas: Wesley Beal, Regina Martin, Christina Van Houten, Patrick McHenry, Mike Mayne, Gordon Johnston, David Davis, librarians at the University of Florida Smathers Library Special Collections, and the network of supportive scholars who regularly attend the conventions and sponsored conference sessions of the Society for the Study of Southern Literature.

An earlier, abbreviated version of chapter 1 was originally published in *Mississippi Quarterly*, and an earlier version of chapter 2 was originally published in *American Studies*. Also, an earlier, abbreviated version of chapter 5 was published in *Southern Literary Journal*. I thank the editors of these journals for their permission to include revised versions of these works in this book.

My dear friends Jenni Halpin and Jon Elmore deserve special recognition. They provided feedback in the late stages of my revisions to *Southern Literature, Cold War Culture, and the Making of Modern America*, and they provided the nudge I needed to prevent work on the manuscript from stalling out. Their encouragement and support were important contributions to the completion of this project.

My parents, Tom and Karen, fostered my love of words as soon as I could pick up a book, and they have had only encouragement for any of my ambitions. So have my grandparents, Ed and Shelby. My brother, Kyle, read early drafts of the manuscript, and his perspective was helpful. He also listened to me drone on about it a good bit as I was revising the manuscript. My children, Oliver and Henry, have patiently endured my work on this book.

None, however, have endured, cared, supported, and loved more than my wife, Jessica. It is no exaggeration to say her love and friendship are the best thing to ever have happened to me.

INTRODUCTION

Southern Culture, US Nationalism, Late Modernism, and the Cold War

This book investigates connections between southern literature and culture, the development of formal, scholarly criticism of US southern literature, and US nationalism leading up to and during the Cold War. Early literary scholarship, authors' responses to that scholarship, the pressures of the Cold War, and close reading of primary texts—mostly fiction and some nonfiction—reveal a desire among intellectuals active in American and southern literature and culture to identify a body of literature amenable to the democratic aims of American Cold War hegemony. A result of this desire was the creation of a specifically southern literary canon. The earliest formalized canon of southern literature would not exist without the peculiar social and political conditions during and after World War II: the growth of formalized disciplines in universities, tension between America's global beacon of freedom and failure to provide for its own citizens' full freedom, and the struggle between the American Left and Right. These conditions were the catalysts for the early, formalized definitions and practice of southern letters and link them closely to US nationalism. Although the historical connection between southern literature and culture and US nationalism originated with the Cold War, it endures in current manifestations of the southern identity in cultural and political arenas, particularly in the white identity politics and working-class conservatism that led to the election of a populist, authoritarian president (paradoxically something that cold warriors sought to avoid).

This cultural history through close reading of southern literature reveals the notions of the region and genre as a variety of Cold War nationalism deeply rooted in particular contexts related to American ambitions after World War II, which included the export of American-style democracy to the countries liberated from Nazi rule and from colonial rule. Along with this desire to spread American democracy comes the compulsion among intellectuals to cleanse communism, fascism, and other undesirable politics from all corners of cultural production. Thomas Hill Schaub fully explores this context in his important study *American Fiction in the Cold War* (1991); Schaub traces this cleansing back to a panic among historians and literary critics in the United States that the previous decades' leftist intellectual leanings, coupled with social realism in the arts, led to the totalitarian regimes that sparked war in Europe and that the same could happen in the United States if any form of vaguely radial politics were left unchecked. This new liberalism coming into fashion, Schaub writes, "sought to define an anticommunism that was still liberal, but this was a high-wire act difficult to perform at a time when such distinctions seemed overly subtle to most citizens" (8). The high-wire act he details also features a greater suspicion among intellectuals of the proliferation of mass culture and a more guarded attitude about what counts for serious art and what does not (15–18). The result of this suspicion becomes a closely protected liberalism at the center of American-style democracy, which Schaub terms the "vital center." Schaub borrows the term from the historian Arthur M. Schlesinger Jr., who coined it in 1949 with the title of an article in the *New York Times Magazine* and a book published the same year expanding on the article, *The Vital Center: The Politics of Freedom*. Both of Schlesinger's works expound on the kind of politics required to steer the United States clear of totalitarianism. Hope lies in neither a communist Left nor a fascist Right, Schlesinger argues, but

> in the revival of the Center in the triumph of those who believe deeply in civil liberties, in constitutional processes, and in the democratic determination of political and economic policies. And, in direct consequence, the main target of both totalitarian extremes must be the Center, the group which holds society together. Neither fascism nor communism can win so long as there remains a democratic middle way, which unites hopes of freedom and of economic abundance. ("Not Left, not Right, but a Vital Center," 47)

In Schlesinger's and other Cold War intellectuals' estimation, such cultural vigilance was the only thing that could protect the American way of life from the threat of Soviet communism.

This cultural vigilance of the vital center escalated with the Cold War and migrated through intellectual culture into the arts as formalism and its attempts to divest art of any political content. The art historian Serge Guilbaut chronicles the deployment of American abstract expressionism to assert the United States' artistic and cultural hegemony. Guilbaut identifies what he terms a "de-Marxization" of American artists and intellectuals in the 1930s and 1940s that coincides with a turn to formalism in the visual and literary arts. To rebuff the perceived threats of communism, political leaders and scholars alike required a democratic art exemplifying the great values of the West that did not seem political at all—an art, to use Guilbaut's term, that was "apolitically political." An important example of this thought that Guilbaut points to is Clement Greenberg's 1939 essay "Avant-Garde and Kitsch," which provocatively defines each of its title terms for American intellectuals. The purpose of the avant-garde is "to keep culture *moving* in the midst of ideological confusion and violence" (Greenberg, 36). Kitsch, on the other hand, is artistic productions informed by the avant-garde, but dangerous because they have been processed through commercialization and aimed at the unwashed masses, who are particularly susceptible to kitsch's content. The popularity of such art in the United States and other industrialized nations—especially Germany, Italy, and Russia—was distressing to Greenberg in 1939. In Greenberg's dichotomy, the avant-garde and its emphasis on formalism and pure aesthetics without overt content—especially any political content—are privileged over commercialized, popularized kitsch that could carry dangerous ideological messages. This distinction is important for a region such as the US South, which contained political and social problems that it and the nation would rather ignore in the mid-twentieth century. One way to ignore them was to dismiss any artistic production overtly addressing them as kitsch and not worthy of serious study or enshrinement in a formal canon.

While intellectuals at the time were embracing the apolitically political art that defined a democratic United States against the totalitarian Soviets, the US government was funding that art and deploying it abroad. In *The Cultural Cold War* (1999), Frances Stonor Saunders traces publications in America and abroad back to CIA projects of cultural warfare, revealing the complicity of intellectuals in CIA projects. Saunders profiles the involvement of many important American intellectuals in US projects of domestic and international policy. Arthur Schlesinger himself, she reveals, worked in close contact with members of the Truman administration, sat on the executive committee of Radio Free Europe, and even knew of covert cultural warfare operations, believing that such efforts were necessary to counter similar Soviet efforts in Europe (91). While Saunders's project focuses primarily on CIA funding of *Encounter* (a magazine published in the United Kingdom) through the 1950s and 1960s, she also addresses the participation of American writers and thinkers in conferences and symposiums abroad and grant programs that were designed to promote free American artistic innovation as a balance to Soviet aesthetics. Participants in such events included William Faulkner and Robert Penn Warren, both key figures around whom scholars formalized early canons of southern literature. Furthermore, the *Kenyon*

Review, whose first twelve volumes are the subject of chapter 1, benefited from some CIA funding after Robie Macauley took over its helm from its founding editor, John Crowe Ransom, in 1959 (333–34). Southern culture and literary production get deployed as part of the vital center.

Another important historical context for understanding the emergence of a formalized, academic literary study of southern literature at the dawn of the Cold War is racism and poverty, the great challenges of the US South that threatened the proliferation of American democracy and capitalism abroad. Thomas Borstelmann argues that race was simultaneously the greatest domestic and foreign policy problem facing the country. World War II honed what was already a sharp category of difference within the United States. On the one hand, having the Japanese as an enemy in the Pacific theater created a "racially coded conflict" that was not replicated in the European theater. Borstelmann quotes a black resident of Harlem who was disgusted with American dependence on racial difference: "All these radio announcers talking about yellow this, yellow that. Don't hear them calling the Nazis white this, pink that. What the hell color do they think the Chinese are anyway!" (30). (Indeed, the government did recognize the color of Japanese immigrants in the United States, confining thousands of Japanese Americans in internment camps during the war.) American soldiers, especially ones from the South, took this racial discord with them to their barracks in Europe. In one particularly telling anecdote that Borstelmann relates, General Dwight Eisenhower wrote in 1942 to Washington brass about frequent altercations among soldiers stationed in England that typically involved white soldiers attacking black soldiers who went out with white English women, who did not harbor the same anxieties about race that many Americans did. In his letter, Eisenhower—sympathizing with his (white) men's concerns—explained that these women were of "perfectly fine character," but the white soldiers often deemed it "necessary to intervene even to the extent of using force, to let her know what she's doing" (Borstelmann, 34).

Mary L. Dudziak recognizes that during this period, "civil rights reform came to be seen as crucial to U.S. foreign relations" (6). After all, World War II and the Holocaust had made racial equality a global issue. As victory in World War II led the nation to take a greater role on the world stage, international interest in lynchings and racial oppression in the United States grew. Newspapers from Fiji to Ceylon ran stories picked up from Reuters on race problems in the United States (30–31). Jim Crow caused great difficulties for American foreign policy, especially in Africa, where the United States attempted to foster American-style democracy while at the same time maintaining good relations with the former colonies' imperial oppressors in

Europe. How could Africans count on America as a democratic ally when the population of African Americans in the United States lived under oppressive racial discrimination? It was the most damning contradiction in the American program, one identified by both Soviet diplomats and American writers in the mid-twentieth century, including southern writers from Lillian Smith to Alice Walker.

The pressures of the Cold War led presidents Harry Truman and Dwight Eisenhower to willingly overlook racial inequality in the United States. Dudziak demonstrates that, during Truman's presidency, he signaled support for civil rights legislation because he sought African American votes in the 1948 election as well as to signal to potential allies around the world his commitment to equality (26–27); Truman did issue an executive order requiring equal treatment of everyone in the armed forces in July 1948, but the order did not explicitly address segregation (86). Dudziak further notes that, in a similar move, Eisenhower appealed to national unity and patriotism in a televised speech about the Central High School desegregation crisis in 1954, evoking patriotism because "the nation, the national image, and national security were at stake. Patriotism required that the needs of the nation be placed ahead of sectional loyalties" (133). In his appeal to patriotism, Eisenhower forgoes pressing for any federal action against Jim Crow as a strategy to maintain national unity against what he saw as the real evil: communism. On the other hand, politicians such as Georgia senator Richard Russell frequently equated civil rights with communism. How, then, do writers and thinkers in a country attempting to assert its new power on the world stage during such a tumultuous time reconcile a democratic, vital center with racial and economic inequality within its own borders? This is where a formalized canon of southern literature emerges and serves a function similar to the one Guilbaut identifies for abstract expressionism. Southern literary studies serves in part to obfuscate these setbacks for the American agenda by creating a space to contain these ills within an apolitically political art. It also accomplishes this task by cleansing racism of political implications in formalist interpretations of literature, ignoring historical and social contexts. Such heavy emphasis on literary representation in the construct of southern literature construes discrimination as a moral problem as opposed to a political one. Its portrayals, scholars argued, showed individuals dealing with the personal, moral struggles of discrimination, and to them such was the mark of great, wholesome, American, democratic art.

The notion that there is artificiality in the canon of southern literature is not a new one. Michael Kreyling proposes in *Inventing Southern Literature* (1998) that southern literature is an invention of white masculinity and its particular notions of history and place, and even more recently suggests in *The South That Wasn't There* (2010) that many notions of the South may not exist at all. Leigh Anne Duck explains in *The Nation's Region* (2006) that by 1950 the liberal consensus—that vital center—dominating the intellectual scene in the United States described the race problem not as a legal or institutional problem but as a cultural problem of a backward region beyond the purview of government in an otherwise democratic nation (214–15). Building on Kreyling's and Duck's work, I argue that southern writers' and intellectuals' concerns for political issues at both the local and global scales occur in their writing as concerns for or questionings of traditional values and morals. These writers also frequently depicted poverty and racism, two weighty flaws of American society. Yet their literary expressions are compatible with the terminology of the intellectuals who were framing the tenets of American democracy as a system of universal values uninformed by politics. In his work on southern intellectual history, Michael O'Brien identifies an insistence among New Critics—many of whom were southerners—that literature "embod[ies] a special and superior order of knowledge." Furthermore, O'Brien argues that among New Critics, "to note that a literary production was caused by and aimed at local social issues seemed to diminish its universality" (161). In light of this, authors' southern settings and themes allow their work to serve a paradoxical purpose for literary critics during the Cold War. These works at once compartmentalize America's social ills to a single region of the country while universalizing the notion of racism and poverty as moral problems best dealt with by intellectuals, not political problems under the purview of governments, national or otherwise. The organization of southern authors into a field of study serves as an academic amelioration of a serious domestic and foreign policy conundrum facing the United States.

Besides its compartmentalization, the emerging field of southern studies had other values that became useful to the vital center from the 1930s onward through the Cold War. Such a dating is atypically early when addressing the Cold War, but key trends that inform Cold War ideology take shape during that decade. One of these is the perennial staunch anticommunism of white southern intellectuals. Although Lillian Smith is the only one I address in this study, other unabashedly progressive southern intellectuals were stringently anticommunist, such as William Terry Couch and Ralph McGill. Daniel Joseph Singal describes Couch's anticommunism as being so fervent that it led him to have more or less a shouting match with Communist Party members at the April 1940 Southern Conference for Human Welfare over amending a resolution to condemn Soviet aggression as well as Nazi aggression (295–96). Paradoxically, white southern progressives were anticommunist even though they lived in a region of the country that to the Communist Party and its fellow travelers in the late 1930s offered a perfect storm for a communist base: a regimented system of both economic and racial class within which to build a base. On the other hand, white southern intellectuals' position is not representative of a homogeneous anticommunism in the region. Robin D. G. Kelley shows that communists who ventured south during the 1930s expecting backward workers found instead (particularly in Alabama) a receptive following among black workers who became members of the Communist Party. Kelley writes: "The prevalence of blacks in the CP earned it the epithet 'nigger party' throughout the South," and the party found a new audience ready to assimilate communist philosophy into their own culture (92–93). This is no doubt a reason for many white southerners' hostility toward communism.

The upshot of understanding the southern literary canon and increasing interest in its institutionalized study as a component of Cold War culture is that it reveals southern literature as a variety of late modernism. Fredric Jameson theorizes late modernism as a moment separate from modernism proper, calling it the "ideology of modernism," that is, a codification of modernist features in art and literature with emphasis on formalism and the divorce of politics from art in the specifically American context of the Cold War. During the moment of modernism proper, artistic production held revolutionary power, according to Jameson, who quotes Adorno's point that "in order for the work of art to be purely and fully a work of art, it must be more than a work of art" (160). In other words, the purely aesthetic cannot be purely art unless it crosses over into other contexts and content, including revolutionary and utopian possibilities. The Cold War, however, closes those possibilities within the American context, and the ideology of modernism emerges:

> Politics must therefore now be carefully monitored, and new social impulses repressed or disciplined. These new forms of control are symbolically reenacted in later modernism, which transforms the older modernist experimentation into an arsenal of tried and true techniques, no longer striving after aesthetic totality or the systemic and Utopian metamorphosis of forms. (166)

The late modernist aesthetic is highly formalist (Guilbaut might call it "apolitically political"), and the Cold War provides a situation ripe for US cultural nationalism and imperialism, Jameson insists. The codification of a southern literary canon during this historical period is part of the late modernist moment that delineates certain artistic practices and values in an effort to protect the vital center.

Jameson also argues that authors and New Critics alike play an important role in preparing a space for late modernism. His specific example is Wallace Stevens, whose "poetry can be seen as literature and as theory alike; his practice is essentially what he himself, along with the influential New Criticism, made theory of: which is to say that both Stevens and the New Criticism prepared the space in which an ideology of modernism could emerge" (168–69). The New Critics considered historical and social contexts irrelevant to the meaning of texts. Any art or literature containing overtly political content they considered propaganda, not art—a repudiation of Adorno's maxim about art. As noted earlier and has long been recognized, many practitioners of New Criticism were southerners, but also important is that two of the figures addressed in this project were university professors and full-time poets, fiction writers, essayists, and critics: Ransom and Warren. Their work functions in the manner Jameson describes for Stevens, as both art and theory of the southern literary studies, and I contend the same is true for other writers, too, especially William Faulkner and Eudora Welty. Therefore the New Criticism is thoroughly connected to the institutionalization and formalization of southern studies. Its rise to power coincides with the spike in college enrollment caused by the GI Bill after World War II and the establishment of modern literature departments in the United States. Successively, they established a canon consisting of formally sound and politically safe democratic literature that they taught to the great influx of students, cementing their methodology as the dominant one in the academy.

Moreover, Cold War culture is a field that has long held the attention of historians and literary critics. I have already mentioned Thomas Hill Schaub's significant work in connecting literature (especially fiction) to the vital center. Also important is Alan Nadel's *Containment Culture: American Narratives, Postmodernism, and the Atomic Age* (1995), in which he shows the ways that hegemonic narratives in American culture emerged parallel to, and in support of, the United States' political policy of containment in dealing with the perceived threat of communist expansion. Nadel argues: "The American cold war is a particularly useful example of the power of large cultural narratives to unify, codify, and contain—perhaps *intimidate* is the best word—the personal narratives of its population," yet the many dualities related to social and political identity make this a task that metanarratives can never complete (*Containment Culture*, 4). These two works, along with Elaine Tyler May's social history of the influence of international politics on American domestic life, *Homeward Bound: American Families in the Cold War Era* (1988), focus on the rhetoric of containment and form what Steven

Belletto and Daniel Grausam identify as the first of two distinct phases in literary studies and cultural histories of the Cold War.

The second phase that Belletto and Grausam note in scholarship on American literary culture of the Cold War is a shift at the beginning of the twenty-first century to global or transnational frameworks rather than emphasizing containment (6). For example, both Christina Klein and Leerom Medovoi recognize how American literary culture helped readers of the midcentury understand the United States' relationships with the noncommunist world and with its newest allies, the new nations that gained independence from their former colonial rulers. In *Cold War Orientalism: Asia in the Middlebrow Imagination, 1945–1961* (2003), Klein theorizes a "global imaginary of integration" that presented a vision of the United States and its noncommunist allies worldwide rapidly "construct[ing] a world in which differences could be bridged and transcended" (41). Also examining how cultural production built bridges between the United States and other nations, Medovoi's *Rebels: Youth and the Cold War Origins of Identity* (2005) locates the genesis of identity through race, sexuality, and generational divides in the Cold War. Medovoi further posits the figure of the rebel, which emerges from within American consensus culture, as important both to youth culture in the United States and within independence movements against colonial powers.

More recent scholarship, according to Belletto and Grausam, "[assumes] the global frame of the Cold War while focusing primarily on American or Anglo-American literature" (8). In *Turncoats, Traitors, and Fellow Travelers: Culture and Politics of the Early Cold War* (2008), Arthur Redding demonstrates how a variety of American cultural figures engaged with the expansion of the rhetoric of containment into global discourses. Tyler T. Schmidt continues the exploration of identity in terms of race and sexuality in *Desegregating Desire: Race and Sexuality in Cold War American Literature* (2013) by studying how American poets and novelists portray "desegregation as a compositional and implicitly political strategy that brings sexuality, particularly queer and interracial forms, into new public spaces and broader public consciousness" (6), suggesting limitations to the containment hypothesis of Cold War culture. Kristin L. Matthews also departs from containment in *Reading America: Citizenship, Democracy, and Cold War Literature* (2016) to show how texts of the Cold War portray "literacy and literature represent[ing] freedom and democracy in its best form" (6), and how entities ranging from book clubs to government agencies sought to influence readers and their reading choices. Others extend and revise established narratives about Cold War culture. For example, Greg Barnhisel further refines Serge Guilbaut's and Frances Stonor Saunders's theses about the role that American literature and art—specifically literary modernism and abstract expressionism—played in the export of American values. In *Cold War Modernism: Art, Literature, and American Cultural Diplomacy* (2015), Barnhisel brings together Cold War culture and artistic modernism by theorizing "Cold War modernism" specifically as a "rhetorical reframing" rather than a trope or periodization (4). He further claims:

> The success of Cold War modernism wasn't just a matter of promoting an American variety of the movement as the pinnacle of modernism; Cold War modernism *redefined* modernism as an affirmation of Western bourgeois liberal values that were considered particularly integral in the American self-construction. The international character of modernism . . . served to knit the West together, with the Unites States leading the way. (10–11)

The codification of modernist aesthetics and canon that Jameson defines as late modernism become part of American foreign policy as it seeks to unite the emerging Third World under the banner of liberal values.

My project in this book attempts to bring together these approaches while shifting to a more regional focus. Understanding southern literature as a late modernist phenomenon and a significant component of Cold War culture is important because it so clearly demonstrates the political function of literary and cultural production in the twentieth-century United States. From before World War II through today, the American South has been portrayed in print, popular, and political culture as an economically and socially backward place compared to the rest of the United States. In 1938 Franklin Roosevelt characterized the region's poverty as the gravest economic problem facing the country. His claim implies a perception within the American public sphere at the time that the South needed rehabilitation, both the region and its literatures. The means and opportunity arrived with the formalist turn and the Cold War. Critics and authors sensed a need to resolve the contradictions that made the South seem a problem at a time when a distinctly American culture was required for unity at home and the promotion of American ideals abroad. In this light, the southern canon that was celebrated for its transcendence of political and social ills to investigate the conditions of humanity becomes the American literary canon; many important authors of the early Cold War period who are candidates for inclusion in an anthology of American literature are just as likely to be included in one of southern literature. This conflation leads to broad popular notions of the US South as a cultural unit finally having little geographical meaning. And so the South as it is broadly conceived and identified with today—a fiercely patriotic, honorably working-class, populist, white, politically and socially conservative ideological and cultural identity that is extremely marketable—is actually a product of the Cold War. In short, the result of late modernism is an America divided not by the geographical binary of North and South but by the ideological binaries of blue states and red states and other demographic binaries such as urban and rural, elite and working class.

My claims about understanding the South more as a cultural identity than as a region add to an extensive discussion among scholars on what has been termed the "postsouthern" and more broadly to work on the South in American popular culture.[1] Among the most important works on the post-South is Martyn Bone's *The Postsouthern Sense of Place in Contemporary Fiction* (2005). Like Kreyling, Bone also reckons with the Agrarians, arguing that there was a break with the Agrarian's definition of place that resisted capitalistic commodification in literary and cultural production about the US South; yet paradoxically it was this resistance to commodification that also made it ripe for such appropriation. "Postmodern capitalist abstraction" has wrested the monolithic "South" from both "material, sociospatial reality" and the "Agrarian political-poetical imagination," Bone contends (51). Much of that capitalist abstraction has been carried out in popular culture in the twentieth century, which has been extensively examined by literary critics and historians alike, such as Tara McPherson in *Reconstructing Dixie: Race, Gender, and Nostalgia in the Imagined South* (2003) and Karen L. Cox in *Dreaming of Dixie: How the South Was Created in American Popular Culture* (2011). Despite thorough analysis and critique of the US South in popular culture, the fact remains that these imagined places remained tethered to, for lack of a better word, a *real* place, and Scott Romine explores this tension in *The Real South: Southern Narrative in the Age of Cultural Reproduction* (2008), noting that what is at stake is not notions of the "authentic" and "real" but the "understanding [of] how individuals and groups *use* these concepts in a region and an age compelled by them" (10). Romine argues that the narratives can transform the fake South into the real South because they have "the capacity to record and transmit social values and meanings, to improvise and secure the boundaries of group identity, to fashion and mobilize what Appadurai calls the 'diacritics of difference'" (26). In other words, the real South can be found somewhere in between stories about its inhabitants, how they imagine (or idealize) themselves, and how those narratives get used by southerners and nonsoutherners alike to confirm their own identities and notions of the South.

My particular contribution to ongoing debates about the material South and southern identity is locating an origin for these tensions in Cold War politics. Few books in the field of southern studies have specifically sought to understand the US South's role in Cold War culture and politics since Jon Lance Bacon's provocative study *Flannery O'Connor and Cold War Culture* (1993). Bacon examines O'Connor's work in the strict context of Cold War culture, arguing that she was a writer who offered a critique not of the actual political conflict between the superpowers of the day but of what happens to characters living in a world "dominated by one political worldview" (3). Bacon identifies O'Connor's use of several tropes of Cold War literature, namely, portrayals of invasion in which the regional South stands in for the whole of the United States as a nation; religious doctrine serving an anticommunist, consumerist society; and racism as the primary obstacle to the international success of American-style democracy. Acknowledging that, before his study, O'Connor's work had not really been explored along these avenues, Bacon states that this shortsightedness is the result of reviewers and critics writing about O'Connor's work during her life and just after her death:

> Once they had categorized O'Connor as a religious writer, readers both sympathetic and unsympathetic to her worldview could overlook the political dimensions of her art. During her career, after all, American religion seemed political only to the extent that it valorized and reinforced the Cold War consensus. Although there were significant exceptions, the adoption of a religious voice usually signaled political quietism or superpatriotism. (140)

Although Bacon is not interested in southern tropes, his reading of O'Connor's fiction in the Cold War context reinforces an apolitically political function for her fiction, indicating the significance of late modernism in the evolution of the "South" from an object of formalized, institutionalized study to a cultural identity and practice prevalent in society.

After being appropriated as a weapon in the cultural Cold War, southern identity endures in popular culture and politics to transmit social values, especially patriotism and US nationalism, which at times enable the rehabilitation of its Confederate flag–waving segments. What once was a vital center of political moderation seems to have shifted right—or has been conservative all along. Country music readily demonstrates this shift. Robert Altman parodied overt patriotism among country performers in *Nashville* (1975), yet the patriotic sentiments remain in country music and other cultural production rooted in images and ideas of the South and the rural to this day. More recently the Zac Brown Band interrupted their upbeat 2008 homage to fried chicken, sweet tea, pecan pie, and the simplicity of things that matter more than the "price tag on your clothes" with a somber verse driven by a military marching cadence. The verse's lyrics thank God for the "Stars and Stripes" and the ones who "gave their lives so we don't have to sacrifice all the things we love." Presumably veterans made sacrifices to protect more than just pecan pie and fried chicken; some would argue this includes protecting the freedom to discriminate. For instance, the Confederate concept of states' rights, the reason often given by supporters of the Lost Cause as the real reason for the Civil War, seems to be making a comeback in the second decade of the twenty-first century. Despite the extension of due process and equal protection to same-sex couples through US Supreme Court rulings in *United States v. Windsor* (2013) and *Obergefell v. Hodges* (2015), in early 2016 the chief justice of Alabama's Supreme Court, Roy Moore, defied the US Supreme Court by ordering judges in his state to not issue marriage licenses incompatible with state law, preventing the issue of licenses to same-sex couples (Blinder).[2] Moreover, the governments of some Sun Belt states have enacted statutes designed to counteract illegal immigration on the basis that the federal government was not doing enough to protect their states' borders and that they have the right to do so themselves. Arizona's Support Our Law Enforcement and Safe Neighborhoods Act, enacted in 2010, is the first and the model for its successors. Many of these measures enable local police to question suspects about their immigration status even though immigration control falls under federal purview. Frequently lawmakers who support such measures claim that the federal government is shirking its responsibility. Upon signing Georgia's Illegal Immigration Reform and Enforcement Act of 2011 into law, Governor Nathan Deal said, "Illegal immigration is a complex and troublesome issue, and no state alone can fix it.... We will continue to have a broken system until we have a federal solution. In the meantime, states must act to defend their taxpayers" (quoted in Brown). Deal frames his support of the harsh immigration measure within the familiar framework of states' rights, emphasizing a dysfunctional federal government that does not adequately support the states. But such laws run the risk of infringing on the due process afforded undocumented immigrants under federal law. Alabama, South Carolina, and Utah also passed similar laws (Archibold; Fausset). The states' rights to own slaves have been replaced with the states' rights to discriminate. The appeal to states' rights is at its core framed by supporters as an appeal to freedom and liberty. These trends reflect a powerful alignment between American nationalism and white southern identity politics that was also appealed to by Cold War intellectuals. These connections are not simply a historical artifact but influential forces in American culture and politics today.

Southern Literature, Cold War Culture, and the Making of Modern America explores this alignment by examining southern literature's development from a formal academic discipline to its seeping into tropes in the popular imagination. I address a variety of literary and cultural texts—periodicals, essays, novels, short stories, television, and memoir—since the 1930s, emphasizing how authors' representations of political anxieties related to communism, totalitarianism, racism, and poverty reflect their political sympathies and how their work comports with or challenges late modernist aesthetics. The consequences can be either canonicity or obscurity. For example, the earliest developments of late modernism emerge through the ideological disagreement regarding the political function of regionalist and nationalist art in society between two publications of the 1940s: *South Today* (1936–45) and selected volumes of the *Kenyon Review* (1939–50). These two publications had highly disparate programs; one ceased publication within ten years of its launch, and the other went on to define the aesthetic sensibilities of an entire generation of critics and educated readers of literature. I also associate primary texts with trends in American intellectual culture, for instance, by examining Robert Penn Warren's winning of the Pulitzer Prize and Ralph Ellison's winning of the National Book Award.

Chapter 1 investigates how the nearly concurrent runs of Lillian Smith and Paula Snelling's *South Today* and John Crowe Ransom's *Kenyon Review* develop two possibilities for the formation of a southern literary canon at the moment of American involvement in World War II. *South Today* is concerned with the political efficacy of literature that is more openly activist and concerned with addressing material conditions; the *Kenyon Review* promotes a highly formalistic, apolitical literary vision. The ideological conflict between *South Today* and the *Kenyon Review* lays the groundwork for institutionalized literary canons in which later critics and authors will participate. It is the *Kenyon Review* that succeeds, and its successful agenda has much to do with institutional backing.

In chapter 2, I consider William Faulkner's meteoric rise in critical acclaim and suggest that the study of his work as model American and southern literature leads to an area studies of the US South. Formerly dismissed as overly violent, grotesque, and formally confusing, Faulkner's critical reputation was transformed by Malcolm Cowley and other New Critics into that of an author who showcases individuals committed to democratic morality against an increasingly alienating modern world. Rather than simply rehashing the tale of Faulkner's rise in scholarly esteem, I examine how recasting Faulkner as the cornerstone of a formalized study of southern literature also forms the basis for a kind of area studies. Area studies emerged in universities after World War II as disciplines used to produce knowledge about global regions to inform policy decisions. Similarly, a southern area studies assists literary critics and intellectuals in determining how best to use the most savory values of southern culture and history to assert American cultural dominance. I turn to the first major collection of scholarship on southern literature, *Southern Renascence: The Literature of the Modern South* (1953), edited by Louis D. Rubin Jr. and Robert D. Jacobs, to scrutinize Faulkner's role in their formulations of a southern literary canon parallel to an American canon. I also read Faulkner's novel *Intruder in the Dust* (1948) as an indicator of the late modernist turn.

Chapter 3 argues that Robert Penn Warren's *All the King's Men* (1946) and Ralph Ellison's *Invisible Man* (1952) depict individual moral responsibility for the upkeep of American democracy and that their awards represent an affirmation of these depicted values. In this chapter, I make three distinct claims. First, the peculiar political developments of this pair of authors and friends—Warren was a former segregationist and Ellison a former communist—indicate their commitments to the American vital center, and likewise, their protagonists ultimately give up on their political extremes. Second, in winning major literary prizes, *All the King's Men* and *Invisible Man* signal that they were key representations of American values for intellectuals who aimed to protect the vital center, and the novels' solid status as canonical works sheds light on the formation of the late modernist canon. Finally, the novels' portrayals of distinctly southern political conundrums universalize their protagonists' experiences as American experiences and therefore suggest a preservation of American values. This point is significant because it connects the previous chapter's reading of southern studies as area studies with the formation of the American literary canon and shows how the canons are one and the same.

Chapter 4 marks a turning point in the book and begins addressing authors who more explicitly acknowledge the political nature of the southern ideals adopted by intellectuals as the body of work began to be canonized. Here I investigate one of the most explicit agents of paradox in southern literature, Eudora Welty, who is famous both for her essay "Must the Novelist Crusade?," in which she claims that writers cannot and should not get involved in political activism, and for her story "Where Is the Voice Coming From?," which is a quickly written and published fictional account of the assassination of Medgar Evers, told from the first-person perspective of the killer. I contextualize Welty's story with details regarding Evers's mandated Jackson, Mississippi, television appearance to show the immediate, real-world sociopolitical engagement of literature, which supports my argument that Welty's story marks an unavoidable reappearance of social consciousness to the canon, despite Welty's own pleas to refrain from crusading fiction.

Chapter 5 examines Alice Walker's *Meridian* (1976) and Walker Percy's *Love in the Ruins* (1971). I argue that the two novels portray a post-South in which the category of "southern" as defined by geography has completely given way to one of sensibilities appropriated by the Cold War thinkers and the culture industry. Walker and Percy provide visions of the US South in which communities are measured by how well their values measure up against those serving the preservation of American-style democracy. Through a treatment of the specific historical contexts of these novels, the civil rights movement and Richard Nixon's victory in the 1968 presidential election, I argue that these values, grouped together in the service of preserving the freedom and liberty of the vital center, morph into the modern conservatism that emerges at the end of the 1960s, marked by the proliferation of a suburban politics informed by segregationist sentiments. The end is a nation no longer divided by North and South but riven by political sensibilities: blue states and red states, located in every geographic corner of the country.

I conclude with an epilogue that that shifts from the book's historical project into ongoing interpretive work. Here I address the survival of these earlier political deployments of southern texts and cultural values into the twenty-first century by addressing portrayals of the southern/national paradox in two popular texts: A&E's *Duck Dynasty* (2012–17) and J. D. Vance's *Hillbilly Elegy: A Memoir of a Family and Culture in Crisis*. These and other southern- or rural-themed popular texts (especially television) showing how working-class identity and populism have become closely associated with the South have attained a great deal of currency among a national audience. This suggests that the values portrayed are much farther-reaching than the region portrayed on the screen. Moreover, the political conservatism of the program aligns with the ascendancy of Donald Trump to the presidency. The first major foreign policy conflicts facing the United States during his presidency are eerily similar to Cold War conflicts; the stakes are high for America to maintain its influence on the world stage.

In his address at the award ceremony where he was presented with the National Book Award for *Invisible Man*, Ralph Ellison described his purpose in writing the novel: "Whenever we as Americans have faced serious crises we have returned to fundamentals; this, in brief, is what I have tried to do" ("Brave Words for a Startling Occasion," 154). While at its outset *Southern Literature, Cold War Culture, and the Making of Modern America* was not a response to any particular crisis in US politics or the academy, recent history and discourse have shaped it into a response. It attempts to continue the revision of narratives on the history of southern literary studies by offering another way to deconstruct southern (and American) exceptionalism, connecting literature and how it is written and understood to ideology. It also strives to provide an innovative, different perspective from which to understand the literature and culture of the Cold War in America in general. It points toward an "end" of southern studies that is not an end but rather a renewed academic discipline that confirms that it and American studies might be better understood as two sides of the same coin rather than the former existing as a subset of the latter. And while this project explores the ways that white southern identity gets conflated with white American nationalism, it also seeks to continue the work of showing how these are constructed fantasies. Cold War culture may have been effective at oppression, but it ultimately failed to totalize. As Jon Smith cautions in *Finding Purple America: The South and the Future of American Cultural Studies* (2013), most folks in the United States live in neither a hillbilly hinterland nor a hip, diverse urban center, but rather somewhere in between that may or may not have some qualities of both. Much recent work in southern studies seems aware of this. Still, Smith claims that sometimes scholars working on the US South have such strong affinities for their own southern identities that they "wind up reinscribing kinds of essential southern identity that the books' own arguments work strenuously and productively against" (17). Smith might characterize my project here as part of the strains of southern and American studies avoiding closure, "endlessly agitated about the loss of . . . 'identity'" (4). While my project does revisit this territory, it does so to more fully think through connections between southern literature and culture, American literature and culture, and the Cold War, which are overdue for an investigation. "A new Southern studies," Baker and Nelson say, "welcomes intellectual, multiparticipant, and revisionary complexity. It welcomes the complication of old borders and terrains, wishes to construct and survey a new scholarly map of 'The South'" (243). To borrow Ellison's words, such, in brief, is what I have tried to do.

PART I
SOUTHERN CANONS AND THE VITAL CENTER

★ ★ ★ ★ ★

1

Reviewing the South: Competing Canons in *South Today* and the *Kenyon Review*

While classrooms of universities and colleges seem the front lines in the academic study of literature, literary and critical periodicals have also served an important role in forming dominant ideas about American literature and culture. At no time was this truer than during the years leading up to and during World War II, when English departments as we know them today began to emerge, influenced greatly by the model of scholarly discourse conducted through the literary quarterly.[1] Many successful quarterlies found university backing, and some, such as the *Kenyon Review* (1939–present), were edited by English professors who promoted the New Criticism. Given access to widely read publications, New Critical tenets unsurprisingly became the dominant mode of literary analysis in classrooms and in published scholarship for a generation. However, attempts to influence the way a broad group of readers engage with literature have not been limited to large quarterlies with strong circulation numbers. Smaller, nonacademic periodicals have certainly had agendas concerning the best purpose for literature, its scholarship, and canonicity. This becomes relevant to literatures of the US South in the particular case of *South Today* (1936–45), a small literary magazine edited and published by Lillian Smith and Paula Snelling out of Clayton, Georgia, which ran concurrently with the early issues of major critical quarterlies. The concurrent publication of *South Today* with the *Kenyon Review*, which was edited by Smith and Snelling's fellow southerner John Crowe Ransom, demonstrates important divergent trends in how intellectuals and authors in the United States were thinking about the canonicity and the institutionalization of literary studies before and during World War II. *South Today* is unique because of its attention to global political and social issues in a regional literary context. Considering *South Today* in this light along with the *Kenyon Review*, an example of a larger, university-supported quarterly, is significant because during their concurrent publication there arises a scholarly interest in a canon of southern literature that coincides with a collective desire for a national literature of democratic values. This desire leads *South Today* eventually to obscurity, while the *Kenyon Review* has lengthy success.

Placing *South Today* in dialogue with a more recognizable quarterly such as the *Kenyon Review* and the larger magazine culture of the early to middle twentieth century in terms of their purpose, editorial policy, and scholarly approach is quite fruitful, especially in terms of revising predominant narratives of the modern as related to the formalization of the study of southern and American literature. Indeed, as George Core stated at a conference on southern letters celebrating the fiftieth year after the founding of the *Southern Review*:

> The critical quarterly as we know it was largely founded in response to modernism—to the work of writers like Ford, Yeats, Pound, Eliot, and Joyce. At first, magazines such as Ford's *English Review* and his *Transatlantic Review* were intended primarily to provide outlets for fiction and poetry; then increasingly the emphasis turned to criticism—a criticism that would explain the obscure and pithy indirections of the modernist manner and style by penetrating its masks, illuminating its shadowed modes, and translating its muted voices.
>
> The major American literary quarterlies since 1935—the *Southern*, *Kenyon*, *Sewanee*, and *Hudson* reviews—therefore have existed largely to explain modern literature. (190)

This suggests that the advent of scholarly literary reviews is a definitive early indicator of late modernism, that is, the codification and canonization by intellectuals, art critics, and literary critics of the artistic practices and works of prewar modernists, especially high modernists. Such emphasis in art and literature became significant in the postwar years for America's battle against communism because it enabled the intelligentsia to keep leftist and progressive politics in check. For late modernism, as Fredric Jameson explains, "high literature and high art mean the aesthetic minus culture, the aesthetic field radically cleansed and purified of culture" (179). Art and literature with all their contexts—political, social, or otherwise—stripped become democratically safe, but only about technique and forms. The purging of contexts comes on the heels of a leftist turn in American culture during the Great Depression, as union membership increased, and artists, writers, and intellectuals became more active in leftist politics. At nearly the same moment that publications such as *Partisan Review* and the *New Masses* began to define and extol to aspiring young writers a proletarian literature that joined working-class realities, radical politics, and artistic innovation (Denning, 201–3), *South Today* commenced publication as a welcoming forum for beginning southern writers with espoused progressive ideas. *South Today* advanced a desegregationist agenda by encouraging those new writers to stop relying on stock portrayals of blacks, and one early issue included an article on the Federal Writers' Project in Georgia.

With this under consideration, *South Today* seems a branch of this literary Left, and the principal differences that emerge between *South Today* and many of its larger contemporary quarterlies are most evident in editorial policies related to representations of social problems in art and treatments of contemporary politics. Smith and Snelling, both attuned to developments in southern letters, reflect through their editorial policies a unique understanding of the US South's relationship to international political turmoil, as well as US involvement in it. *South Today* developed a presentation of the South as a region with high stakes in political conflicts on the global stage. As a result, Smith and Snelling's little magazine becomes an instrumental indicator of the moment of late modernism and attempts to influence ideas about the southern literary canon in two distinct ways. The first is the magazine's tempering of political extremism, especially communism or fascism besieging Europe and elsewhere, by publishing editorials and other writing condemning such politics. The second is Smith's critique of racism as political extremism and how the United States overlooks these racial and economic inequalities. Nowhere was this gap in American democracy more visible than in the South. Smith and Snelling made it their life's work to expose the discrepancy between that vision and the realities for African Americans living in the US South. Consequently they faced serious institutional resistance to their project. Smith and Snelling saw this cultural battle against racism as an important duty of literature, and such is evidenced in their editorials, essays, and editorial policies.

New Critical quarterlies such as the *Kenyon Review*, on the other hand, were focusing strictly on the aesthetics of literature and art and not social or political representations. The flourishing of formalist principles in literary criticism in the twentieth century shows just how influential Ransom's writings and editorial policies for his magazine became. Through them, he became a key figure in articulating the tenets of the New Criticism. By the end of the 1940s, his review was one of the most influential academic periodicals in the United States. Ransom's ambitions for the *Kenyon Review* were anything but modest from its inception. Upon being offered the editorship, Ransom wrote his friend Tate on October 29, 1937, to suggest he become his assistant editor, saying, "I have an idea we could really found criticism if we got together on it" (*Selected Letters*, 229). Emphasizing the need for a "new" criticism, Ransom reviewed Cleanth Brooks and Robert Penn Warren's new textbook *Understanding Poetry* in the first issue. In his review, Ransom draws a conclusion concerning the book's equally rigorous and stirring analyses of both old and contemporary modernist poems, saying, "What can this mean, but that criticism as it is now practised is a new thing? We do not possess anything like a critique of our own major poets" ("The Teaching of Poetry," 83). For Ransom, his review provided a space for that critique, and consequently he became the arbiter of taste for an entire literary generation and championed America as the center of (apolitically) democratic art after World War II. Ransom and his *Kenyon Review* did so with the backing of universities, which provided the institutional foundations for the earliest canons of literature that rendered Smith and Snelling's more politicized vision irrelevant.

South Today and the *Kenyon Review* had one thing in common at their outsets: they both published articles about Thomas Wolfe. Otherwise the two publications were quite different. At twelve pages, the first issue of *Pseudopodia*, as *South Today* was called when it began in the spring of 1936, was extremely small compared to most critical or literary quarterlies, and the quality of its poetry and fiction indicated the contributors were beginning writers. But whereas regional concerns might be present yet subdued in larger journals, the few pages of the inaugural issues of *Pseudopodia* openly exhibit the deep regional concerns of its editors. Smith and Snelling indicate that they had a specific audience and purpose for their magazine in mind from their first editorial, concerning themselves with present conditions and what they meant for the future of the South: "We are not interested in perpetuating that sterile fetishism of the Old South which has so long gripped our section. We believe that the saline state which befell Lot's wife did not come by divine whim" (6).[2] They promised to encourage developing artists and writers, but "in the many places where we see vapidness, dishonesty, cruelty, stupidity, we wish to expose rather than gloss over" (6). While the progressivism that characterized *South Today* had early roots in the magazine, those same early issues did take a primarily regionalist perspective, though often a critique of that regionalism. Its purview would expand soon enough.

In the meantime, Smith and Snelling went straight to work on tearing the veneer off works they deemed vapid, dishonest, and cruel, and with a methodology that emphasized social, psychological, and economic criticism. From the beginning, they took aim at a few obvious (and perhaps easy) targets. The group drawing most of Smith's ire in the early issues was Ransom's Nashville Agrarians, against whom Smith defined her literary career and likely had in mind when she dismissed the romanticized visions of the Old South. In her first "Dope with Lime" column (a soda jerk's term for Coke with lime juice), Smith called Allen Tate's essay in *I'll Take My Stand* "brilliantly untenable" (*Pseudopodia* 1, no. 1 [1936]: 7). Following her opening salvo, the lead of the second number was a review by John D. Allen of *Who Owns America?*, the second volume of essays from the Agrarians. Although Allen does take a moment to praise the talent the Agrarians have for making their position appealing, he focuses his critique on their unrealistic "us versus them" paradigm—capitalism's and modernism's encroachment on morally and traditionally sound regional cultures. While Allen's summary of the book's argument is reductive, he sums up his own critique well: "It is a pity that a program so futile, a social philosophy so warped and partial, can be urged with a charm and vigor so dangerously seductive" (14).

Another author winning attention in the same issue was Erskine Caldwell. Snelling's critique of Caldwell's work is not as sharp as Allen's critique of the Agrarians, yet she takes issue with the fact that Caldwell portrays the worst of the South without including a call for help for southerners living in abject poverty. The region re-created in Caldwell's books, Snelling says, is "just about as good a picture of the South as the old fashioned returned missionary gave us of China." But there is hope for him yet, she says, "if he would give himself time between books; would return to a continuous first hand study of his people as he matures": essentially, if he could incorporate a constructive criticism of the South (Snelling, "Ground Itch," 13).

While Snelling wrote many of the early review pieces,[3] relegating the editorializing to her partner, Smith did forcefully present her perspective on southern literature, its merits, and its downfalls. An important example of Smith's literary criticism from the early days of their magazine is her review panning Margaret Mitchell's *Gone with the Wind* in the fall 1936 number, not just for its demonstration of Smith's critical tendencies. The review's tone is harsh from the outset and reveals Smith's unwillingness to forgive what she considered bad politics for strong artistic production: "We too had long looked for the 'great novel of the South' and hoped that this was it. It isn't" ("One More Sigh," 6). While she commends Mitchell on her factual knowledge of Reconstruction Atlanta, she takes her to task for nostalgically clinging to the plantation economy as the best way to understand the society and culture of the Old South. Smith's criticism of the novel's sentimentality—it seemed to her ready-made for transformation into film by Hollywood—demonstrates her resistance to caricatures of the South being commodified.

Another factor influencing Smith's negative review may also be an unhelpful visit with Mitchell for an interview on the writing of *Gone with the Wind* and a brief, flippant correspondence thereafter. Darden Asbury Pyron, a Mitchell biographer, tells this story with reference to letters written by Smith and the review itself, unfairly calling Smith disingenuous and "capable of vengefulness, resentment, and fierce jealously, however veiled in gauzy flattery and ideological earnestness," and a "Southern lady, and even 'fine ladies' practiced bitchiness and cattiness as a refined, if intuitive and unselfconscious art" (327). Pyron concedes that Mitchell held the same qualities, pointing to a letter Mitchell wrote to her editor, Harold Latham, complaining of the visit, Smith's request for three hundred words, and her poor interviewing skills. However, he does so with only passing reference to letters written by Mitchell to Smith in the relevant correspondence.

The extant correspondence begins with Mitchell writing to answer a request from Snelling for the interview, suggesting that she and Smith visit her. Mitchell indicates that she would like to talk with them about *Pseudopodia* and how they got the idea for it; she also mentions that though she used to be a newspaper reporter, she had never been interviewed before, which seems unlikely, given the publicity *Gone with the Wind* received before publication (letter to Lillian Smith, May 4, 1936). The editors visited Mitchell at her home in Atlanta with the intention of conducting an interview for *Pseudopodia* during May 1936 and were among many callers Mitchell had in the weeks leading up to her novel's publication. According to Pyron, the editors "basked in Mitchell's hospitality, attentiveness and good talk" (326); but when Smith found herself unable to write the article because she had not gotten the information she desired from her host, she "laid her burden on the harried novelist in Atlanta" (326) by asking Mitchell for three hundred words about how she wrote *Gone with the Wind*. Smith's acknowledgedly flattering request is written in the folksy voice she used for the "Dope with Lime" columns:

> But wouldn't you prefer really to write us 300 words (or more) about the writing of the book, its inception, how it grew, its background, rather than trust it to come out right at second-hand? We'd feel terribly honored if you would, and perhaps our four hundred readers would talk enough about GONE WITH THE WIND throughout the long summer to add another thousand to the many thousand readers you will surely have anyway. Oh yes, I'm baiting—and I know you don't need it, but I hope you will do this. If you do, I shall simply add a sketch of our interview using the biographical material you gave me. (Letter to Margaret Mitchell, May 16, 1936)

Pyron says Mitchell declined the request; however, a handwritten note to Smith shows that Mitchell actually does not decline outright. Rather, she replies that she does not know when she would be able to write it because the task is difficult for her now that she would need a deadline. This is perhaps a halfhearted refusal, but she goes on to say: "I wish I could think of some thing entertaining or interesting to write but I can't as all writing seems a god-awful bore and I loathe writing and the profession of the novelist seems the most wearisome and lonely one an addled mortal could choose" (letter to Lillian Smith, May 19, 1936).[4] Mitchell's morose response elicits the following reply:

> Far be it from me to tell a successful author who has written a book probably destined to be read by as many people as Anthony Adverse how to write 300 words for little Pseudopodia, but I would like to suggest that you crawl up on your divan, drink another cup of that delicious black coffee you gave me, and just let it write itself, as you talked. (Letter to Margaret Mitchell, May 18, 1936)[5]

The correspondence ends when Mitchell replies and explicitly declines the request but tells Smith, "I just can't do anything about the three hundred words for you and I beseech you to use whatever you got when you were here. I know you can do it better than I" (letter to Lillian Smith, May 21, 1936).

And Smith does just that: in the summer 1936 number, the issue before the one containing the *Gone with the Wind* review, Smith writes of the visit with Mitchell in one of her "Dope with Lime" columns and presents a rather unflattering portrayal of an author unwilling to discuss her own work, worth quoting at length:

> A very small keen-eyed red-headed attractive person asked, "Which is which?" said immediately, "I'm scared to death. Do come in." But curled up on a divan, drinking black coffee, she really did not look scared but very alert and intelligent and vivacious with the situation well in the hollow of her hand, and seemed far more interested in discussing Faulkner, Cabell, Emily Clark, Wolfe, and some mutual friends than her own book. "I'm sick to death of it," she groaned. (11)

Smith goes on to write that Mitchell said during the interview, "I didn't write of the past . . . but of contemporary happenings. Time has stood still hereabouts" (11).

Considering this correspondence in its entirety is significant because it provides a more complete context for understanding the nature of the exchange, the negative review in question, and Smith's approach to literary criticism. First, the complete correspondence reveals the excessive self-deprecation and dismissiveness in Mitchell's replies and her attitude toward the profession of writing, indicating that she seems never to have taken Smith's interest in writing, the novel, the interview, the request, or even *Pseudopodia* seriously. As their involvement and writing in the magazine indicate, Smith and Snelling were sincerely concerned with matters of southern letters. While revenge may play a role in the portrayal of Mitchell as an anxious, flighty woman in the aforementioned "Dope with Lime" and "One More Sigh for the Good Old South," the review cannot be reduced to vengeful, jealous "cattiness," as Darden suggests. Second, Smith clarifies in "One More Sigh" how artists serve as commentators on society's understandings of history and the dangers of romanticizing the past: "An artist comprehends the social-economic-intellectual assumptions of a period, their implications and effect upon personality but surely he must remain detached and critical of them" (6). By Mitchell's own admission, she saw herself writing about a past in the present, and her levity about her own work indicates that Smith and Mitchell did not see the same ramifications for art. Smith suggests that such a perspective could manifest as extremism in contemporary times. In her review of *Gone with the Wind*, she argues that such a single-minded focus on "capitalistic (or of Marxist) ideology" is no different from the emphasis on the defunct plantation economy, the emphasis of Mitchell's novel ("One More Sigh," 6). Nearly a decade before the beginning of the Cold War, Smith recognizes the impending ideological conflict. Her dialogue with Mitchell and review of *Gone with the Wind* are significant because they recognize the power of romanticizing a past without regard to politics to influence a present; in characterizing the politics as dualistic (capitalist or Marxist), Smith prefigures the middle ground of the subtly apolitically political vital center.

The review's attention to historical context and social and material conditions places Smith and her magazine in opposition not only to romanticized versions of the South, such as Mitchell's, but also to the New Criticism that began to coalesce in the late 1930s. Indeed, the bulk of Smith's literary criticism is socioeconomic or psychological. The influence of leftist literary thinkers such as V. F. Calverton, Granville Hicks, and Michael Gold (the latter two both editors of the *New Masses*), whom Smith seems to have actively read, shines through in her critique of *Gone with the Wind* (Blackwell and Clay, 27). Smith was well traveled and well educated (she spent three years as a teacher at a missionary school in China, as well as time in New York attending Columbia and teaching in Harlem) and held clearly leftist politics and literary sensibilities. However, Smith expressed dissatisfaction with what seemed to be communism's requirement of strict party lines, and outside literary circles, she had little familiarity with Marxism. She did not align herself with "Communists, even during the Popular Front years when other southern reformers such as Lucy Randolph Mason and Claude Williams cooperated with them," nor did she trust communists (Loveland, 60–61). Smith's anticommunism was the one thing she had in common with many of the southern liberals she critiqued. However, she found particularly strong political allies in southerners who also supported desegregation: Howard W. Odum, whose sociological works she reviewed favorably in *South Today*, maintained an extensive correspondence with Smith as a consultant to the magazine. W. J. Cash, who was just as anticommunist and antitotalitarian as Smith and Snelling, was also a supporter of the magazine. He contributed an excerpt of *The Mind of the South* for the issue that included the review of *Gone with the Wind*, and he even visited Smith and Snelling at their home in Clayton in late February or early March 1941 (letter to Lillian Smith, February 26, 1941). Given these associations, Smith's lack of interest in communism coincides with the de-Marxization of American intellectuals toward the close of the 1930s.

John Crowe Ransom's concerns with the US South—or at the least issues of southernness—are much more veiled in the *Kenyon Review*. These considerations mostly lie in the figure of Ransom himself. The motives for his move from Vanderbilt to Kenyon were probably primarily financial (he got a substantial raise and a rent-free house on campus). However, the move and his acceptance of the editorship of the *Review* suggest that Ransom sought to depoliticize himself. By the end of the 1930s, the Agrarian thought experiment had been carried too far for his liking and was criticized by nationally recognized thinkers, such as Howard W. Odum, as well as regional ones, including Smith and Snelling. Ransom attempted to distance himself from it, beginning with his contribution to the aforementioned and highly criticized *Who Owns America?* The volume was imagined by members of the original Twelve as a sequel to *I'll Take My Stand* but morphed into something else when it fell to Allen Tate and Herbert Agar to edit the collection. Ransom confided to George Marion O'Donnell in 1936 that he was "determined to write no more economic essays," and the two agreed: "Agrarianism . . . is now passing into a second phase—the political" (quoted in Young, 261). This phase of Agrarianism was better left to politicians, they concluded. He also expressed his falling away from the movement in letters to Tate. Furthermore, in planning the *Review*, university president Gordon Keith Chalmers seems to have more or less overlooked Ransom's prior ideological associations, and the pair came to an implicit understanding that the magazine would not be a soapbox for Agrarian issues. Marian Janssen suspects that this is reflected in Chalmers's choice of Philip Blair Rice, a left-leaning philosophy professor, as the journal's associate editor to counterbalance Ransom's Agrarian past when Tate could not accept the position. But she perceives Ransom as having been "not at all disturbed by Rice's leftism, which was only political and 'not a literary matter.' Clearly, Ransom, as in his Agrarian days, was not interested in everyday active politics" (21). Ergo politics would no longer be a focus of Ransom's work. Additionally, the move to Ohio physically removed him from the politics and culture of the South. This self-insulation made him capable of the work he did with the *Kenyon Review*.

With this in mind, the choice of John Peale Bishop's retrospective on Thomas Wolfe to begin the magazine becomes more significant in at least two ways. To be sure, "The Sorrows of Thomas Wolfe" was the lead essay in the first issue because, as in Janssen's estimation, it was the best one at Ransom's disposal upon the launch of the magazine. However, Bishop's emphasis on the structure of Wolfe's novels foreshadows the formalist tendencies that would be prominent in the later volumes of the *Review*, tendencies that reflected Ransom's own critical bent. Second, Thomas Wolfe was a southern author, born and educated in North Carolina before he moved to New York, and his novels featured protagonists with backgrounds similar to his own. Ransom's own southern background suggests that a lead essay featuring a southerner in the new review would be no coincidence. Yet Bishop's essay makes no mention of Wolfe's origin and does not address his southernness. This would be a continuing trend for the *Review*. The absence of discussions about the South, and race, is conspicuous. The need to disregard deeply rooted racism and poverty in the South at the center of the region's problems merged concerns that were both regional and national. The *Kenyon Review*'s apoliticism, along with the pressures on Ransom to keep the magazine unsouthern, made it a convenient site for this convergence.

One of Ransom's first editorial conundrums concerning regional topics for his journal resulted also in the convergence of regional issues with the apolitical politicism characteristic of formalism. The event was Lionel Trilling's enthusiastic request to review James Agee and Walker Evans's *Let Us Now Praise Famous Men* (1941), which chronicled in prose and image the difficulties faced by three families of white sharecroppers in Alabama during the late 1930s. Ransom initially wanted to deny Trilling's request because upon his first glance at Evans's photographs in the book, he figured it to be a "leftist tract about the South" (Janssen, 56). However, Trilling insisted, so Ransom relented. Ransom ended up liking Trilling's essay so much that he ran it as the lead review for the winter 1942 issue. As do many of the reviews accepted for publication, Trilling's piece focuses on the form of the book, though he addresses its moral content with significant results. He sees a failure in Agee's inability to point out the faults of the sharecroppers, specifically their hatred of blacks. Trilling says, "[Agee] writes of his people as if there were no human unregenerateness in them" (102). But ultimately he calls the book "the most realistic and the most important moral effort of our American generation" (102). Trilling is willing to ignore, and quite explicitly at that, the book's unsavory elements so as to convert any political engagement with its subject to an ethical imperative. What need is there for activism when "the relatively fortunate middle class that reads books and experiences emotions" can read Agee and Evans's account and, like Trilling, "feel sure that this is a great book" (99)? This facet of Agee's work, according to Susan Hegeman, was immediately identified by Trilling as "conformity with that classic ethical position of the Cold War intellectual: liberal guilt" (187). Thus the book became not one about cruelties of poverty and the abuse of tenants by the landowners in the South, but a book about "the condition of the self": the self of the middle class and the other of the impoverished (188). This dynamic demonstrates a contribution of the *Kenyon Review* to showing a congruency between southern literature and American culture and ideals more broadly. With Trilling's review, the seeds are sown for the beginnings of a more formalized southern studies, as it came to be known.

Other authors with southern backgrounds were featured in Ransom's magazine as subjects or as authors with regularity, but rarely were southern issues explicitly discussed. Robert Penn Warren wrote a piece on Katherine Anne Porter that appeared in the same issue as Trilling's review of *Let Us Now Praise Famous Men*, yet Warren makes no comment about Porter's southernness, opting instead to draw comparisons between her short fiction and that of authors in the modernist canon, which was coming into being in the pages of the *Review*. Porter would make her own contribution later in the special Henry James number in autumn 1943. Warren would also bring Eudora Welty some of her first critical attention with an essay in the *Review*'s spring 1944 number, but there is no treatment of her as a regional writer. However, nothing makes the lack of southern issues as conspicuous as the lack of critical attention paid to certain authors, especially those addressing racial politics.

A key feature of the move toward the liberal consensus of the postwar United States is that it does not accommodate critiques of the racist status quo. So, as Leigh Anne Duck notes, "By the late 1940s, activists suggesting that US apartheid reflected broad and intractable problems with the nation-state and its purportedly liberal structures were pronounced subversive and subjected to harassment and substantial penalties" (214). How this relates to *South Today* becomes all too clear in Smith and Snelling's battles with the KKK and local Georgia authorities. The magazine's publication even led the Federal Bureau of Investigation to open a file on Smith.[6] On the other hand, that certain authors related to the South and the topic of race went unreviewed or unaddressed by the *Kenyon Review* is also a likely indication of this phenomenon. This is not to say that Ransom was actively censoring radical critiques, but certain works and authors most likely went unconsidered because of his aversion to politics altogether. These simply were ignored. For example, Carson McCullers's work is reviewed or critiqued only once in the first twelve volumes of the *Kenyon Review*, and the work reviewed is not *The Heart Is a Lonely Hunter* (1940), her first significant work and the one critics today might expect to receive attention. Instead, the winter 1947 issue features a review of *The Member of the Wedding* (1946). Quite possibly, her first novel's blatant treatment of union politics and racial inequality could have been intense subject matter in Ransom's eyes and too closely related to the subject of current politics.

Unsurprisingly, an author who does not even appear in the *Kenyon Review*, save a couple of advertisements, is Lillian Smith. No doubt, her 1944 novel *Strange Fruit* and its explicit story of an interracial love affair that takes racial prejudices in the South head-on proved too controversial and politically radical for review. Given the notoriety the book enjoyed after being banned in Boston and its status as a best seller, one might think that it would have commanded treatment in one of the nation's leading literary quarterlies. Smith received so many letters with questions about *Strange Fruit* that she published several of these letters with her responses to them in the final issue of *South Today* and later printed a pamphlet, "Lillian Smith Answers Some Questions about *Strange Fruit*," to deal with letters that came after the end of *South Today*. Smith's status as one of the first white southerners to speak out against segregation probably made her too much of a lightning rod for Ransom's liking, but her novel does get a veiled critique in 1946. Quentin Anderson's "Notes on the Theatre" reviews dramas running in New York, and he begins by saying that the current season was "badly cluttered with ideas and problems" (477). Anderson soon turns his attention to a production called *Deep Are the Roots*, which is about the "Negro 'problem'" (478). He refers directly to the novel *Strange Fruit*, suggesting that the play attempts to do the same kind of work that Smith's novel does. In a critique typical of the New Critical dismissal of political art as propaganda, Anderson says the cost of this portrayal of social problems is flat characters. Concerning *Deep Are the Roots*, he concludes, "The effort to account for a situation as you present it is the task of the historian, not the playwright. It is a curious fact that the history of ideas which is the burden of much of our bad scholarship threatens to become a blight in the arts as well" (478–79). No doubt this is a jab at the work of raising awareness that Smith attempted in her novel, as well.

Otherwise, the *Kenyon Review* paid little attention to issues of race as they related to the South. Gordon Hutner notes that it was "as sorry as any other mainstream publication in apprehending the claims of minority cultures" (108). One significant treatment of the "Negro problem" comes in a 1941 symposium called "The American Culture: Studies in Definition and Prophecy," which featured the anthropologist Clyde Kluckhohn. In his statement, Kluckhohn says that assimilation is the answer to the Negro problem, if Americans truly believe in racial equality, but he says so in a solitary, understated sentence (162). His essay also offers a reconciliation of sorts between the ideas of regionalists like Smith and those who were ready for American intervention in international affairs. In the same breath that he praises the city, "which makes possible that greatest of all paradoxes: unity in diversity" (164), he praises regional sentiments at the roots of America's cultural origins. In the same vein as Trilling's later review of Agee and Evans, Kluckhohn resolutely opens a space for a southern studies when he quotes the historian and critic Lewis Mumford: "So far from being archaic and reactionary, regionalism belongs to the future" (165). Such a statement represents an endorsement of the kind of regional work done by *South Today*, work that Lillian Smith believed could change the nation and the world.

Ransom's lack of interest in issues related to race may be elucidated with a brief survey of not only the appearance of works directly addressing racism but the appearance and contexts of related terminology. The phrase "Jim Crow" appears only once in the first twelve volumes of the *Kenyon Review* (in a 1948 book review), and the term "racism" also only appears twice, in essays by Meyer Shapiro in 1945 and Philip Blair Rice in 1950. Even more symptomatic of this general unconcern with racial issues is the infrequency with which African American authors were reviewed. Ransom's magazine paid as little attention to writers of color as it did to the color line. Zora Neale Hurston's *Of Mules and Men* was briefly reviewed by Stanley Edgar Hyman in his featured review in the summer 1948 number. Malcolm Cowley briefly mentions Richard Wright in a summer 1947 essay on American naturalism. (Wright appears in a few advertisements, though, including one for a volume called *Primer for White Folks*, described as "a collection of the nation's most understanding stories and articles about the Negro in America." According to the advertisement, he shares the pages of this collection with Lillian Smith [xiii].) Lying beyond the first twelve volumes, though, is Richard Chase's review of *Invisible Man*. The review is a favorable one, calling the novel "significant." Yet it takes the same strategy as Trilling's review by supplanting any political agenda within the novel with morality using the New Critical apparatus. Chase calls "invisibility" the novel's greatest symbol, but it is not the invisibility of African Americans he highlights:

> By extension, this invisibility is in our time the fate of all individuals. And this idea is not only a social comment, for Mr. Ellison is able to give it metaphysical, psychological, and moral meanings. Invisibility becomes for the hero both a plight and a device, like Hamlet's madness. (682)

Chase effectively generalizes the condition of black Americans in a way that evokes affect rather than action; their plight is one that can be legitimized only because it is an experience common to modernity.

However, given Smith's belief that art can bring about social and political change, *South Today* did not shy away from addressing real-world conditions, even in the early issues published as *Pseudopodia*. An editorial called "From Lack of Understanding" notes the poor standards of both secondary and higher education among the southern states, especially the disparate amount of funding devoted to white schools as opposed to black schools. This marks one of the magazine's first concerns with broader social issues beyond their relevance to literature. Yet it also reveals the magazine's early clinging to regional subject matter even while addressing problems of national import. The fourth issue announced a series of writing contests open to college and high school students that invited essays on topics from "a formulation of the primary problems which the United States must face in the next ten years" and "a statement of the political theories of Communism, Fascism and Liberalism" to "the problems of tenant farming" and "a sketch of some person or group in the writer's hometown" ("Prize Contest Announcement," 11). The issue also included a rave review of Howard W. Odum's *The Southern Regions of the United States* and continued the publication of poetry and sketches by previously unpublished southerners.

Smith and Snelling changed their publication's name to the *North Georgia Review* with the spring 1937 issue in an effort to signal their regional subject matter, but it is with this name change that the magazine begins heeding more national and international concerns, especially racial concerns. Smith emphasized this with "Along Their Way," the lead article of the first issue under the new title. In this review of a biography of Paul Laurence Dunbar and an autobiography by Claude McKay, Smith praises the works of McKay, James Weldon Johnson, W. E. B. Du Bois, Zora Neale Hurston, and Jean Toomer. She differentiates herself from the majority of southern liberals by indicating her belief that the fight for civil rights is worthwhile and can be influenced through the arts (3–4). Many of Smith and Snelling's peers, though, did not support desegregation and civil rights, not because they objected to them but simply because they saw them as futile in the shadow of the nostalgic visions of the Civil War and Reconstruction (Sosna, 181). Still, the *North Georgia Review* began reviewing more and more works by black and women authors, including a favorable review of Hurston's *Their Eyes Were Watching God* and a detailed critical article on Evelyn Scott by Snelling, with whom Smith corresponded. Smith believed Scott to be one of the most important ignored novelists of the time. Their literary activism extended not only to their own writing but to their editorial policies as well, which could not abide any work that did not adhere to their editorial program. In a draft of a May 1937 letter to Lucy Winn, author of a short piece that was submitted to (but did not win) one of the *North Georgia Review*'s various contests, Snelling articulates the magazine's stance on the race question as related to its editorial policy:

> It is our purpose in the little magazine to treat the Negro always with as deep respect as we do the white. . . . The traditional attitude of the white towards the Negro is to treat him, at best, as an end-man; to laugh down at him in a kindly way; to assume that he is more absurd that we are, instead of merely revealing his absurdities in ways which we can see, while we remain comparatively blind to our own unlogical and childish acts. This tradition having been established, the burden of proof that one does not accept it is upon the writer of each new manuscript dealing with them. (Letter to Lucy Winn, May 17, 1937)[7]

When the *North Georgia Review* announced the contest winners, no winners in the fiction or poetry category were chosen because of the prevalence of stories similar to the one critiqued in the foregoing comments. "Most of the contributions were mere paper and typewriter ink," Smith laments in her summer 1937 "Dope with Lime," but she goes on: "We say it frankly because we know the South can do better than this and while our slice of its literary output was thin we believe it was representative. We are still fixated to our Lost Cause" (2).

Snelling also pressed the issue of stereotypical portrayals of African Americans in the literature of the South within the pages of the *North Georgia Review*. She heaped her own criticism on *Gone with the Wind*, and other works as well, for maintaining the typical portrayal of whites as aristocratic individuals served by faithful, demeaned black servants and sidekicks. No better were works that ignored the presence of black culture in the

South: "The black segments of southern life can no more be ignored than can the black squares on a checker board: they are as indubitably prevalent and integral to the pattern. To ignore them is to exemplify pathological blindness" (Snelling, "Southern Fiction and Chronic Suicide," 6). Not only did the *North Georgia Review* advocate respect for all people; it went so far as to acknowledge the inevitability and necessity of integration. This was the focus of the magazine's regional concerns: to harry white southerners into abandoning the Lost Cause and to raise social awareness and opportunities for all living in the South. The editors continued to define their regionalism against former Agrarians, and at times adopted the mode of discourse used by critical quarterlies. For example, in a symposium including John Allen, Hortense Powdermaker, and Paula Snelling, Powdermaker unfavorably reviews Donald Davidson's *The Attack on the Leviathan*. She argues that rather than a "regionalism based on an awareness of historical and social processes" (the regionalism of improvement that Smith and Snelling advocate in the *North Georgia Review*), Davidson's regionalism is "based on a number of fears. The objects of these are a strange medley and include Charles A. Beard, H. G. Wells, Walter Page, Arthur Raper, Freud, Marx, the southern liberals, social planning, Roosevelt's new appointees, Teachers College of Columbia, equality for the Negroes, 'science to the limit,' the *New Republic* and the Future" (Powdermaker, "Disunion in Dixie," 15). This concern with equality, an issue that would in coming years become more global than regional, confirms that Smith and Snelling, despite their publication's size and circulation, believed they were making a big difference with their little magazine.

Smith and Snelling maintained their deep devotion to regional (and domestic) political issues as long as they did, suggests Robert Brinkmeyer, precisely because of the international political climate of the late 1930s: "Smith's concern about America's entry into another world war intensified as the political situation deteriorated; steadfastly refusing to acknowledge Nazi Germany's threat to Europe and, more generally, to democratic societies throughout the world, she kept her eyes focused on domestic issues, fearing that the nation's internal problems would be overlooked in the rush toward armament" (124). Yet at the end of the 1930s, the global stage could no longer be ignored, and Smith's regionalism forced her to defend what seemed an isolationist position. The *North Georgia Review* looked abroad toward these problems in the winter 1937–38 "Dope with Lime." Smith subtitled this column "A Catechism," and its text takes that form. The piece solidifies the magazine's priority for domestic issues and, more importantly, how if we are not vigilant, troubles abroad can become troubles at home:

IS THERE ANY EVIL ON EARTH GREATER THAN FASCISM?
YES. ITS PROGENITORS.
WAR?
YES.
POVERTY?
YES.
HATE?
YES.
STUPIDITY?
YES.
AND YET WE HAVE NO PROGRAM?
NO.
. . .
AREN'T WE A BIT OLD FASHIONED?
YES.
PERHAPS A LITTLE PROVINCIAL?
PERHAPS.
MAYBE "INNOCENT" AFTER ALL?
MAYBE. (32)

Fighting domestic fascism requires fighting conditions that breed and are fostered by totalitarianism; therefore correcting social ills at home should be the first step in facing down political ills in Europe. The editors certainly knew how easily fascist ideology could be accepted. In the summer 1937 number, they published as an honorable mention from their essay contest the article "Apologia of a Dictator," by Morrison Colladay, which defended the practices of the late governor of Louisiana, Huey Long. An editors' note warns the reader that the article "also presents the case for fascism in a most persuasive manner" ("Editor's Note," 3). The white, fascist power structures in place in 1930s Europe struck awfully close to home for Smith and Snelling, and they saw their fight for equality in the South as the best strategy to ensure that such persuasive ideology did not take root in the United States.

Gradually, Smith and Snelling's editorial stances and practices became more activist in regard to politics. Smith began going to even greater lengths in "Dope with Lime" and her general editorials to express her ire with the rumors of war permeating journalism in the time leading up to World War II, as well as the connections she saw between the global political strife and regional racial discrimination. Smith's earliest commentary on the war called for America to remain uninvolved. She saw an alliance with Britain not as an effort to sustain democracy around the globe but as one to hamper it:

aiding England would allow it to maintain its oppressive rule over colonies in Africa—Jim Crow on a global stage. She criticized American politicians in her winter 1940–41 "Dope with Lime" for "toadying to England" (4). Yet in the same breath, Smith saw a way for the United States—and necessarily the South—to lead the world to a new era of democracy. "If one were not squeamish about Messianic talk," she admits that the United States is in a position to lead the world:

> We are already a nation of nations in a democratic framework. Already on a small scale we have untangled the most irritating problems of States' Rights—which would be the first overtly hard step for nations to take toward an international democracy (a framework which surely is the only rational alternative the world now has to endless nationalistic wars). If we wanted it, we could go a long way on the new road by unifying this hemisphere not according to imperial patterns of spheres of interest (the interest being ours), but in a genuine democratic way. (5)

Smith implies two significant points in her comment. First of all, the South is necessarily part of that contingent in the United States capable and ready to lead. Smith is convinced that the South, for better or for worse, stands on the verge of having an important presence on the global stage. The second is an optimistic parallel between the US South and the nations of the world in terms of their participation in democracy. If other nations could possibly be persuaded to join a supranational collective, perhaps then southerners could finally be aware of themselves as global citizens in the same way that Smith and Snelling thought of themselves.

Yet Smith remained acutely aware that international efforts to spread democracy were subject to the same problems that democracy in America faced. As Brinkmeyer points out, Smith's writing in the *North Georgia Review* and *South Today* indicates her belief that black soldiers in the United States would experience the same kind of subjugation that minorities from the colonies of the British realm would: being compelled to fight a war for the nations oppressing them (126). Smith makes her concerns explicit in an editorial called "Mr. Lafayette, Heah We Is—." Its beginning opens an essay contest on the causes of war but restricts from consideration "the war cries of 'democracy' and 'fascism,'" suggesting that for an editor of a regional magazine, Smith was well aware of the complexity of the political situation in Europe and America's stake in it (14). The heart of the editorial is, however, a satirical critique of calls for democracy abroad while democracy was not even offered to all of America's citizens. She imagines what a group of African

American troops would say to Allied command of their home and mission upon arriving in France:

> We live in Gawd's country en that's a fact, en it's a fine place to live in ef yo knows yo place, and we knows our place, yeah Lawd! Now we'se come to lay down our lives for those Jews Mister Hitler's been pickin' on. We hear tell he takes their property and their money and kicks them about and spits on 'em and burns their books. An' all that makes our democratic blood boil over. Yas suh! . . . And it sho must be an awful sight to have yo books burned—hit's a lot better never to learn how to read and write like us, we'se telling you. (15)

Scholars are of two minds concerning this editorial. Loveland finds it not all that effective because it seems insensitive to the serious issue of the Holocaust while at the same time being patronizing toward African Americans, the group for whom Smith was advocating fair treatment (35). On the other hand, Brinkmeyer sees the editorial as one of Smith's most persuasively bitter attacks on the status quo (126). Yet the editorial's significance does not lie in its efficacy. More importantly, it exhibits Smith and Snelling's understanding that regional problems are at once international problems: their activism could be helpful because these seemingly different problems were yoked together by the fact that the first step in reaching the solution was to persuade individuals, namely, southerners, of the contradiction.

On the other hand, the *Kenyon Review* rarely explicitly acknowledged political issues, national or international. Such issues were ignored in New Critical literary analysis, and Janssen argues that during its first decade, the *Review* presented the New Criticism primarily as the answer to a call for a new approach to literature (though Ransom did frequently include critical essays from other perspectives). More telling are Janssen's comments on the political ambivalence of the magazine: "Political and regional issues were avoided; reading *Kenyon* of the early 1940s, one has virtually no sense that World War II was being fought" (7). This contrasts starkly with *South Today*, which increased its focus on politics as the war escalated. The extent to which the *Kenyon Review* did dabble in subjects beyond literature was at the behest of President Chalmers; these subjects were not a priority for Ransom. Chalmers insisted that the publication he dreamed of would raise the reputation of his college and have a scope that included some visual art, politics, and culture. But when Ransom's magazine did address political issues, it did so in anticipation of cultural dominance for the United States. Significantly, one of the few articles that mention the war is one that addresses the arts and the role that America must play in their survival.

In his contribution to the aforementioned symposium featuring Clyde Kluckhohn, John Peale Bishop said of art surviving the war:

> Without waiting for the outcome, or even attempting to predict it, it is possible even now to say that the center of western culture is no longer in Europe. It is in America. It is we who are the arbiters of its future and its immense responsibilities are ours. The future of the arts is in America. (Bishop, "The Arts," 183–84)

With this statement, Bishop plants the seeds of America's claim to cultural and artistic hegemony that drove the Cold War even before American involvement in World War II. His statement also links, as Serge Guilbaut also observed, democracy and the arts to American exceptionalism—an exceptionalism that, according to Kluckhohn, was rooted in the diversity provided by America's various regionalisms.

But this is not all that Bishop had to say about art. In the first volume, he provided notes on the 1939 World's Fair at Flushing Meadows, New York. His notes comment on the pavilions set up by the powers of the world, and in particular those of Mussolini's Italy and Stalin's Russia. Of significance are Bishop's statements on the merit of art used as propaganda by these two countries:

> Mussolini's compositions of disparate photographs pasted together are good, not because of what he has to say, but because whoever did them learned his collage in a good school and because . . . classical materials lend themselves admirably to collage. The Soviet Worker is bad, not because of what soviet workers are, but because it is done by a sculptor badly trained in a bad tradition. (Bishop, "World's Fair Notes," 247)

This criticism indicates that he perceives a difference between art and politics; Bishop judges these works based not on the merits of the political ideologies they support but on their merits as works of art. Such stringent formalism, again, isolates politics from art. Any sense of urgency that came from this and similar treatments of fascist art in the *Kenyon Review* came not from the need to combat the political ideologies of such art, but from an imperative to dismiss the artistic merit of such works so as to prepare the way for the American artistic hegemony that Bishop, among others, laid claim to. The causes of World War II and the actual conflict itself may never have been taken up as a principal topic for the *Review*, but what it did make clear was that a place drowning in political turmoil as Europe was in the late 1930s and early 1940s was no place for art.

Conversely, the war spurred Smith and Snelling into further extolling the South and America's place in a democratic world rather than its place as the cultural and hegemonic leader of it. Their efforts resulted in an expansion of the magazine's readership. Despite its modest circulation, the subscription correspondence of *South Today*, as their little magazine was finally named, shows that it boasted readers as far away as California, New York City, and Chicago and as diverse as college students, TVA officials, and soldiers in boot camp. The change of title marked the beginning of some of their most directed efforts at editorial activism, stressing repeatedly that the war abroad could not be won at the cost of losing ground on the civil rights issue at home. The most politically charged issue of *South Today* is the autumn–winter 1942–43 number. Smith explained the challenges the issue faced in a response to H. C. Nixon, who sent a postcard inquiring about his very late issue. "The KKK or Vigilantes are after us and the magazine," Smith wrote.

> A large number of copies were stolen and circulated among the most vicious groups of anti-Negro Georgians. They are urgin[g] the governor to have the legislature investigate us. . . . And lately there has been prowling around Clayton according to reports from local friends a GBI [Georgia Bureau of Investigation] man trying apparently to "get something" on the magazine's editors. (Letter to H. C. Nixon, February 3, 1943)

The KKK's efforts to discredit the magazine also hindered the editors in obtaining the second-class mailing permit necessary to send issues to subscribers. Smith hoped that her regular readers and supporters would not be her only audience for this particularly stirring issue, but hoped to reach out to her fellow southern liberals who felt their hands tied on the issue of race. A common criticism leveled against Smith by southern liberals was that ending segregation, while the right thing to do, would never be practical because of the violence such drastic measures would bring about. These explanations were unsatisfying for Smith, and she went about dispelling them in two key essays—perhaps the most important essays of the magazine's entire run—"Buying a New World with Old Confederate Bills" and "Addressed to Intelligent White Southerners." The two pieces certainly drew the attention of a larger-than-normal audience: based on purchase orders, Smith sold tens of thousands of reprints of the two essays to churches and activists across the country (Lillian Smith Papers).

The most striking feature of "Buying a New World with Old Confederate Bills" is its treatment of racial tensions at home and the racial politics surrounding the war as two sides of the same coin. Smith's principal targets in the essay are southern liberals who fold their hands when the social conditions have been made pliable by political turmoil. Smith begins by extending the currency metaphor to a comparison between the South and its global neighbors: what really is the difference between old Confederate bills, British pounds, and German marks? They all place a premium on white supremacy ("Buying," 9). Despite naysayers who argue that neither world war nor legislation does much to alter human nature, Smith argues that the world is ripe for reform, since the war effort sheds light on the contradictions in the allied British imperial system and segregated America's claims of fighting for democracy the world over. She places special emphasis on understanding regional problems through global problems and vice versa:

> We, the whole world, are going in new directions; and we, the South, must not lose our way. We must *learn to read our maps*. Unless we keep the world map open before us we shall slip back into the old, bad habit of looking down at our own feet, and if we do we shall find ourselves at the same place where we first began. We must learn to read our maps simultaneously: regional map, national map, world map. As time goes by, perhaps we shall find it more and more important to read and know our regional and world maps; less and less important may become our national map. That is possible. ("Buying," 12)

In following this maps model, one can only understand progress in the South as progress when it is progress in relationship to global conditions. Peculiar here is Smith's suggestion that the national map may become unneeded. In the aforementioned profiles of herself and Snelling for *South Today*, the editors consider themselves just as much citizens of the world as they do citizens of the South. Moreover, her suggestion de-emphasizes the role of national governments in creating real change. Smith seems not to completely dismiss the federal government or the governments of other nations as incapable of solving the problems her magazine addresses, but she does acknowledge that the problems can be solved through the collective action of individuals driven to action. Her system of maps de-emphasizes the role of government, even if only accidentally, thus casting southern segregation as a cultural issue beyond the purview of government.

Collective action becomes a key point again in the essay when Smith addresses the contradictions within the antiunion South. Despite her avowed anticommunism, she offers a compelling argument for a more prolific organization of labor among southern wage workers, both white and black: "Why do we fight organized labor when strong democratic unions are a most potent lever by which to lift the burden of southern poverty?" ("Buying," 18). Imagine how strong unions would be, she muses, if white and black workers organized together as opposed to against each other. She effectively links the problems of poverty in the South to the race problem, and not through the traditional North-capitalist/South-agrarian axis that began losing traction in the 1940s. Rather, she points to the greed of individuals—whether factory owners or the landlords of tenant farmers—as a factor in prolonged racial inequality. In either case, "human exploitation" is the problem ("Buying," 20). Yet she faults most the liberal intellectuals in the South who squander the opportunity for change. She tells them how direly their leadership is needed, for "changes can come to the South *without group violence*, only by the liberals' using the leadership now theirs, to prepare the people psychically, to give them understanding of the urgent necessity for these changes" ("Buying," 24). For Smith, the intellectual and the activist must play the same role when effectual reform is a moral imperative. Her critique of those who believe they would do more harm than good in advocating equality by stirring up racial violence is among her most scathing. This person's objections are "not so much to evil means (as evidenced by many liberals' enthusiasm for war as a means to democracy) nor even to evil ends when they are sufficiently remote and beclouded, nor to deriving profit indirectly from them, but to the soiling of his own hands, the turning of his own stomach, from too close contact with them" ("Buying," 25). Smith closes the essay by reiterating her point that the circumstances of the war provide the opportunity for significant changes to improve the world, not only for its citizens today but for its future citizens: "The price will be high; but it will be a good bargain, a fine 'buy' for us, and for all the earth's children" ("Buying," 30).

Smith pushes the point of activism beyond only intellectuals in "Addressed to Intelligent White Southerners," and this essay was more popular in reprint than "Buying a New World with Old Confederate Bills," topping 250,000 copies sold (Loveland, 80). As its subtitle, "There Are Things to Do," suggests, the essay further reaches out to readers, listing things they can do in their everyday lives and interactions with individuals to combat racism, and calling for dialogue and mutual understanding between races. Smith calls on Rotary clubs, Kiwanis clubs, and similar social and civil organizations to invite black members. Churches must integrate; leaders must be open to labor unions. And again she makes clear to her readers that their successes regionally have global implications. Every act in defiance of segregation, Smith writes, "is a triple victory for racial democracy, for Christianity and for the United

Nations in this war. It is also in the best southern tradition of Jefferson and Robert E. Lee" ("Addressed," 40). And in the vein of her work with the Laurel Falls camp, Smith stresses the centrality of educating children about racial equality in bringing about a truly democratic world: "We can all begin to train our children now to be, not little Nazis, but democratic world citizens. We owe this to them, in order that they may adjust harmoniously and without psychic conflict to the new world democracy which we now dream about and know is coming towards mankind" ("Addressed," 39). Smith's final point of the essay is that such activism has never been more important because, in her estimation, the question is not whether the South will integrate, but *when* and with how little violence. She is convinced that the South is necessarily beginning to desegregate because of the changing economic order caused by industrialization and the war. "The choice is ours only in *what we do about it*; not in the changes themselves" ("Addressed," 43). The obvious plan of action Smith and Snelling framed for their readers was to work to the best of their abilities to usher in not only a harmonious South but a new democratic world. Brinkmeyer amplifies the essay's power in noting that it ultimately considers southern traditionalism as the worst enemy of democracy (136). This would necessarily apply to racial injustice the world over.

South Today ceased publication with the winter 1944–45 number, a special issue on the role of men in the church; the lack of institutional backing left the magazine dependent on subscriptions, and therefore financially unsustainable. Although Snelling's literary career effectively ended with the magazine, Smith's took off with the success of *Strange Fruit*, which became a controversial best seller upon its publication. Through her novels and her memoir, *Killers of the Dream*, and her continued participation as one of the most prominent white southern women in the desegregation movement, Smith continued the legacy of *South Today*'s political activism. She became more anticommunist during the 1950s and 1960s: as Brinkmeyer argues, "It is finally the South's anti-Communism that provides Smith with a ray of hope for the future. She believes that if southerners could ever break free from the binding chains of totalitarianism . . . [they] would not be seduced again by other forms of authoritarianism" (144).

Strange Fruit and *Killers of the Dream* garner most scholarly energy focused on Smith, yet *South Today* and its important work remain overlooked. Its editors' activism was prolific—editorial policies that respected minorities, a reprint program for its articles as viable as any tract ministry, and several trips to conferences across the South further extolling the importance of racial equality. But *South Today* also reveals itself to be ahead of its time. In emphasizing a canon of southern authors and literature that it deemed important on the basis of their political aims and awareness of global issues, the magazine includes figures who would not receive scholarly attention until more recent decades. Also, Smith and Snelling argued that regional, and specifically southern, literature plays an important role as a local barometer for global issues, perhaps even as the internal conscience for a nation waving democracy's flag abroad while its citizens suffered at home. Yet despite her strong political preferences, Smith does so with a literary mind. For her positive reviews of books that offered meaningful and constructive critiques of the South and all of the United States, W. J. Cash complimented Smith as "one of the ablest book critics in the country" (letter to Lillian Smith, February 26, 1941). The essays and reviews of the little magazine published from the mountains of northern Georgia are certainly important documents from the trenches of the earliest moments of the civil rights movement, but the most significant work of *South Today* was providing an outline for what a more complete canon of southern literature based on criteria outside of New Critical tenets might look like: one that did not allow readers to comfortably identify with what they read, but rather pushed them to grow unsettled by the injustices of a too-romanticized, fantasized southern past and democratic present.

On the other hand, the *Kenyon Review* was successful (and continues publication today). The magazine and its reviewers and critics mostly ignored the political issues arising in the South and its literature, focusing instead on aesthetics and form. Southern literature, especially the work of Faulkner, became the wild card in the New Critics' hand as they made a play for America's status as the new home for democracy and art as World War II wound down. The nation could move forward from the New Critical perspective because southern literature acknowledged the moral injustices of segregation and poverty domestically and internationally, and such an interpretation absolved them of any guilt in making such a power play to aid America and its colonialist allies. The result is the creation of a space in which the works of the so-called Southern Renascence could be canonized even before the phrase "southern literature" finally appeared in the *Kenyon Review*. Leslie Fiedler first used the phrase in 1948 in his review of Truman Capote's *Other Voices, Other Rooms*. Fiedler argues that the book's conviction lies in its success as an anthology of southern literature. Fiedler writes: "Poe is there first of all, in the ambivalent image, half fairy-tale, half psychopathic revelation; Faulkner does the décor; the young girls are by Carson McCullers, the freaks by Eudora Welty" (522). Fiedler was no New Critic, but what he does here, even if facetiously, is outline a nascent canon of southern literature, but with different criteria from those of *South Today*. The phrase does not appear again in the *Kenyon Review* until 1955 in a book review, but no matter. By this time, an anthology of southern literature and the collection of essays from which the Renascence got its name had been published. This is the work of late modernism: codifying a canon of modern literature and its characteristics. This nascent canon of southern literature therefore readily met the requirements of the cultural Cold War, capable of presenting democratic virtues even if not overtly political in its aesthetic concerns. Ransom may have tried his best to distance himself from the South professionally, but as the United States emerged from World War II victorious and entered the Cold War, it was still his periodical that prepared the way for its myth.

2

Southern Studies as Area Studies: Faulkner and Provincial Nationalism during the Cold War

Arguably, the establishment of southern literature as an academic discipline has been influenced by scholarly interest in William Faulkner more than interest in any other author. His well-documented critical recovery at the hands of the New Critics in the 1940s and early 1950s is integral to the formalization of both American literary studies and southern literary studies. Indeed, the advent of southern studies can be understood as the creation of area studies for a regional literature and culture within the United States and a nationalistic project of the Cold War. In this usage, "area studies" denotes interdisciplinary academic fields that proliferated during the mid-twentieth century at American universities that studied geographic regions, nations, and cultures that generally "correspond to the new areas of political and economic influence being sought by the United States" (Pletsch, 588). Faulkner's prominence in Louis D. Rubin Jr. and Robert D. Jacobs's volume of literary criticism *Southern Renascence: The Literature of the Modern South* (1953) and his own political and social commentary in the novel *Intruder in the Dust* (1948) demonstrate how southern studies becomes a kind of area studies through his inescapable associations with regional literature and the ease with which he is interpreted as an author concerned with morality and individualism. Formalist scholars transformed Faulkner from an author of regional oddity and the literature of his region into subjects of national import because they were able to identify parallels between the South's racial conundrums and the moral challenges facing American democracy in light of Soviet diplomatic ambitions. In this manner, Faulkner became important to the American modernist canon and formed a way by which the recovery of his work could be extended to an entire southern literary canon, making the study of southern literature simultaneously a provincial and a nationalistic project.

Few would dispute Faulkner's importance to the southern or American literary canon, but he serves as an important figure in my argument about the formation of southern literary studies not because he is a prototypical southern writer, nor because southern literature began with him, though this is the mythology that developed around him in the final decade of his life. Rather, Faulkner appears in the canon as a key figure among the development of southern literary studies because his work served the same important political and ideological purposes for formalist intellectuals, especially New Critics. Moreover, even Faulkner's own work engaged the notion of American exceptionalism through southern exceptionalism, the ideological causes that required a southern area studies. This is the starting point for Lawrence H. Schwartz's *Creating Faulkner's Reputation* (1988). While Malcolm Cowley and others would argue that Faulkner became great because he was a literary genius who would eventually have attained proper honors, Schwartz counters that Faulkner "became one of the beneficiaries of an aesthetic created by an intellectual elite committed to the survival and preeminence of the United States" (28). During the late modernist moment, both New Critics and the New York Intellectuals recuperated Faulkner from his prior reputation—a realist author countering modern society with tales of the barbaric, violent, and corrupt South—to a modernist literary master dealing with the moral challenges of an irrational modern world and as key as T. S. Eliot and Jackson Pollock, whose achievements were products of the "preservation of freedom of expression under the democratic traditions of the West" (Schwartz, 36). What happens to Faulkner and southern literature during this time parallels what Guilbaut says happens to abstract expressionism. Rather than a school of art, however, intellectuals turned to a regional literature in which they could identify a useful aesthetic and divorce it from all political contexts and weed out unsavory political positions associated with the Far Left, socialism, and Marxism. The interest in rehabilitating Faulkner begins at the time, Schwartz explains, when scholars interested in southern literature were looking for "a great literature rooted in the regional consciousness, but one that also transcended provincial nationalism to achieve universality" (94). Faulkner provided just such a convenient New Critical paradox: simultaneous concern for humanity and the peculiar customs of the US South. His distance from "literary radicalism" in the 1930s and containment of history and current events made him politically safe compared to leftist authors such as John Steinbeck.[1] Rather than endorsing the New Deal, associating with suspected Marxists, and encouraging collectivism, Faulkner's perceived southernness emphasized a rugged, sacred individualism and self-determination that was the centerpiece of America's arsenal in the cultural Cold War, and so he became a literary figure on whom intellectuals of the vital center for which Schlesinger called could compromise.

While Schwartz is concerned mainly with Faulkner, this chapter offers a corollary to his argument regarding how Faulkner's recuperation affects the formal study of southern letters. Focusing on Faulkner as an exemplary American writer also raises the question of exemplary southern literature and writers and their relationship to the national canon, providing a pathway to formalizing southern studies. Southern studies emerges as a peculiar manifestation of area studies—not a regional genre—within which unsavory elements of American democracy could be housed as moral problems as opposed to political challenges tarnishing America's image abroad. As Carl E. Pletsch notes, area studies are "academic specialties created during the Cold War to supply governments with advice about policy making" (582). African studies, European studies, and Asian studies are all key examples. This chapter does not propose that southern studies formed as a way for the US government to better understand how to exert its influence within the South; rather, I propose that southern studies, as the field was initially practiced, provided a way for literary critics to better understand America's newfound hegemony and to achieve, through Faulkner and other authors, international cultural influence: provincial nationalism achieving universality. Organizing a canon of southern literature and formalizing its study became tools for such influence. This earliest formal framing of southern literature as the segment of national literature containing America's problems also indicates global contexts because it equipped warriors fighting in the cultural Cold War to better understand the challenges facing American democracy abroad and to counter Soviet attacks on the unsavory political elements of American society. The US State Department directly put this critical work to use in its cultural Cold War offensives: after Faulkner won the Nobel Prize, they recruited him to be a cultural ambassador.[2]

Thomas Borstelmann argues that, going into the postwar period, the greatest foreign policy issue facing the United States was a domestic problem: the existence of segregation among its own peoples while attempting to spread democracy abroad to areas formerly under colonial rule, especially Africa. The Soviet Union told the colonized world that wherever the United States went, along with its money it would also bring Jim Crow, and US tolerance of European colonialism in Africa could be attributed to racial ideas that were held in common between Europe and the United States (70). American attitudes about race were being scrutinized in the international arena, and after World War II efforts were made to shove Jim Crow to the fringes of American society (i.e., locate it only in the South). Nevertheless, racial violence in the South went overnight from being local news rarely heard to big international headlines. "The elemental problem for America's first Cold Warriors in dealing with race," Borstelmann says, "was their inability to wall off white American racial attitudes and practices from the rest of the world and its nonwhite majority" (74–75). The formalized study of southern literature, though, allows just that: literary works portraying racism in which ultimately democratic and American ideals wall off these problems from the real political situation facing the United States during the Cold War. Through the lens of southern studies as area studies, the peculiar ethical challenges of the South paralleled in a less immediately dangerous way America's challenges abroad. Segregation became a cultural difference within American literature and culture beyond the purview of national and, by extrapolation, international law.

Faulkner saw his work and southern literature mobilized to support democracy on all stages of the Cold War, and he participated in this mobilization, thought reluctantly at first. His understanding of literature's ethical influence is perhaps nowhere clearer than in his Nobel acceptance speech:

> I believe that man will not merely endure: he will prevail. . . . The poet's, the writer's, duty is to write about these things. It is his privilege to help man endure by lifting his heart, by reminding him of the courage and honor and hope and pride and compassion and pity and sacrifice which have been the glory of his past. The poet's voice need not merely be the record of man, it can be one of the props, the pillars to help him endure and prevail. ("Address," 120)

Faulkner saw his own writing and others' as not merely an account of (an assumedly westernized) humanity but a key element in its survival because it reinforced certain values—courage, honor, hope, pride, and so on. Later in his life as a cold warrior, though, in 1956, Faulkner wrote to David Kirk, "There are seventeen million Negroes [in the United States]. Let us have them on our side, rather than on that of Russia" (*Selected Letters*, 395), indicating that a turn toward communism among blacks because of its integrationist sympathies was an outcome he thought plausible and one he wished to avoid. Given his anticommunism, one might also interpret the comment to mean that for Faulkner one of the best reasons to address civil rights concerns is simply so that blacks would not become communists.[3] Read together, Faulkner's comment to Kirk (a firmly established conservative) and the earlier remarks in the Nobel acceptance speech show a perceived disconnect between the values of courage, honor, hope, and pride and the immorality of communism compatible with the Cold War vital center. Deborah Cohn states that Faulkner's Nobel win and critical recuperation made him a "simultaneously American and universal writer" (394); I would add to that list, of course, southern. Moreover, the themes of his work had great international appeal. Cohn further notes that this was one of many features that made Faulkner a useful figure for US diplomatic interests. He was "the representative of the center and its hegemonic designs; the vocal proponent and sometime critic of the United States and its democracy; and the author whose work resonated in postcolonial nations and those facing U.S. encroachment" (396). Audiences abroad found him quite affable, too, despite his introverted personality and heavy drinking. Via this complex amalgamation of literary themes, critical recognition, and personality quirks that makes up William Faulkner, the Cold War purpose for southern literature and its study in part emerge as the portrayal of values that also happen to be claimed by the United States in its championing of capitalistic democracy as an alternative to communism abroad. Furthermore, in understanding the conflict between the South's minorities and their oppressors, the United States could better understand its role as the disciple of democracy among nations newly freed from colonial rule.

With Faulkner as the author around whom southern area studies organizes, Louis D. Rubin Jr. and Robert D. Jacobs emerge as important critics organizing it. Fred Hobson calls *Southern Renascence: The Literature of the Modern South*, the volume of essays Rubin and Jacobs edited, "the origins of modern southern literature as an academic discipline" (743). Michael Kreyling echoes that sentiment, specifically about Rubin's career, saying, "Few will dispute the claim that Rubin is the primary architect and developer of southern literary study" in the twentieth century (*Inventing Southern Literature*, 41). The clearest marker of Rubin's agenda for southern literature is a stringent formalism through which he plays, as Kreyling describes, guardian of the southern canon, preserving the vision of the South held by the twelve Nashville Agrarians in *I'll Take My Stand* (1930), which omitted its explicit political trappings, namely, racism (48). Yet the real import of Rubin's interpretive balancing act between the South's history and its literature is that he seems to have a certain purpose in mind for the field: an area studies of the South. The preface to *Southern Renascence* explains that he and Jacobs originally conceived of the book as a special issue of the *Hopkins Review*. After gauging the response to the special issue proposal, "it was realized just how widespread was the *latent* interest in southern writing, and how potentially important a thoroughgoing survey and analysis of the literature of the modern South might be" (vii; italics mine). Rubin and Jacobs indicate that there has been a present but undeveloped critical interest in the literature of the US South. Presumably this latent interest lay among their formalist colleagues in literary criticism; this suggests that literary critics busy positioning America's national literature as the best artistic examples for the free world saw potential for but did not realize how southern literature fit into any nationalist canon. Rubin and Jacobs help to provide just that by leveraging Faulkner into their area studies of the South, acknowledging in their preface that they sought to provide southern literary studies as a way for scholars to better understand American literature.

For scholars, Faulkner is the most important figure included in Rubin and Jacobs's project, but also significant are correlations drawn between distinctly southern themes and the national zeitgeist of the Cold War. Walter Sullivan, in his contribution, argues that a recurring theme in southern fiction is the Civil War's disturbance of the moral concurrence of the public and private spheres, in which the traditional family falters (119). Sullivan additionally states, referring directly to Faulkner's opus:

> Because in the Old South the honor and the pride were there, not as individual virtues in isolated men, but as a part of the public consciousness, the moral basis on which the culture was constructed. This is the reason that the [Civil] War has been used so often by so many Southern writers. It is the grand image of the novelist, the period when the "ultimate truths" with which Mr. Faulkner says the writer must deal, existed as commonly recognized values within a social framework. *It is the only moment in American history when a completely developed national ethic was brought to a dramatic crisis.* (125; italics mine)

Sullivan's explication of the southern writer's relationship to the Old South through the Civil War certainly fits what has been a cornerstone of southern studies, yet he presents his version of the southern experience and understanding of history and ethics as commensurate with the national experience. From this point, it follows that southern literature reveals for its scholars how a commonly held morality centered on pride and honor confronts and endures a challenge to its integrity. In Sullivan's depiction, comparisons beg to be drawn between the southern ethic he describes and a similar American ethic developing during the Cold War: belief in God in the face of godless communism, the self-determination of the individual, the nuclear family. Given these comparisons, scholars at the time could learn from southern literature's portrayals of its ethical and moral challenges (the simultaneously political problem of slavery, for example) and its confrontation with crisis how best to promulgate and protect America's ethics abroad in an equally precarious and challenging climate.

Of particular importance to the collection is an essay by a figure who would play a significant role in the shaping of southern studies. C. Vann Woodward, then a professor of history at Johns Hopkins, contributed his well-known essay "The Irony of Southern History" to *Southern Renascence*. In it, Woodward argues that studying the South as an "eccentric" segment of the United States is important not because doing so will enhance our understanding of the South, "for from a broader point of view it is not the South but America that is unique among the peoples of the world. This eccentricity arises out of the American legend of success and victory, a legend that is not shared by any other people of the civilized word" (63). Implied in his comment is that the study of the South, its literature, and place in history is paramount for understanding America and its literature and place in history. To make that connection, he draws parallels between the economic situation facing the United States in the 1950s and that of the US South during the nineteenth century, as well as comparing the world opposition and resentment of American successes with southern attitudes about the South's defeat in the Civil War. Most powerful and significant in the essay, however, is his comment about what history is and where the history of America is located.

Early on, Woodward comments that history is commonly regarded as the bad things that happen to other people, implying that America's history has been obscured by the comparison of Europe's recent turmoil with the legendary status of the Founders and Revolutionary War heroes. Moreover, the comment implies that because most Americans have not suffered a major military defeat and the world wars were not fought in North America, they are disconnected from their history, as opposed to southerners, who did suffer military defeat, and Europeans, who witnessed war firsthand. He declares, "With all her terrible power and new responsibilities combined with her illusions of innocence and her legends of immunity from frustration and defeat, America stands in greater need than she ever did of understanding her own history" (78). He ultimately proposes in "The Irony of Southern History" that the way for Americans to connect to their history is to study the South because southerners know from firsthand experience that "history has happened to our people in our part of the world" (79). The United States can best understand how to lead the free world from its own precarious position of power through the South's historical circumstances and its literature's representation and interpretation of that history.

Where Woodward's essay calls for a greater emphasis on studying the history of the South—which could be extrapolated as part of the emerging area studies of the South—the rest of Rubin and Jacobs's book answers. As the clearest guiding principle of the book, the call is answered by studying the South through the lens of William Faulkner's work and the circumstances of its composition. Faulkner is the primary focus of five individual essays and appears as a point of comparison in nearly every other entry in part 3, "Novelists of the South," and in all four pieces in part 2, "The Themes of Southern Literature." (In contrast, Robert Penn Warren and his fiction are the focus of only two essays.)[4] Rubin and Jacobs make this explicit in their editors' note to a symposium that opens the book's second part. The symposium features the sociologists Howard W. Odum and John MacLachlan, and in their note, the editors emphasize a question posed by Donald Davidson in an address to Mississippi State College in 1950:

> I turn to sociology and ask whether it can account for the appearance in Mississippi, of all places, of William Faulkner, in the three decades between 1920 and 1950.... Can sociology also explain why William Faulkner, or some novelist of comparative stature, did *not* appear, during this period, somewhere north of the Ohio—say, in Massachusetts or Wisconsin? (Rubin and Jacobs, editors' note, "Literature in the South," 83)

In hindsight, Davidson's pondering seems a little preposterous, unanswerable outside of intangible speculation and perhaps irrelevant; yet it raises "a root question," according to Rubin and Jacobs, "one which must be thoroughly considered in any serious attempt to understand the modern literature produced by Southerners" (83). Their use of Davidson's question as a key point of inquiry bears a couple of significant implications for *Southern Renascence*. It more pointedly than other passages of the collection establishes an area studies project, especially in Davidson's call for sociology—a discipline closely associated with other area studies—to answer what was for scholars at the height of renewed interest in Faulkner's work a burning question. Most importantly, the question all at once binds together the perceived supremacy of the southern regional, the hegemonic aspirations of American national literature, and the figure of William Faulkner.

Yet Odum seems dubious regarding Davidson's question. In his contribution to the seminar, Odum casts doubt on whether Faulkner's southernness has anything to do with his greatness. Odum addresses the problems with Davidson's understanding of sociology, then explores how different variables—socioeconomic, political, and otherwise—could be construed as factors in not just Faulkner's southern origins but the origins of any other author from the South or other US region. He even mentions the literary importance of H. L. Mencken, whose influences within the publishing industry opened the door for many southerners (99–100). His co-respondent,

MacLachlan, on the other hand, readily accepts Davidson's assertion that the South has something to do with Faulkner's greatness. In "No Faulkner in Metropolis," MacLachlan contends that Faulkner's familiarity with the rural allowed him in his fiction to create a place, unlike urban landscapes, where "there is nothing between its folk and the elemental forces of the universe, no canopies, walls, clinics, ranks of professionals and bureaucrats to stand between them and life and death" (107). The distinction between Odum's and MacLachlan's responses is significant because the former provides a coy critique in highlighting the challenges sociology faces in undertaking such a question, whereas the latter unquestioningly embraces southern exceptionalism and area studies of the South as the best method for understanding the moral, existential plight facing the individual in modernity.

Race does not take center stage in the area studies formulation of *Southern Renascence* until Irene C. Edmonds's "Faulkner and the Black Shadow," which is the book's last essay directly addressing southern studies' founding figure and the only essay written by a black scholar for the collection. Rubin included his former student in the collection despite resistance to her inclusion.[5] Regardless, his gesture toward inclusivity did not prevent the book from being charged by some reviewers with, as Kreyling put it in *Inventing Southern Literature*, "parochialism and special pleading" (48). Edmonds begins her essay by quoting Shreve McCannon, who asks his roommate at Harvard, Quentin Compson, to tell about the South in *Absalom, Absalom!* (1936). Her essay seems to stand in for Quentin's response; Edmonds indicates in her consideration of black characters in Faulkner's work that understanding blacks and their relationship with their oppressors is vital to understanding the South. She declares that the South's fall has roots not so much in "a death struggle between decadent Sartorises and materialistic Snopeses" as in claiming to be Christian, yet not behaving as such, particularly in regard to race relations (192). Faulkner rarely attempted such an understanding, she argues, pointing to Lucas Beauchamp of *Go Down, Moses* (1942) and *Intruder in the Dust* as the only black character whose inner thoughts are revealed through narration (201). However, Edmonds's critique does not so much present how Faulkner's presentation of race could be a model for intellectuals grappling with racial discord in the United States as it demonstrates how best to avoid a treatment of the problem altogether. In pointing to disparities between the character of Dilsey in *The Sound and the Fury* (1929) and the strong-willed Lucas Beauchamp in *Intruder in the Dust*, Edmonds concludes that Faulkner's fiction as a whole does not contribute a solution to the race question in the South. And though she concludes that Faulkner deems slavery the cause of the South's failures and struggles, she says, "What Faulkner has done is to present situations and reserve any personal judgment. He does not write social protest" (206). So if the archetypal author of southern literature and culture takes no activist stance on improving conditions for minorities in the South, why should its scholars and intellectuals?

It is precisely this kind of formalist posturing that *Southern Renascence* features: praising works by framing their significance within questions of aesthetics, morality, internal conflict, or individual worth as they relate to a grand American society modeled on Faulkner's Yoknapatawpha County, the fictional setting for many of his novels and microcosm of idealized southernness, rather than addressing any collectivist or progressive narrative advocating change within the real world. While the collection does devote essays to other authors in its pages, the figure of Faulkner is what makes possible the area studies paradigm of southern studies. This is significant not only for southern studies but for Faulkner, as well, who was alive and witnessing this mobilization of his novels and stories and found himself in a position to participate in it.

A critical project such as Rubin and Jacobs's thus bears significance not only for understanding the inception of southern studies as an area studies in Pletsch's theorization of area studies and the development of Faulkner's critical history, but also for Faulkner's own attitude toward the South. Without a doubt, he felt the intellectual pressures that scholars of the emerging canons of American and southern literature placed on him. Frequently an audience to interpretations—political or otherwise—of his own works, he maintained a distance. Kreyling argues, "Faulkner had few or partially formed ideas and judgments on many of these issues, and he was normally reluctant to divulge, and never willing to debate, most of them," requiring a critical "fabrication" of the larger-than-life figure, "Faulkner" (130). Kreyling further comments, "William Faulkner was sincere when he said he wanted anonymity, that he resented imprisonment in the role of representative author, that his later work is marked by the desire to unwrite or subvert his public image" (132). On the other hand, *Intruder in the Dust*, a novel from just past the midpoint of his career, assists in the formulation of Kreyling's "Faulkner" who became integral to the nascent southern studies rather than separating the individual Faulkner from the public figure of "Faulkner." The novel does so in its representation of racism facing the US and South after World War II and its suggested solutions.

Intruder in the Dust, which predates Rubin and Jacobs's *Southern Renascence* by five years, departs from Faulkner's previous work in both genre and direct political content. Faulkner himself referred to the novel as a "mystery-murder" (Blotner, *Faulkner*, 1246). Moreover, Faulkner's main motivation for writing it seems mostly financial; he had asked his agent, Harold Ober, to seek magazine serial publication to maximize his profits on the manuscript, even acknowledging that he could leave out a chapter to make it more suitable for "popular consumption" (1252). Beyond its detective story form, *Intruder* differs from earlier work in that the novel not only serves as a case history of the nascent civil rights struggles but provides pointed commentary on solutions to the problems in contemporary southern race relations. Prior works certainly address race relations—even Gavin Stevens speaks about race in *Light in August* (1932)—but usually in a summary, descriptive manner as opposed to prescriptive: Shreve McCannon speculates at the end of *Absalom, Absalom!* that blacks will "conquer the western hemisphere" through racial assimilation (302), and Ike McCaslin in *Go Down, Moses* proclaims the South cursed for slavery and landownership (266). It is not until *Intruder in the Dust*, however, that any character proposes solutions to the real-world problem of racism and deliberately casts the problem as anything but a political one.

Intruder in the Dust centers on Lucas Beauchamp, a black man who frustrates the folks in the fictional Yoknapatawpha County because he has white ancestors and refuses to behave in the way blacks were expected to in the 1940s. Lucas is wrongly arrested for the murder of Vinson Gowrie. At Lucas's request, the sixteen-year-old Charles "Chick" Mallison and his black companion, Aleck Sander, search for evidence of the real murderer. Lucas had rescued Chick when he fell into a frozen creek on a rabbit hunt four years earlier (Chick attempted to pay for Lucas's care but was refused). Their efforts exonerate Lucas, whose legal representation, Gavin Stevens, Chick's uncle, is barely a party to the activities.

Early reviewers immediately noticed a political tinge in the novel. Calling it a "tract," Edmund Wilson, in his frequently cited 1948 review, surmises *Intruder in the Dust* "seems to have been partly inspired by the crisis at the time of the recent war in the relations between white and Negroes and by the recently proposed legislation for guaranteeing Negro rights" (122). Yet few later critics who refer to Wilson go on to include his more polemical comment on Lucas's rescue from the lynch mob. He says of the would-be lynchers leaving in their cars to return to Beat Four, the community in the outlying areas of Yoknapatawpha County where the murder took place, "There has been nothing so exhilarating in its way since the triumphs of the Communist-led workers in the early Soviet films" (124). The description importantly compares *Intruder in the Dust* with propagandistic art, framing the coalition of Chick, Aleck, Stevens, and Miss Habersham (a spinster who assists Chick and Aleck) as having specific collective political aims beyond simply rescuing Lucas. Wilson is not alone in detecting the political content of Faulkner's detective novel. Another early reviewer, Elizabeth Hardwick, perceives Gavin Stevens's expressed views on the race issue to be nothing more than a "want [of] violence in order to prove themselves right" that immediate integration would cause more harm than good (1133). She, too, evokes Cold War apprehensions, suggesting that the position held by *Intruder in the Dust* could cause the continued popularity of communism among African Americans.

Some years later, however, Cleanth Brooks, in the first extensive scholarly treatment of *Intruder in the Dust*, discounts both Wilson's and Hardwick's political readings of the novel. Being the consummate New Critic, Brooks could not accept a simple dismissal of the novel as political, for doing so acknowledges political content. "A more cogent objection to this novel," he declares, "is the incoherence of the plot," with the speeches providing that political content being one of the incoherent elements (280). Alternatively, Brooks reads *Intruder in the Dust* as the story of a boy growing into manhood through conflict with his community. Chick's own ethical compass, which spurs him to accept Lucas's request and extend justice and equality to Lucas, steers him through the storm of racial discontent. Stevens's ramblings are, in Brooks's understanding, "subordinate to the main matter: Charles Mallison's development toward wider sympathies and a sharper ethical conscience" (288–89). Such a reading of Chick's moral individuality as the solution to what is really a rampant political problem within the South is not only a classic New Critical perspective but another move offering a palliative for racial unrest that does not solve the underlying issues of discrimination (such as the poverty and vigilantism of the Beat Four lynch mob).

Most scholars regard *Intruder in the Dust* as one of Faulkner's lesser works, perhaps following Brooks's lead, citing Stevens's moralizing speeches as poorly connected to the narrative. Jean E. Graham suggests that critics have applied a double standard to *Intruder in the Dust*. Other characters—Graham gives Quentin Compson and Jason in *The Sound and the Fury* as examples—have extended dialogues guilty of the same transgressions levied against Stevens, yet one finds no prevalent dismissal of them as characters in the scholarship (78–79). Graham ultimately argues for Stevens's importance to the novel as a tutor attempting to instruct his nephew concerning their southern community's long-held racism. The interaction between the two results in a complex dialogue between uncle and nephew. Indeed, to dismiss the novel altogether on the basis of Gavin Stevens is a terrible mistake and a great irony. Stevens's pontificating is what makes *Intruder in the Dust* at the same time a significant point of departure for Faulkner (no character of his before had so directly addressed current events) and a difficult text for literary scholars of his day to deal with. The novel presents Faulkner's understanding of how the South at the start of the Cold War fit the discussion taken up by critics such as Rubin, Jacobs, and Brooks who founded formalized southern studies, yet it is this same school of criticism that passed over the novel because it was too overtly political.

The keys to this are, of course, Stevens's long monologues, which fall short of any kind of meaningful action. Such comes to light even better when considering Faulkner's own description of Stevens in an October 1948 conversation about *Intruder in the Dust* with Malcolm Cowley during a visit at Cowley's home. According to published notes Cowley scribbled down about the visit after Faulkner's departure, "Stevens, he explained, was not speaking for the author, but for the best type of liberal Southerners; that is how they feel about Negroes. 'If the race problem were just left to the children,' Faulkner told me, 'they'd be solved soon enough'" (*The Faulkner-Cowley File*, 110–11). The latter assertion plays out in the pages of *Intruder in the Dust*, for it is through the efforts of Chick, Aleck, and Miss Habersham that Lucas is exonerated, and certainly not through any lawyering or philosophical waxing on Stevens's part. As Noel Polk explains, Stevens is mostly a smoke-blower where race is concerned (and so is Faulkner). Polk points to the number of times Stevens lights his corncob pipe at the end of speeches and the way he reaches for the offensive abstraction "Sambo" when addressing the broad issues of the race problem as opposed to actually naming his client, Lucas Beauchamp, and addressing legal methods by which to defend him. Moreover, *Intruder in the Dust* was not the first time Stevens had appeared in Faulkner's work to speak about race. Near the end of *Light in August*, Stevens, described as a "Harvard graduate, a Phi Beta Kappa," makes a brief appearance in the capacity of district attorney to provide commentary on the lynching of Joe Christmas, a man of uncertain racial origins accused of murdering a white woman (444). Stevens concludes that the root cause of Christmas's troubled past and violent demise is the dueling sensibilities and identities within him caused by the simultaneous presence of white and black blood, thus suggesting an antimiscegenation stance (448–49). Even here when Stevens does not address the impact of racial tensions of the South or even the whole nation, he seems a man of lofty ideals, not meaningful action.

Despite Faulkner's denial to Cowley that Stevens spoke for him, critics have long regarded the character as the author's political mouthpiece. More importantly, Stevens's commentary in *Intruder* serves as an instrument of southern area studies: a critical framework for understanding southern racial redemption that obscures and depoliticizes the problem by emphasizing individual moral responsibility and duty to country. If not outwardly, his statements support certain values key to American ambitions for global democracy during the Cold War. Most telling are Stevens's claims about defending an American "homogeneity." He tells Chick they are defending it as opposed to tradition or "politics or beliefs." He also states, "I'm not speaking of Sambo right now; I'll get to him in a minute" (150). The white South stands alone, Stevens claims, for "the rest of the country has had to surrender voluntarily more and more of its personal and private liberty to continue to afford the United States. And of course we will continue to defend it [homogeneity]" (150). Here, through Stevens, Faulkner reveals and endorses one of the great paradoxes of southern political sensibilities of the twentieth century: individual, provincial pride that is also nationalistic. As his comments go on, Stevens seems to be lecturing to a wider audience than just his nephew: "Only a few of us know that only from homogeneity comes anything of a people or for a people of durable and lasting value—the literature, the art, the science, that minimum of government and police which is the meaning of freedom and liberty, and perhaps most valuable of all a national character worth anything in a crisis" (151). If democratic art and values are what Cold War intellectuals seek to enable the US fight against the contagion of communism, then the South ostensibly has all these things to offer. But how can homogeneity be preserved?

In Stevens's analysis, it is a delicate balance. Reasoning similar to that used by Stevens in his homogeneity comments appears again in his argument about northern interference in the race question. In his famous remarks toward the end of *Intruder in the Dust*, he states, "I only say that the injustice is ours, the South's. We must expatiate and abolish it ourselves, alone and without help or even (with thanks) advice" (199). In other words, the problem can be solved through methods he has mentioned before, such as "character," and with little intrusion from the federal government, a "minimum of government and police" (151). When comparing these statements with Faulkner's later essays, Stevens does appear to speak for the author. In a response to the *Brown v. Board of Education* ruling, "On Fear: Deep South in Labor; Mississippi" (originally published in *Harper's*, June 1956), Faulkner issues a dire warning to his fellow white Mississippians who have ignored opportunities for economic growth because of their intent to prevent blacks from achieving social and economic equality. Part of what white Mississippians have done is accept federal assistance, such as cotton subsidies ("On Fear," 98). Faulkner characterizes being beholden to the federal government as antithetical to freedom, more akin to a "caste system" (106). He concludes:

> We must be free not because we claim freedom, but because we practice it; our freedom must be buttressed by a homogeny equally and unchallengeably free, no matter what color they are, so that all the other inimical forces everywhere—systems political or religious or racial or national—will not just respect us because we practice freedom, they will fear us because we do. ("On Fear," 106)

On the first level, Faulkner's essay echoes Stevens's refusal of outside assistance in solving the region's race problem. This essay also echoes what Stevens goes on to say regarding political and moral homogeneity. Stevens uses as an example minority individuals who share the same values of whites and take the "long view" of civil rights (152). He claims that "he" (blacks who share values with whites and are patient in their hope for equal rights) and "us" (Stevens's homogeneous white southerners)

> should confederate: swap him the rest of the economic and political and cultural privileges which are his right, for the reversion of his capacity to wait and endure and survive. Then we would prevail; together we would dominate the United States; we would present a front not only impregnable but not even to be threatened by a mass of people who no longer have anything in common save a frantic greed for money and a basic fear of failure of national character which they hid from one another behind a loud lipservice to a flag. (153)

It is preposterous, of course, to suggest that contentious racial relations over hundreds of years built character among white and black southerners and that their differences can be solved once and for all through an economy of generosity in which white southerners give black southerners their rights in exchange for all the brutality endured. Yet we can interpret Stevens's claim here, considered with his earlier direct comments on homogeneity, to suggest dual meanings for the homogeneity the rest of the country lacks: a separation of equal races that remain homogeneous and a moral homogeneity valuing national pride that crosses race and geographic region within the United States and runs deeper that "lipservice." Joe Karaganis assists in clarifying that in Stevens's logic, the protection of this homogeneity is crucial for the protection of the United States. Furthermore, he claims: "*Confederation*, in this respect, is not just a regional solution to the race question, but a model of national redemption in which the white South stands, unexpectedly, in the vanguard" (121). Karaganis's presentation of Stevens's assertions presents this confederation as southern area studies: the South leads with a model for the best management of national—and international—tensions. Faulkner then repeats this rhetoric in "On Fear."

As argued in Stevens's foregoing comment, Chick, Aleck, Miss Habersham, and Lucas *confederate* through their efforts to solve the murder. Their motivation is framed not as an interest in racial justice or civil rights but as an interest in the moral right of preventing the lynching of an innocent man. Their confederation demonstrates their valuing of honor, pride, hope, and courage, which Faulkner would go on to mention in his Nobel acceptance speech. Given such emphasis, the argument in *Intruder* is, and Karaganis agrees, that individuals who honor these values in particular circumstances are necessary to make meaningful changes to race relations in the South and the United States. Progress begins with individuals and spreads virally rather than from outside influence and agitation (124–25). Faulkner's model is therefore not one of collectivity, which would be too closely associated with communism during the Cold War. Here Faulkner divulges one of his great political fears within his art. Polk notes that the notion of any group acting collectively, in Faulkner's mind and the collective consciousness of Cold War intellectuals, is unappealing precisely because collectivism most frequently manifested itself as communism after World War II. This also applied to the new government programs that "in Faulkner's view, were depriving individual man of his capacity and of his right to depend upon himself" (175). Stevens's lectures may be nothing but smoke blown at Chick, but these lengthy talks suggest more broadly what southerners and Americans can do to combat these unsavory political developments in the United States and abroad. Polk further explains:

> Southern whites and blacks, he [Faulkner through Stevens] argued, had more in common with each other than any Southerner had with any Northerner; therefore, Southerners, black and white, had better stick together to stave off any outsider's challenge to their way of life. By the same token, he felt all Americans, black, white, southern, northern, needed to stick together in order to present a united front to combat the menace of communism. (176)

Faulkner's vehement anticommunism as a context for *Intruder* is important for two reasons. First of all, the novel does, in this light, transmit Faulkner's political sensibilities regarding issues newsworthy in 1948: discrimination and communism. Second, it shows how Faulkner's sensibilities are complicit in Rubin's and his fellow New Critics' organization of the nascent field of southern studies: America can learn how best to contain its political ills by watching how the South labors to contain its own. *Intruder* becomes a literary text contributing to area studies of the US South.

Elizabeth Hardwick's aforementioned excoriating review of the novel also notes these gestures toward area studies. "The sickness of *Intruder in the Dust*, the fear and despair," which she sees driving the political agenda of southern resolve in solving its own shortcomings,

> are intimately connected with the future of Faulkner's career, *a career which demands that there be a South*, not just a geographical section and an accent, but a reasonably autonomous unit, a kind of family ready, and even with a measure of geniality, to admit the existence of the people next door and to cooperate in the necessary civic responsibilities, . . . but beyond that unique and separate, not to be reproached, advised, or mourned for the goings on behind the door. (1131; italics mine)

We can read a double meaning in Hardwick's statement. Initially she seems to say that a career such as Faulkner's required there to be a South to use as subject matter. (To say that Faulkner's career would not exist without the South is, perhaps, reason enough to be run out on a rail from English departments, given the sheer quantity and depth of scholarship produced on his work and life.) Of greater consequence is the second interpretation of Hardwick's remark, and what I believe she intends: Faulkner's career and the study of it *command* that there be a South. His works foster the theorization of the South as a discrete unit for twentieth-century historical and sociological study (if even in the least by way of Donald Davidson's misguided question that Howard Odum was forced to answer) and the formal study of its literature (for which Faulkner has been taken as the supreme example and starting point). And in the case of *Intruder*, the South must maintain its independence by being allowed to lead itself to whatever destiny after a sordid and brutal history of racial injustice, even if that destiny includes the secret hope for violence to prove all nonsouthern meddlers wrong. But because of the entangled, unique history of white and black in Faulkner's South, it can lead the way as the model for the management of such tensions.

William Faulkner never escaped the "Faulkner" figuration posited by Kreyling, and neither *Intruder* nor the increased amount of attention his work would receive in the years after his Nobel win and prominence in *Southern Renascence* would assist him in gaining any more distance from it. Instead Faulkner became not only the rallying point but a participant in the founding of southern literary studies as an area studies by which intellectuals better understood what it meant to be American—to value tradition, history, the individual's moral initiative and ingenuity in solving problems, and to be uninvolved in the affairs of others (or at least maintain the appearance of being uninvolved)—and how to further contain unsavory national political problems by making them into an object of formalistic literary study. The emerging field of southern area studies enabled what Matthew Lassiter and Joseph Crespino have termed "color-blind myths of American innocence," in which racial unrest and the civil rights movement happened only in the South, where they did not harm narratives of exceptional American leadership during the Cold War (7).

In the wake of the emerging southern studies, the South's unwavering self-determinism seems to influence the United States in its dealings with European allies regarding its colonial holdings. Borstelmann recounts that, to maintain good working relationships and free commerce with European nations and their colonies, the United States allowed its distaste for outside rule (akin to the South's distaste for meddling) to slow down its pressing for colonial independence even as its own cultural influence expanded (68–70). During the 1950s, President Eisenhower and his administration were satisfied with the "political containment of racial problems rather than their solutions" both domestically and internationally (Borstelmann, 86), even after President Truman had desegregated the armed forces and *Brown v. Board of Education* had nullified "separate but equal." By 1954, Faulkner himself was making his first voyages abroad at the behest of the State Department as a cultural ambassador, which he began with an understanding that "the need to resist Communism took precedence over his concern that domestic racisms undermined the democratic system" (Cohn, 398). His first assignment was to an international writers' conference in São Paulo, Brazil, with legs through Lima and Caracas; the purpose of the trip was "improving relations between the United States and the countries of South America" (Minter, 232–33). The mission was a success when Faulkner was not debilitated by his heavy drinking, which prompted State Department officials to keep a close eye on him to avoid bad international press. Faulkner earned enough respect from the US government to be assigned to a US-sponsored seminar in Nagano, Japan. This seminar was part of a larger effort to "promote American studies abroad" (Cohn, 401), enhancing the reputation of American ideas, culture, politics, and ideology. While participating in the seminars, Faulkner drew comparisons between the military defeat of Japan and the US South, suggesting that from the ashes of both could emerge a literary tradition espousing the "universal truth" of freedom via democracy. The seminar proved a huge success for US objectives in Japan (Cohn, 400–401). His participation in the seminar further closes the gap between Faulkner and "Faulkner"; that is, the Nagano seminar solidly correlates Faulkner's literary and political ambitions and activities with the aims of New Critics refounding democratic art on American (and southern) soil.

In 1966, four years after Faulkner's death, Malcolm Cowley attempted to sum up the writer's career. Cowley claimed that Faulkner retained his "genius" as a writer late in his career despite the challenges of isolation, provincialism, and sudden stardom—all of these related to his southern origins. Cowley admires Faulkner the most "among the great dead" because "he was the proudest man I knew. The pride made him act by his own standards, which were always difficult ones" (*The Faulkner-Cowley File*, 175). Faulkner is no longer, or perhaps never was, judged by those exacting personal standards of his but is judged today by a knowledge community much less interested in him than in "Faulkner," the area study that his fiction demanded for his canonization, and how its politics framed America's unique situation entering the Cold War.

3

American Canons, Southern Fiction, and the Institution of Literary Prizes

The evening of January 28, 1953, found the authors of two decorated and highly regarded novels at the same dinner party. The day before, the National Book Foundation had presented Ralph Ellison with a National Book Award for *Invisible Man*. Although it was only the fourth presentation of the award, the ceremony drew much attention and provided Ellison with the opportunity to mingle with other acclaimed American authors: William Carlos Williams, Eudora Welty, and William Faulkner, to name a few. The dinner party, however, gave Ellison time to do more than simply mingle with Robert Penn Warren, whose *All the King's Men* had won the Pulitzer Prize in 1947. The two quickly developed a professional relationship at this dinner party. Warren asked Ellison that very evening to collaborate with him on a television documentary on American history (Rampersad, 272). This professional relationship developed into a friendship when their families spent time together in Rome in 1956. Other professional connections between the two include working with the same editor, Albert Erskine, at Random House; Warren later interviewing and featuring Ellison in *Who Speaks for the Negro?* (Warren's edited interviews and commentaries on the leaders of the civil rights movement, published in 1965); and their service in several academic positions throughout their long careers. Their friendship ended with Ellison delivering a eulogy for Warren at his memorial service in 1989 (Blotner, *Robert Penn Warren*, 500).

It is in the context of these connections that I reexamine the roles that Robert Penn Warren's *All the King's Men* and Ralph Ellison's *Invisible Man* played in the formation of literary canons in the United States and the conditions for the formalization of the study of southern literature during the postwar period. Warren's and Ellison's abandonment of extreme political views serves as an example of the commitment among writers and intellectuals at the dawn of the Cold War to hold fast to the politically safe and savory. Three factors support my historicization of these novels. The first is Warren's disavowal of Agrarian political views and Ellison's rejection of communism, which both illustrate the commitment among writers and intellectuals to hold fast to Arthur Schlesinger Jr.'s vital center. The commitment to centrist, safe politics makes both *All the King's Men* and *Invisible Man* examples of late modernist fiction in their humanist or moralist agendas despite their deeply politicized settings. Second, the recognition of these novels by prize committees, each charged with conferring their award on a work of American fiction of the highest artistic—and politically amenable—merit, indicates that these works were held in the highest regard by their contemporaries as representations of American values, and that the persistent treatment of these works in the scholarship on American literature suggest an importance to the late modernist impulse for canon formation. Finally, these novels' separate portrayals of political conundrums perceived as distinctively southern universalizes them as a part of the American experience by emphasizing the US South's valuing of the individual as a key component in shoring up the vital center in American political aspirations. This reinterpretation of the place of *All the King's Men* and *Invisible Man* in American letters is significant because it reveals the treatment of southern literary studies as a kind of area studies that is necessarily one and the same with the formalization and institutionalization of American literary studies.

In the decades that followed the publication of *I'll Take My Stand* (1930), its most visible and most critically acclaimed contributor was Robert Penn Warren, who won three Pulitzers and a National Book Award for his poetry and served as poet laureate of the United States. Warren was also a respected critic and author of textbooks that fundamentally changed the approach to literature in the college classroom. Perhaps his success can be attributed to the fact that no other Agrarian seems to have recanted his segregationist beliefs faster than Warren, nor perhaps—along with John Crowe Ransom and Allen Tate—clung to formalism so tightly. Most telling of Warren's commitment to New Critical formalism is his application of it to his past in the opening pages of *Who Speaks for the Negro?* (1965). He reminisces about an essay he wrote—a "cogent and human defense of segregation"—during the winter of 1929 and admits not reading the essay in its published form for concern of it making him "uncomfortable." Going on, Warren states, "In fact, while writing it, I had experienced some vague discomfort, like the discomfort you feel when your poem doesn't quite come off, when you've had to fake, or twist, or pad it, when you haven't really explored the impulse" (10–11).

No doubt the essay to which he refers is "The Briar Patch," his contribution to *I'll Take My Stand*. What is most notable about his recollection of the essay is the nature of the uneasiness it gave him. Warren seems concerned with neither the ramifications of being a committed segregationist nor his audience's reaction to Agrarian politics. He certainly does not seem concerned about the future and welfare of those whose fate his essay most pointedly addresses. Rather, the essay makes him uncomfortable because it reads like a bad poem. While one could interpret Warren's statement as a deployment of figurative language to suggest that any argument in support of segregation holds its basis only in imagined supportive points about the conditions of the US South, this is nonetheless an instance in which Warren attempts to depoliticize his former associations and beliefs. According to his reminiscing about the essay, the gross inhumanity of segregation is nothing worse than an overwrought poem.

Warren's retreat toward the center seems to have more basis in his artistic and critical commitments than his political sensibilities, though they become one and the same. This is repeatedly evident in the progression of his literary career. One significant marker in particular is his essay "Literature as Symptom," which he provided for *Who Owns America? A New Declaration of Independence* (1936). This sequel of sorts to *I'll Take My Stand* was intended as a deep criticism of finance capitalism. Of the essay, Joseph Blotner warns, "Any reader seeking a political-literary program would have been disappointed, finding there instead a brilliant discourse on literary history capped by the adjuration to the artist to his own self to be true" (*Robert Penn Warren*, 153–54). That is, an apolitically political program instead.

Warren eased into the center over the course of a decade. On the other hand, Ralph Ellison bungeed from the left to the center over a shorter period than Warren. Ellison departed the Tuskegee Institute for New York City in 1936 to escape the Jim Crow South but found racism still in the North. Arnold Rampersad suggests that it may have been Ellison's brief employment as a lab technician at the A. C. Horn Paint Company during 1937—where his white coworkers resented him as the only black employee at the factory, and which no doubt served as the inspiration for the Liberty Paint Company in *Invisible Man*—that springboarded him toward the radical Left and the Communist Party, of which he became a member (91–93). Ellison participated in political events, agitations, and picketing; he toed the party line so tightly that he even supported a plank in the party's platform that would create an autonomous nation for African Americans in the South (122–23).

The principal records of Ellison's involvement remain the essays, reviews, and stories he contributed to the *New Masses*, the most famous communist publication, between 1938 and 1942. Some of these essays were pointedly about African Americans' struggle for equality, such as Ellison's account of attending the Third National Negro Congress in Washington in a piece called "A Congress Jim Crow Didn't Attend," which also advocated trade union membership among blacks. His contributions to the magazine ceased upon his service in the Merchant Marine during the winter of 1943–44, but his lack of involvement was more closely tied to his altering political beliefs. Before departing New York that winter, he had already begun his quiet break with the Communist Party. When the *People's Voice*, another publication with close communist ties, asked him for a special piece for its May Day issue in 1943, Ellison declined—or possibly never acknowledged the request (Rampersad, 162). Even during his work for *New Masses*, Ellison did not feel politically aligned with the publication or its editors in terms of writing. Rampersad quotes Ellison at length, reflecting later in his life on his involvement with *New Masses*:

> "I never wrote the official type of fiction," he later insisted. "I wrote what might be called propaganda—having to do with the Negro struggle—but my fiction was always trying to do something else.... I never accepted the ideology which the *New Masses* attempted to impose on writers." (121–22)

Ellison attempted to maintain a separation between ideology and literature in essays he wrote after his involvement with the *New Masses*. In "Twentieth-Century Fiction and the Black Mask of Humanity," Ellison addresses the problem of unsophisticated or grossly exaggerated, inaccurate portrayals of blacks in American fiction with a particularly moralistic emphasis on the virtues of American democracy rather than the political implications of such portrayals. After establishing that the renderings of black Americans in fiction by Twain, Hemingway, and Faulkner have a basis in the context of slavery and oppression, Ellison asserts that not history but fiction is his concern. He then questions how America's literature, "one of the most vital bodies of twentieth-century fiction, perhaps the brightest instrument for recording sociological fact, physical action, the nuance of speech, yet achieved—becomes suddenly dull when confronting the Negro" ("Black Mask," 83). Never does he deny that American fiction has served as a kind of barometer for race relations in the United States. On the other hand, Ellison favors addressing the issue in terms of individualism and morality instead of emphasizing politics or political action. The fiction of prejudice "forgets that a democracy is a collectivity of *individuals*" and "its function is no less personal than political" ("Black Mask," 84). The greatest purpose in analyzing this stereotype in literature is to understand that it is a "key figure in a magic rite by which the white American seeks to resolve the dilemma arising between his democratic beliefs and certain antidemocratic practices" (85), namely, discrimination and de jure segregation in the US South. Ellison recasts the greatest foreign policy and domestic issue facing the United States during the escalation of the Cold War as a problem of morality: the national crisis reduced to immorality, specifically in the denial to African Americans of the greatest virtues that the American way of life has to offer.

These examples from the lives and works of Warren and Ellison significantly reveal their commitment to the apolitical politics. These politics deemed necessary for American-style democracy and freedom can be located in Schlesinger's vital center. He envisions it as a democratic and distinctly American political center that would prevail because the "non-Communist Left" and "non-Fascist Right" both have a tremendous stake in the perseverance of American capitalism, the free market, and civil liberties—"a faith that the differences between them over economic issues can be best worked out by discussion and debate under law" rather than through violence or, perhaps worse, political radicalism ("Not Left, Not Right," 47). The vital center influences the late modernist turn in the arts because it uses a closely monitored aesthetic to protect the sanctity of these American politics-turned-values, namely, "civil liberties," "constitutional processes," and "democratic determination" (47).

Schlesinger further develops his ideas in *The Vital Center: The Politics of Freedom* (1949), a book that Thomas Hill Schaub says attempts to understand history only "within ahistorical and moral categories" as opposed to political ones (10), especially in Schlesinger's repeated references to the "faith" that American intellectuals must have in liberalism for the country to succeed on the world stage. The book also repeatedly ties economic success to the success of individual liberty within society. The moral category with which Schlesinger seems particularly obsessed is none other than the evils of communism. In a chapter on the virtue of American civil liberties, he celebrates the Constitution's protections of free speech and the Supreme Court's espousal of the "clear and present danger" doctrine when dealing with inflammatory rhetoric. This celebration cannot include manifestations of communism in free speech, for when "Communist activities do present, not just a potential threat . . . we must act swiftly in defense of freedom. Civil liberties do not deny society its right of self-protections" (218). Not discussed, however, is how civil liberties might defend civil rights, a category he mentions but fails to discuss at length. At the beginning of the civil liberties chapter, Schlesinger comments briefly on President Truman's Committee on Civil Rights and its 1948 report, stating merely that "most Americans accept, at least in principle, the obligations spelled out in the Civil Rights report" (190). Yet he, too, recasts the social conditions of prejudice as a moral conundrum in writing that "the sin of racial pride still represents the most basic challenge to the American conscience" (190). The challenge is so basic for Schlesinger that he addresses it in all of one page. It is such a nonissue for him that he suggests that even the South understands that the civil rights agenda is a valid program, "even though it may have serious and intelligible reservations about timing and method" (190). His gross understatement of the realities of the predominant southern attitudes toward desegregation indicates an attempt to refocus intellectual attention on what he deems greater threats to American democracy: fascism and communism.

If vehement antifascism and anticommunism are the markers of the vital center, then *All the King's Men* and *Invisible Man* certainly situate Warren and Ellison within its area on the political continuum. The markers are strong in both books although both authors claimed that their novels were not at all about politics; this, too, is arguably a marker of late modernist literature. In an introduction that Warren wrote for the Modern Library edition of his novel, he says that even though readers interpreted the novel to be an "apologia" for Huey Long—the wildly popular but paranoid and tyrannical senator from Louisiana—or a "rousing declaration of democratic principles and a tract for the assassination of dictators" (v), politics were not what he had in mind. *All the King's Men* "was never intended to be a book about politics. Politics merely provided the *framework* story in which the deeper concerns, whatever their final significance, might work themselves out" (vi; italics mine). In Warren's view, the political content of *All the King's Men* is not content at all. Willie Stark's platform and method of governance serve merely as a formal aspect of the novel on which hangs the novel's larger questions of personal responsibility and morality. Yet politics were no doubt on Warren's mind. As he described in his introduction, the characters and story of *All the King's Men* find their genesis in *Proud Flesh*, a verse drama about a character inspired by Huey Long, which Warren finished work on in the late 1930s. The preponderance of the work on the play was completed in Rome during the time of Mussolini's rise to power (i–ii). Robert Brinkmeyer identifies this fact to be of critical importance in understanding Warren's work during this time, especially considering the opportunities Warren had to see the specter of fascism with his own eyes during his long stays in Europe:

> Almost all of Warren's writing from the mid-1930s to 1950 show him wrestling in one way or another with this dark enemy [fascism], though not with the patriotic clarity that many critics demanded. Straightforwardly instructive

literature for Warren was not a defense against totalitarianism but the voice of totalitarianism, and the best way to silence that voice was to write contested, complex, and ironic literature whose very form embodied an affirmed intellectual freedom and democracy. (279)

Essentially Brinkmeyer outs Warren as a late modernist; his works during these years had no outward political warnings against the trappings of charismatic political leadership and totalitarianism (that would be propaganda), but his works had a political agenda nonetheless. The agenda was more concerned with that "affirm[ation of] intellectual freedom and democracy," the American morals of utmost importance.

Just as telling as the proto–Willie Stark from *Proud Flesh* regarding political trappings are the early drafts of *Invisible Man*.[1] At no point in his life did Ellison ever broadcast his involvement in the Communist Party, especially not when he won the National Book Award. Barbara Foley describes the novel as "unequivocally, a text of the Cold War" because of its anticommunism and "antipathy to the organized Left" (164). Yet in her study of the drafts of *Invisible Man* (held by the Library of Congress), Foley notices a pattern in which the presence of the Communist Party diminishes as Ellison made progress on the novel. The first manifestations of Ellison's invisible man were of a figure much more invested in organized radical political activism on the left and much more enamored with the Communist Party. Foley comments, "His hero's encounter with the organized Left is hardly that of a Cold Warrior and in fact suggests considerable admiration for various facets of the Communist activity in Harlem with which Ellison himself was quite familiar" (178–79). Also according to Foley, the shunning of communism in the pages of *Invisible Man* did not happen overnight: Ellison excised the radical leftist politics in a "process, not a single act"—a process she terms "anticommunistization" (179). The deradicalization of *Invisible Man* makes it no less a political novel despite Ellison's claims to the contrary. He described the novel as an "attempt to return to the mood of personal moral responsibility for democracy" ("Brave Words," 151). The moral responsibility for democracy again recalls the vital center, treating American democracy not as a political program but as a sound, moral, and highly valued principle.

Literary prizes by their design seek to reward certain qualities in literature. Indeed, the celebration of certain qualities in American literature was of the utmost importance to intellectuals and critics in the late 1940s and early 1950s. In the particular case of the Pulitzer Prize, the initial prize criteria and later revisions to them supplied a convenient organ by which to reinforce American values. The prizes were established at Columbia University upon the death of the shrewd journalist and businessman Joseph Pulitzer. The prizes mostly focused on awarding outstanding journalism, but there were also categories in letters, including one for the best American novel. Pulitzer's will stipulated, "Annually for the American novel published during the year which shall best present the whole atmosphere of American life, and the highest standard of American manners and manhood, One thousand dollars ($1,000)" (quoted in Hohenberg, 19). Pulitzer's will also stipulated that the advisory board for the prize may revise the criteria as necessary to keep the prize relevant, which the board did with frequency. Soon after the first prize was awarded in 1917, the board, under the control of Nicholas Murray Butler—the conservative president of Columbia—replaced the word "whole" with "wholesome" (Stuckey, 7). By 1928, "wholesome" reverted to "whole," and the words "manners" and "manhood" were dropped from the criteria; they were revised again for 1930, when the prize was given for "the best American novel published during the year, preferably one which shall best present the wholesome atmosphere of American life" (9–10). The insistence on wholesomeness—most likely the work of Butler—deeply frustrated literary critics and writers because such a qualification severely limited what subjects serious, meritorious novels could broach.[2] Moreover, in the method by which the prizewinners are determined, the final decision lies not with the jurors but with the advisory board, who have ignored the wishes of the jurors on more than one occasion.[3] In the ultimate act of capriciousness, almost immediately after awarding Warren the prize for 1947, the advisory board changed the word "novel" to "fiction in book form" in the anticipation that they would give the following year's prize to James Michener's collection of stories *Tales of the South Pacific*.

The consequences of the advisory board's capriciousness and obsession with wholesomeness resulted in the selection of novels that are often highly accessible and safe in regard to their portrayal of politics (or lack thereof) and the passing over of novels that scholars today look back on favorably. J. Douglas Bates points to the repeated exclusion of both Hemingway and Faulkner from the award (123). Of particular relevance is the 1937 award, for which Faulkner's *Absalom, Absalom!* was eligible. Instead Margaret Mitchell won for *Gone with the Wind*. Rather than choosing a technical and difficult novel weaving a sexually explicit story of probable incest and cold-blooded murder that confronted southern (and American) obsessions with racial purity, the advisory board honored a best-selling novel ripe for film adaptation and featuring an ameliorated portrayal of plantation slavery and honorable Confederates. The novel's adherence to idealized tradition and social mores (i.e., wholesomeness) also made it a safe choice. The journalist John

Hohenberg, a longtime secretary to the advisory board, reports in his history of the prizes what the selection of *Gone with the Wind* accomplished:

> With the passage of time, Margaret Mitchell's story became a part of American folklore—a novel that was read by millions of people inside and outside the country, a movie that was shown and reshown, and shown on television to a new generation, even a musical drama that originated in Japan with an all-Japanese cast singing a score by the American composer, Harold Rome. Whatever the critics may have thought of the book's sentiment and magnolia-scented romance, the public loved it and still does. *Gone with the Wind* was an eminently defensible choice. (140)

As secretary of the advisory board, Hohenberg had an interest in defending the board's decisions concerning winners. But while his comments suggest that, because of the success of *Gone with the Wind*, the Pulitzer went to the right novel that year, there is no accounting for the effect that winning such a prestigious award had on the future successes of Mitchell's novel. Also revealing is that Hohenberg points to the novel's worldwide success as a part of "American folklore." The implication is that the most defensible winners of the Pulitzer Prize in fiction are works that serve as ambassadors of idealized culture and that the prize can influence what passes into the American mythos.

The choice of *All the King's Men* in 1947, however, is the selection that cements the prize's commitment to promoting literature of the vital center, a choice on which the advisory board and jurors could agree. W. J. Stuckey argues that Warren's novel was a natural choice for the award because his conservatism was a trait he shared with previous Pulitzer novelists, with slight differences:

> Whereas his predecessors' outlook is primarily social and economic, Warren's is primarily philosophical and moral. [Booth] Tarkington, [Edna] Ferber, [Louis] Bromfield, [Margaret Ayers] Barnes, [T. S.] Stribling, Mitchell, [Martin] Flavin, and the others are concerned mainly with the individual's allegiance to certain rules of conduct having to do with money, work, and sexual behavior; Warren is concerned with the total problem of individual responsibility and the individual conscience. (134–35)

But what is the real difference between being socially and economically conservative and philosophically and morally conservative? *All the King's Men* is all too aware of social and economic mores, given Jack Burden's project of digging up dirt on Judge Irwin. The better way to express Stuckey's perceived differences is that Warren ameliorates the political problems of social, racial, and class differences with a novel that focuses on "individual responsibility and ... conscience." The novel is a literary manifestation of the vital center that depicts democratic values as indicative of a geographic and cultural region integral to the survival of the nation as a whole.

Invisible Man was eligible for the Pulitzer Prize in 1953 and, similarly being a novel of the vital center, would have been more than a worthy target. The Pulitzer for fiction that year went instead to Hemingway for *The Old Man and the Sea*. But another award for literary merit had appeared since the Pulitzers: 1950 saw the reestablishment of the National Book Awards, which were founded and first administered by the National Book Foundation (an association formed by publishing firms) in the 1930s. These awards in the categories of fiction, poetry, and nonfiction were intended to be conferred on writers by other writers and quickly became the more lauded honor because of the awards' novelty and close associations to practicing writers and editors. Moreover, unlike the Pulitzers, the founders of the National Book Award provided no criteria: the judges each year could make their selection based on whatever criteria they deemed appropriate.[4] For the 1953 award, *Invisible Man* was an easy winner. A Harvard professor, an editor, and three writers (Alfred Kazin, Saul Bellow, and Irving Howe) sat on the committee that year; Ellison's novel won the votes of all but the professor (Rampersad, 269). In only the fourth year of the award, Ellison found himself in the company of William Faulkner, who had won in 1951 for *The Complete Stories of William Faulkner*, and in the subsequent year would be joined by Saul Bellow, whose *The Adventures of Augie March* won the fiction award.

Even at such an early point in the granting of the awards, these selections indicate the qualities of literature held valuable in the United States in the early 1950s. Although the selection committee did not have criteria as specific as those of the Pulitzer, the manner in which Ellison himself seems to have understood the significance, and apolitically political importance, of being selected (over Hemingway's *The Old Man and the Sea* and John Steinbeck's *East of Eden*) indicates what criteria writers and literary thinkers held in highest esteem. In his acceptance speech, Ellison stated: "That my first novel should win this most coveted prize must certainly indicate that there is a crisis in the American novel" ("Brave Words," 151). He went on to clarify the nature of the crisis:

> I felt that except for the work of William Faulkner something vital had gone out of American prose after Mark Twain. I came to believe that the writers

of the period [of Twain] took a much greater responsibility for the condition of democracy and, indeed, their works were imaginative projections of the conflicts within the human heart which arose when the sacred principles of the Constitution and the Bill of Rights clashed with the practical exigencies of human greed and fear, hate and love. (152–53)

Somehow American values had made their way out of American fiction, and Ellison strove to restore those values and make the American literary tradition part of the vital center. Beyond the tinge of patriotism in his naming the Constitution and Bill of Rights, referring to their principles as "sacred" aligns with Schlesinger's repeated references to faith in American values in *The Vital Center*. Ellison's speech corroborates Richard Chase's review of *Invisible Man*: the experience of the alienated African American in the United States becomes generalized into the alienation of the modern man in a politically dangerous world. Confirming this as the extent of late modernist interest in the plight of minorities in the United States, it would be another thirty years before another black writer won the National Book Award for fiction (Alice Walker for *The Color Purple* in 1983).

The selection of *All the King's Men* and *Invisible Man* for prestigious literary prizes actually reveals much more about the aims and societal functions of such prizes than the prizes teach later generations anything about a text's merit. Of course, this statement does not preclude the fact that many novels that have won awards are in fact texts deserving of scholarly attention and have provided enjoyment for casual and serious readers alike. However, the function that the Pulitzers, National Book Awards, and other literary and cultural prizes in the twentieth century largely have is to recognize creative works that preserve the American mythos and national identity. This function does not begin in the American context but began with the grandfather of all cultural prizes, the Nobel Prize in Literature. James F. English emphasizes that, from the Nobel's beginnings, it has retained an emphasis on the Swedish national identity. The prize itself is awarded by the Swedish Academy, which was founded by the Swedish monarchs to "defend the purity of the Swedish language," and to this day the Swedish king presides at the awards ceremony and personally confers the medals on the recipients (55). Although the Nobels carry an air of cosmopolitan goodwill, English argues, "The prize remained recognizably a nationalist initiative on the European model, designed to raise the cultural profile and broaden the cultural authority of a self-consciously minor European nation-state" (55). In the cultural disruption of World War II, the Pulitzer and National Book Award for fiction became part of the attempt of the United States, self-consciously one of two major players on a shifting world stage, to raise its cultural and political profile. The same may be argued for the barrage of awards devised within the culture industry beginning around 1930 and lasting through the 1950s, which include the Oscars (1929), Tony Awards (1947), Emmys (1949), and the Grammys (1958). Throughout the Cold War, these awards, along with the literary prizes, began honoring creative works as successful cultural products of American society just as much as, if not more than, works of high artistic merit and integrity. Sometimes it is not necessary for a Faulkner or a Robert Frost to be a cultural ambassador; award-winning products, such as *Gone with the Wind*, its film adaptations, and popular culture can be effective carriers of American values.

Although literary prizes can be dismissed simply as decorations awarded for the cultural reproduction of the American mythos, *All the King's Men* and *Invisible Man* are not so easily dismissed. Prizes or no, Warren's and Ellison's most significant contributions to American letters remain important primarily because they are indispensable artifacts of their era that show depoliticized treatments of race and other political issues.

All the King's Men could certainly be described as the great American political novel despite Warren's claims to the contrary. Yet even if the political atmosphere of the South is merely a framework, to use Warren's word, the novel's designations of desirable versus undesirable political allegiances within Willie Stark's inner circle remain associated with socioeconomic factors. Race and history necessarily pervade the novel. Nearly all of Willie's decisions in the novel are political, but in the reasoning narrated by Jack Burden, Willie exercises his power by influencing an individual's moral character. "You don't ever have to frame anybody, because the truth is always sufficient," he explains to Jack, further elaborating his method of rule: "'I went to a Presbyterian Sunday school back in the days when they still had some theology, and that much of it stuck. And'—he grinned suddenly—'I have found it very valuable'" (508). At the least, the tactics used by Willie and his rivals conflate morality and political viability. When the MacMurfee outfit, Willie's nemeses, approach him about his son, Tom, and the young woman Sibyl Frey, whom Tom allegedly impregnated, the situation is problematic for Willie, but not because Tom broke the rules of polite southern society by having sex out of wedlock. Rather, Tom's breaking of the social mores is a problem because it endangers Willie's political power. It is a problem because Tom's perceived moral baggage makes Willie unelectable.

Essentially every instance of the conflation of morality and political power in the novel is connected to good social standing or honor in white southern society. John Blair argues that honor is the fulcrum on which Jack totters, not knowing whether to trust his friend Adam Stanton, who clings to an honor-enriched identity, or his boss Willie, who sees honor as a political tool. Jack realizes in his historical studies that the notion of southern honor is bankrupt, considering the story of betrayal told in the journals of his supposed ancestor Cass Mastern, the cuckolding of Ellis Burden (called the "Scholarly Attorney" by Jack and his mother's first husband) by his best friend, the Judge, and Adam and Anne Stanton's father's involvement in assisting the Judge in covering up the moves that secure his finances and drive Mortimer Littlepaugh to suicide. Jack finally copes with this construction of southern tradition by acknowledging that it is false and "allowing his heritage of traditional Southern values to affect but not delineate his identity" (Blair, 470). What fills that hollow space in honor is political power and responsibility. Tom's bawdy behavior puts a blight on the Stark name, but only in terms of Willie's political aspirations. The facts Jack unearths about the Judge's money problems and their connection to Mortimer Littlepaugh tarnish the Judge's reputation so much in his mind that the Judge commits suicide, which Blair describes as a flagrant public ritual (464). The suicide also reveals the secret dishonor of Jack's true parentage, but the real impetus it gives to the progression of the novel lies in how it renders irrelevant the chink in Irwin's armor. In an effort to preserve honor, he interferes with Willie's political leverage.

In a novel where respectability is the key to power, southern honor becomes a salient issue. This feature of *All the King's Men* is crucial to understanding the novel as an artistic artifact of late modernism and the immediacy with which it became a part of the American canon and southern studies. When honor equates with political power, not only must it be protected by either hiding or avoiding ethical misconduct, but it must also be used to resist unfavorable political methods and ideologies. Here we have the Cold War context of the novel: the totalitarian Willie Stark will always be linked with the legacy of Huey Long, who could be described as a socialist because of his advocacy of wealth redistribution to alleviate poverty. Even if not a one-to-one correlation with Long, the story of Stark's rise and fall is recognizable as a compelling narrative that suggests the possibility for, and delineates the pitfalls of, fascism or other totalitarian forms of government. This was recognized in the time soon after the novel's publication. In an article on Warren's first three novels (in none other than the *Kenyon Review*), Eric Bentley says that, rather than a "political treatise about Long," *All the King's Men* is about "self-knowledge" (417), about how knowing the virtues of one's self can fight political contagion. "Indeed, to say that we must see politics within a broader frame—the frame being morality and human life in general—is precisely Warren's thesis. Willie Stark, Adam Stanton, and

Tiny Duffy are wrong politically because they are wrong humanly," Bentley insists (417). He expounds on this point by relating it to the larger realm of American culture:

> For the Hollywood movie, just as much as the Moscow edict, takes politics to be a battle between the Wrong People and the Right People. One judges the man not by his nature but by his affiliation. The same action is good, performed by Us, and bad, performed by Them. All war propaganda depends on this morality, and today we live in a perpetual state of war.
> Now there is nothing Warren loathes more than this morality. (417–18)

Bentley interprets Warren as exhorting his readers to not accept the moral relativity offered by the groupthink of any particular faction: one side must be good (American) and the other evil (fascism and communism). The lesson learned by Jack Burden is the same one *All the King's Men* teaches readers: the individual's honor dictates that strict adherence to any ideology is a fallacy, and disagreeable politics must be resisted. Mike Augspurger goes so far as to suggest that Warren's lesson is addressed specifically to citizens of democratic societies, who "must learn through experience that any single idealistic narrative will eventually fail to explain a profoundly complex reality: only by eschewing the certainty of ideological explanations can they function effectively and democratically"; moreover, human connectedness, symbolized by Jack Burden's theorized "spider web," makes all citizens responsible for the welfare of other citizens (52). In protecting democracy for oneself, a citizen preserves it for other citizens.[5]

The novel's emphasis on the culpability of individuals has its limits, though, and makes way for something that Jack Burden calls the "moral neutrality of history," a theory that holds significant ramifications related to the novel's late modernist project. Burden ruminates on the day his best friend assassinates the Boss at the height of his political power: "Process as process is neither morally good nor morally bad. We may judge results but not process. The morally bad agent may perform the deed which is good. The morally good agent may perform the deed which is bad" (*All the King's Men*, 593). The statement comes as Jack considers the good things Willie has accomplished for the impoverished people of the state, but also as an attempt to reconcile Willie's and Judge Irwin's respective deeds. Jack's theory suggests that individuals have a responsibility primarily for the ends, but not necessarily the means, of political outcomes. The theory then also provides the opportunity to ponder who or what is responsible for the means, or the course of history. Willie Stark, after all, begins his meteoric rise to power after the collapse of a shoddily built fire escape at a schoolhouse whose contractor he attempted to block. "People said that God had taken a hand in the schoolhouse business. That God had stepped in on Willie's side," Jack recalls. "The Lord had justified him" (99). And why question an act of God?

Even so, on the day Willie squashes his impending impeachment, Jack looks out at the crowd gathering around the Capitol, drawn by the suspense, and says he "felt like God-Almighty brooding on History" (*All the King's Men*, 225). His comment is the genesis of some philosophical meandering within his narration regarding God's relationship to history in the form of a remembered conversation with the Scholarly Attorney. (He became a missionary when he left Jack's mother, a choice for which Jack holds contempt.) Jack shares some of the facetious reasoning implemented in his sparring with his supposed father but returns again to the image of God brooding over history: "I felt like God, because I had the knowledge of what was to come" (227). In the most literal sense, Jack knows what is to come because, in his telling of the story, he has just delivered the paperwork that ends the impeachment proceedings against his boss. However, the larger meaning contained in his statement is that, as narrator of the entirety of Willie's story, Jack knows it from the beginning to the end, from Willie's trouble as the Mason County treasurer to his shooting in the rotunda of the same building from which Jack looks out in this scene. Jack's brooding over history is a metaphor for his absolute power over the legacy of Willie Stark; in remembering him in the manner he does, intermingled with his own personal history, and refusing to renew the cycle of political tyranny by joining Tiny Duffy's administration, Jack is taking personal responsibility for history and the safety of democracy for his fellow citizens. Yet as the knower of history, Jack is not culpable in its happening, only in its retelling. Thus we may understand the novel's treatment of history and knowledge thereof as an oblique comment on the historical situation of the United States in the 1940s, in the vein of the adage that victors are the authors of history—manifest destiny updated for the Cold War. Allied triumph and the promise of Western democracy's defeat of totalitarian regimes somehow negates the horrors of World War II; American economic supremacy abrogates the class disparity and discrimination that drive massive growth in global capitalism. Individuals within democracy can act according to appropriate understandings of these events.

Despite emphasizing individuality and honor and setting the novel clearly in the South, Warren stops short of naming a specific state as the location for *All the King's Men*. Possibly, in an effort to prevent the politics of Willie Stark from being associated with a particular place, Warren left only clues in his geography and settings. Besides the environment, characters, and idiom-laden dialogue, the novel suggests the South in Jack's indication that the state is a stronghold of the Democratic Party (competing in the Democratic primary for governor, Jack explains, "in our state is the same as running for Governor") (98). The location of Burden's Landing on the Gulf and the ability of Willie, Jack, and Sugar Boy to visit the Judge there and return to Mason City all in one night during in the first chapter suggest Alabama, Mississippi, or Louisiana. Considering the use of "county" rather than "parish" (18), any Gulf state could be a possibility. Mississippi, the home state of Cass Mastern, and Alabama are most likely, yet the novel is inconclusive.

Rather than being a trivial, slippery detail of the novel, its coyness about location creates a universality by decentering the setting as the South. The locale's vague namelessness opens the possibility for it to be any American locale, southern state, border state, or beyond. For instance, in Jack's digging on Judge Irwin, he travels to Savannah to investigate the finances of the Judge's wife, Mabel Carruthers. Jack discovers through conversations that she "married a rich man from the West. Or rather what in Savannah they called 'the West'" (*All the King's Men*, 328). The novel's setting appears outside the South to the residents of a quintessential southern city, adding indeterminacy to the locale. The imprecise location serves as a universalizing gesture of the vital center, supporting a late modernist project within the novel, and is indicative of Warren's own tempestuous relationship with regionalism. As Joseph R. Millichap notes, while Warren retains blatant ties to his southern identity in his writing that he shared with some fellow southern writers, he "moves beyond it to his own regionalism constructed from universal literary themes and artistic meanings" (30). Millichap even goes on to categorize Warren alongside Faulkner as a "universal regionalist" (31).

A social ill of note whose absence is as conspicuous as the specter of fascism in the pages of *All the King's Men* is racism. Indeed, the only black characters appear in a caricature in the novel's opening pages—black men chopping cotton witness Jack's imagined automobile accident, laugh at it, and comment in dialect—and in the character of Phebe, a slave central to the story of Cass Mastern's affair with his best friend's wife. Indeed, Forrest G. Robinson argues that Warren's own unwillingness to address at length or in detail his own conflicted feelings on the issue of race manifest in Jack's muted attitudes toward the subject. Robinson helpfully describes the imagined fatal automobile accident as a "fantasy" in which Jack simultaneously acknowledges but declines to engage in discussion of "the race problem":

> His [Jack's] death—inevitable, as if profoundly deserved or desired—is of little moment to the black field workers save as the occasion for their amuse-

ment. Their laughter is testimony to their secret contempt for white people, a return, no doubt, for all that the word "nigger" has meant in their lives expressed not so much with bitterness as with the resigned levity one might direct toward a madman. (Robinson, 524)

Robinson's interpretation supposes a lack of understanding or even a fear on Jack's part of confronting racism, perhaps in thinking about the awkwardness of being a white man in the South who breaks the stringent Jim Crow codes. This fantasy that Robinson identifies works in tandem with the fantasy of the otherwise homogeneously white South that Jack inhabits in *All the King's Men*.

For a political novel based in the American Southeast, there is certainly very little talk of Jim Crow or discrimination. Jack uncovers some during his career as a newspaper reporter, investigating Willie's ousting as county treasurer for his insistence on using the lowest-bidding contractor for the new school building. The men Jack interviews on the street in Mason City say that Willie "wants 'em to take the low bid and git a passel of niggers in here," which would "put white folks out of work" (*All the King's Men*, 80), and the chairman of the county commissioners and his cohorts call Willie and Jack both "nigger-lovers" (85). This racism is merely a screen for the real issue of political corruption, that the company awarded the contract was given a favor, and is therefore downplayed within the novel. Racism in the form of nineteenth-century slavery is raised directly through Jack's sharing of Cass Mastern's papers and journals. Cass is perhaps the sympathetic activist-of-sorts and ascetic that Jack, and even perhaps Warren, aspires to be. Cass attempts to track and buy the freedom of Phebe, the house slave his friend's wife sold down the river simply because she knew about the affair between her and Cass. When Cass returns to Mississippi from that journey unsuccessful, he frees all his slaves, opting instead to run his plantation on a wage system. Cass Mastern's story is rich in details about the horrors of chattel slavery, from Phebe's treatment to Cass witnessing a Frenchman from New Orleans at a Lexington, Kentucky, slave market procuring slaves to become prostitutes. In sharing such a story with such details, "Jack Burden reveals a deep, though unconscious, concern with racial injustice," Robinson asserts (521). Regardless, it is a concern that Jack cannot deal with because of his commitment to his theory of the moral neutrality of history; he and other politically responsible citizens strive toward the understanding of the implementation of democracy, and not the means by which it is imagined or won. "The novel is studied and approved because it moves us toward a bearable angle of vision on a matter we can neither face for long nor fully forget" (Robinson, 525). In this manner, *All the King's Men* successfully universalizes southern virtue and honor while concurrently compartmentalizing its racism.

Unlike *All the King's Men*, *Invisible Man* is arguably not a story of the South. Ellison is similarly indeterminate in whether his protagonist identifies as southern or northern, and for good reason. Ellison's novel follows the nameless invisible man from his youth at a black college in the South to his deep involvement and then separation from the Brotherhood in the great metropolis of New York City, more specifically Harlem. This is just one way that *Invisible Man* makes the South a universalizing element in American literature: the invisible man fails to escape the racial discrimination so readily associated with the US South even when he moves to the North. One might say the South is everywhere there is discrimination. And given Ellison's commitment to the moralized conception of democratic values, the book is an artistic demonstration that American-style democracy is aware of its own shortcomings and is prepared to face them. The great New Critical irony, though, is that *Invisible Man* suggests a correction through the attempted use of the same set of political values that resulted in discrimination to begin with. The systematic change begins with individuals: individuals who suffer the prejudices of American society, such as the invisible man, must understand that their situation is the same, as Richard Chase observed, as the plight of alienation visited on the modern man in the industrialized global economy. Truly democratic, individual citizens are able to defeat any obstacle to freedom. Rather than simply compartmentalizing racism to the South, I suggest that Ellison instead portrays a serious flaw in what was internationally perceived to be an American foreign policy problem as an immoral discrepancy in the American dream corrected only by the individual, who is fully culpable in his actions based on his willingness to use the knowledge of past events to correct the present.

Understanding *Invisible Man* begins with considering it as an example of migration fiction, which has historical underpinnings in the Great Migration of African Americans from the South to other parts of the United States in the years after World War I through the years following World War II. Several factors spurred this movement, but most noteworthy are the growth in manufacturing in urban centers across the United States; the increased mechanization of agriculture in the South, which eliminated manual labor and forced small-time farmers to seek a living in other ways; and the reluctance of African American veterans to return to the South after experiencing equality abroad. In his history of the migration of southerners in the twentieth century, James N. Gregory notes that Ellison's novel hinges on the sociology of migration. Gregory writes of the protagonist, "This southerner in Harlem is not simply lost in the metropolis and yearning for home. There is no home, not in the South and not in the North" (75). Many individuals hoping for social mobility found none in their moves across the country, but only a fresh version of their former poverty and social inequality. *Invisible Man* confronts this reality, which was rapidly becoming a stark revision of the American dream, by showing not only that hard times lacked geographical boundaries but that discrimination was an unavoidable part of the American social landscape.[6]

One of Ellison's best metaphors for this reality comes during his protagonist's brief employment at the Liberty Paint Company, where a flashy sign near the entrance advertises boldly, "keep America pure with liberty paints" (*Invisible Man*, 196). The sign evokes the Cold War atmosphere in that it suggests that the purity of American ideals depends on consumer capitalism—that "liberty" comes in the form of the free market and also in the form of government contracting with the private sector (the personnel officer at Liberty Paint tells the invisible man that much of the company's paint is sold to the government). He begins his work finishing the production of a color called "optic white," destined for a national monument, by following instructions to add "dead black" to each bucket of paint and stirring. The procedure makes the paint improbably whiter: "as white as George Washington's Sunday-go-to-meetin' wig and as sound as the all-mighty dollar!" declares the supervisor (201–2). The dope added to the paint is the great secret in the myth of American exceptionalism: the necessary exploitation of African Americans brought America to its idealized, racially homogeneous supremacy. George Washington, of course, owned slaves who ran his profitable plantation; before the growth of manufacturing in the United States, the plantation economy, impossible without chattel slavery, brought the country riches through agricultural exports. As Joseph Urgo insightfully notes, the Negro was the first product of American capitalism (6). Alan Nadel connects this whitewashing directly to *Invisible Man* and its place in the American canon. Nadel claims that issues of canonicity are central to the novel because it reckons with "how to speak to and through tradition without sacrificing the speaker's voice or denying the tradition it attempts to engage," since that tradition is one that tried to erase any traces of blacks' contributions to its success (*Invisible Criticism*, xii). Yet the intensity and depth of this injustice do not blemish the American story; they make it whiter, purer, and cleaner. The paint's planned use on a national monument indicates a collective unwillingness to acknowledge the atrocities that went into making the country and its culture great and whitewashes away race as crucial to the conversation about democracy.

The narrator experienced a shrewd manipulation of this reality earlier in the novel while serving as the chauffeur and assistant to Mr. Norton, the white, northern trustee who is visiting the southern college his funds endow (presumably an analogue to Tuskegee Institute). After his initial explanation to Dr. Bledsoe, the college president (presumably an analogue to Booker T. Washington), that Mr. Norton's sudden illness is the result of his desire to hear firsthand the sordid tale of Jim Trueblood's incest with his daughter and the ill-advised attempt to procure whiskey for the swooning trustee at the Golden Day, Dr. Bledsoe gives what reads like a refresher course on how blacks must deal with whites. "Damn what *he* wants," Bledsoe tells the invisible man, "haven't you the sense God gave a dog? We take these white folks where we want them to go, we show them what we want them to see. Don't you know that?" (102). The comment is merely the first in a line of harsh admonishments by Bledsoe that the best way for the minority to survive in America's severely distorted democracy is to provide the construct of blackness to whites in power. The only way to please a white man, Bledsoe says, is to tell a lie (139). Of great consequence is one of Bledsoe's final statements to the invisible man: "If there weren't men like me running schools like this, there'd be no South. Nor North, either. No, and there'd be no country—not as it is today" (142). The cunning Bledsoe reveals his understanding that discrimination is necessary to American democracy. There would be no South as it is without a college such as Bledsoe's that instructs African Americans about their role in society—an unassuming assimilation through which greater resources for black schools and colleges can be procured and predominant constructions of blackness may be manipulated. The other implication is that Bledsoe's school and others like it instruct citizens in the complacency necessary to build the unified nation that would ensure victory in the Cold War. To reveal to whites their prejudices as opposed to exploiting them would be too disruptive.

Bledsoe's model is one of responsibility to a collective ideal. The narrator ultimately learns through his adventures on the Harlem political scene that individual identity and its responsibility to democracy are more important. This realization begins with the man at the yam stand, to whom he says upon rediscovering his love for sweet potatoes, "They are my birthmark,... I yam what I am!" (266). The freedom to fulfill the desire to eat a sweet potato is more important than the stereotype the yams informs, and in a rejection of Bledsoe's model, the narrator imagines the administrator being outed as a secret lover of yams and chitterlings (265). On the heels of this moment and muddying the waters, however, is his recruitment by the Brotherhood, which approaches him because they need "someone who can articulate the grievances of the people" (292)—a mouthpiece for collective representation. Since the novel's publication, critics have understood the Brotherhood to be analogous to the Communist Party; this organization, which the invisible man joins and becomes a representative of, interferes with the individual responsibility to democracy. The narrator joins the Brotherhood because of the opportunity it will give him to finally use his rhetorical gifts, which were an object of disdain to the white folks back home, who more enjoyed the beatings of the battle royal. But before he can give sanctioned speeches, he must learn the organization's view of history and its lexicon for his speech making. This causes the narrator some anxiety at his first official speaking engagement because he "couldn't remember the correct words and phrases from the pamphlet" (342). After a somewhat successful run as an orator and organizer for the Brotherhood, his patience for them runs out when party's directives require that it "sacrifice" Harlem to pursue a larger political agenda.

Danielle Allen homes in on the Brotherhood's lack of understanding of the word "sacrifice" as its greatest weakness in affecting democratic values. She concludes that for sacrifice to be meaningful, those being sacrificed must have some agency in the act, yet the Brotherhood does not give the invisible man or the people of Harlem an option. Doing so undoes the work of democracy, which is to open "a distinction between those who give up their interests consensually and those who do not, between sacrificers and victims, aiming to reduce as much as possible the category of victim" (67). The Brotherhood's action undermines individual responsibility, and the conundrum that Ellison wrestles with, Allen concludes, is that "democratic citizenship ... empowers only to disempower" (74). The narrator feels himself to be betrayed as well in this move, for the refocusing of the Brotherhood's efforts will interrupt the personal responsibility he felt for citizens of Harlem.

How exactly the invisible man goes about navigating the vision of American democracy the novel re-creates—and suggests as a strategy to us as readers—has been at the center of recent critical conversations about the enduring popularity of the earliest readings of the novel as a universalizing force for humanity. The shortcomings of such a reading, as Lesley Larkin points out, is a lack of any true understanding of racialized identities on the part of white readers:

> A postwar white reader might experience an amelioration of the anxieties of modern individuality without having to understand a black experience on its own terms. Crucially, a reader's acquisition of individuality or independence can proceed through transracial identification without requiring the application of "race-free" individuality to a black author. The resulting conundrum

is that "race" is at once excised from such a reader's experience of the text's "universality" and is the central mechanism of that experience. (269–70)

While this reading does little to assist the reader in any real understanding about racial identity and its construction, this approach to the novel, no doubt spearheaded by the New Criticism, is more closely aligned with Ellison's purposes and retains its importance as a tool historicizing the novel and examining its relationship to the ideology of the vital center. Schaub is the most important voice on this point, and he sees the African American experience of being denied equal representation under the law as comporting with the New Critical emphasis on paradox and irony as the great way markers of the shared human experience. Ellison strived to expose this "hypocrisy" about American democracy, Schaub claims, and his effort to portray his protagonist as a figure whose commitment to individual responsibility would "resonate universally for all readers" was typical of Cold War thinkers (92). The narrator's desire to steer clear of the political extremes of the Brotherhood leads to a paralysis, Schaub concludes, which allows the novel to become Schlesinger's political treatise in novel form: "Ellison's effort to situate the grounds of responsible political action within the space between extremes provides the literary instance of similar exhortations in the writings of Schlesinger and Trilling, for *Invisible Man* transforms his paralysis into a 'vital center' through the power of art" (114).

Christopher Douglas observes that it is easy for literary critics to see the resistance to "radical projects" in *Invisible Man* but cautions that "critical works on Ralph Ellison have to grapple not only with his rejection of radical ideologies but with his apparent acceptance of conventional national ones as well" (60). We can make a similar observation of *All the King's Men*. One conventional, national ideology is no doubt Schlesinger's vital center. And these political affinities made these novels prime candidates for the awards they won—prized emissaries of the mythical processes of American democracy. But these novels are also examples of artistic late modernism, which distills the artistic output of the early twentieth century into a set of tenets and features, institutionalized and depoliticized. The framing of America's social problems as the responsibility of individuals endures in Warren's and Ellison's thinking, as evidenced by their aforementioned conversation, which Warren edited for inclusion in *Who Speaks for the Negro?*, published thirteen years after *Invisible Man*.

In a wide-ranging interview covering many issues related to civil rights and America's national values, Warren raises questions on topics ranging from W. E. B. Du Bois to the value of nonviolent protest. Rather than delving into practical matters of race relations, the exchange remains abstracted. For example, when answering a question from Warren about the effects of the long history of violence committed against southern blacks by southern whites, Ellison responds by discussing "personal courage," which "had to either take another form or be negated, become meaningless" (341). Literature was one of those forms. Ellison does state that courage has to be tempered because the consequences of courage against racial violence in the South are typically more racial violence, but Warren guides the conversation through an intellectual investigation of values, heroism, and the psychological effect violence has on blacks living in the South (341–43). The conversation ends with a discussion of universality: "You see, it's a question of recognizing the human core, the universality of our experience. It's a matter of defining value as one has actually lived" (345), Ellison tells Warren when the latter suggests parallels between white southerners being "imprisoned by a loyalty to being Southern" and "the genius of the Negro" being "imprisoned, in the race problem" (344). But the imprisoning that the two writers go on to discuss is not one of economic disadvantage or lack of political agency. Rather, it is the imprisoning of "genius" or the value of their culture. The interview ends with a comment from Ellison:

> There is no Southerner who hasn't been touched by the presence of Negroes. There's no Negro who hasn't been touched by the presence of white Southerners. And of course this extends beyond the region. It gets—the moment you start touching culture, you touch music, you touch dance attitudes, you touch movies,—touch the structure anywhere—and the Negro is right in there helping to shape it. (347)

What will resolve racial discord is art, not politics. Also telling in these comments is that Ellison specifies "white Southerners" but provides no geographical or regional characteristic for the blacks by whom he claims white southerners have been affected. Southern identity remains white identity, just as in *All the King's Men*'s fantasy of a white South. Warren doubles down on this idea in his commentary after the interview is concluded in *Who Speaks for the Negro?* Of Ellison, he writes:

> No one has made more unrelenting statements of the dehumanizing pressures that have been put upon the Negro. And *Invisible Man* is, I should say, the most powerful artistic representation we have of the Negro under these dehumanizing conditions; and at the same time, it is a statement of the human triumph over those conditions. (354)

Warren published *Who Speaks for the Negro?* in 1965, during the thick of the civil rights movement, the same year that Malcolm X was assassinated, police in Alabama beat protesters marching from Selma to Montgomery, and the Voting Rights Act was signed into law by Lyndon B. Johnson. Clearly plenty of socioeconomic and political fights remained in order for blacks to triumph over their dehumanizing conditions. The answer to the rhetorical question in the title of Warren's book about the leaders of the civil rights movement is that Warren steps in to speak for the Negro, and he keeps the topic strictly about morality and art, advocating for the defeat of prejudice through individual commitments to the universality of the human experience.

Indeed, both Warren and Ellison envisioned their novels as telling a universal story as part of an American tradition. As these new works became objects of study during the moment of the institutionalization of literary studies, their universalizing of perceived southern values and southern social ills went a long way toward formulating a response to the threat of fascism and communism within the United States. The novels remind intellectuals that while the circumstances of American cultural and political influence are beyond their control, the nation's culture and politics can last only as long as individuals are willing to be responsible.

PART II
★★ THE ★★ RETURN TO POLITICS

4

Eudora Welty and the Problem of Crusading

Eudora Welty won the Pulitzer Prize for fiction in 1972 for her final novel, *The Optimist's Daughter*, and her *Collected Stories* won the 1983 National Book Award in the short-lived paperback fiction category. She also won the National Book Foundation's Medal for Distinguished Contribution to American Letters in 1991. However, she never won the Nobel Prize in Literature. Rumors exist claiming that she was often nominated but continually passed over by judges because of a perceived "lack of social-political consciousness" in her work (Prenshaw, "Welty's Transformations," 22).[1] The extent to which Welty's oeuvre deals with its social and political contexts, and racism in particular, has been a topic of contentious debate. On the issue of race, Andrew Banecker argues that Welty's fiction provides no way for the reader to make a definitive determination regarding her stance on racism and divides critics, perhaps oversimplifying, into either "Welty apologists" or "Welty bashers" (126). Many scholars, especially those who knew her personally, understand Welty's attitudes toward race to be progressive and argue that her fiction reflects as much.[2] Her own political activities would suggest this, as well. In interviews, Welty professed her admiration of Adlai Stevenson, for whom she canvassed in New York City in 1952. She also sought integrated audiences for lectures and readings at Millsaps College in Jackson in 1963 and 1965. Regarding the integrated audiences at the Millsaps events, Suzanne Marrs contends, "She did not ask that her audience become political activists, but she did ask, implicitly, that they refuse to be part of racist activities, that they recognize the humanity and complexity of all individuals" ("Huge Fateful Stage," 84). On the other hand, it is this *implicitness* that others point to when claiming that Welty's work shows, as Dean Flower argues, an "ambivalen[ce] about racism" (331). Welty's political activities may have been progressive, but Flower claims that "her fiction sometimes keeps that well hidden" (332). The result, he suggests, has been to force Welty's defenders into contortions to use textual evidence and biographical research to claim that Welty was not racist. (Flower's claim has in turn been the target of rebuke.[3])

This chapter shifts the discussion of Welty's fiction and politics toward the Cold War and her place in late modernism. While much of the conversation on the relationship between Welty's fiction, her life, and her politics has examined her connections to the civil rights movement, less has examined her work's Cold War context. Welty appears here as a transitional figure. Even though her published reviews and her essays, such as "Must the Novelist Crusade?," reflect her own commitment to an aesthetic that rejected overt politics in favor of focusing on individuals and moral struggles, her story "Where Is the Voice Coming From?" is clearly a product of its political moment. During the 1960s, media coverage, especially television, made it clear that the struggle for equality could no longer be ignored, and neither could it continue to be discussed in moral (as opposed to political) terms alone. The headlines and unrest became inescapable for writers and other intellectuals of the vital center, who were appropriating southern values as national, democratic ones and disassociating these values with a geographically southern identity in favor of a patriotic, conservative cultural identity. Welty may have argued that good fiction could not be propaganda, yet her fiction was political, as "Where Is the Voice Coming From?" demonstrates. Welty clearly understands the role fiction plays in purveying American democratic values, and she subverts apolitically political late modernism by writing a story (featuring a chillingly compelling character) that makes an argument against racial oppression. Consideration of the Cold War context, the larger context of national coverage of the civil rights movement on television, and, in particular, Medgar Evers's mandated television time in Jackson, Mississippi, shows an immediate, real-world sociopolitical engagement in Welty's stories despite her own advice not to crusade.

"Must the Novelist Crusade?," published in the *Atlantic Monthly* in 1965, was originally delivered as a lecture titled "Words into Fiction" to an integrated audience at Millsaps College in April 1963. Welty also read her 1940 story "Powerhouse" at the same event (Marrs, *Eudora Welty*, 300). This nuanced essay has been a lightning rod for those wishing to criticize Welty's work as not being politically engaged, as well as for those who champion a political awareness in Welty's work. It has most frequently been considered in its context of the civil rights movement, and the essay certainly supports such an analysis. Near the beginning, Welty indicates that she has been questioned by interlocutors outside of the South about how she might help: "'All right, Eudora Welty, what are you going to do about it? Sit down there with your mouth shut?' a stranger asked over long distance in one of the midnight calls that I suppose have waked most writers in the South from time to time" (147). While the essay does not explicitly address current events, many readers have reasonably gathered that Welty means for it to explain why she is not more actively involved in the civil rights movement and why her writing does not directly address it. "Must the Novelist Crusade?" continues the separation between good literature's concerns with timeless values compatible with American democracy and the sins that challenge it and the novelist-crusader-editorialist's concerns with publishing to directly plead for political action. Yet the essay represents more than a simple explanation of why Welty's art is not explicitly political; rather, the essay offers a defense of late modernist aesthetics at the height of the civil rights movement and the Cold War that functions subversively by acknowledges the political nature of fiction.

Reading "Must the Novelist Crusade?" as late modernist aesthetics highlights the essay's Cold War context, a context that scholars have paid little, if any, critical attention to. By the 1960s, the South's treatment of blacks was bad global press for the United States and its diplomatic ambitions worldwide. As the US government deployed writers in the cultivation of Western democracy abroad through promoting their art, Welty imagined what the life of writers in the Soviet Union must be like to draw her distinction between novelists and crusaders. The passage is worth quoting at length:

> The ordinary novelist, who can never make a perfect thing, can with every novel try again. But if we write a novel to prove something, one novel will settle it, for why prove a thing more than once? And what, then, is to keep all novels by all right-thinking persons from being pretty much alike? Or exactly alike? There would be little reason for present writers to keep on, no reason for the new writers to start. There's no way to know, but we might guess that the reason the young write no fiction behind the Iron Curtain is the obvious fact that to be acceptable there, all novels must conform, and so must be alike, hence valueless. If the personal vision can be made to order, then we should lose, writer and reader alike, our own gift for perceiving, seeing through the fabric of everyday to what to each pair of eyes on earth is a unique thing. We'd accept life exactly like everybody else, and so, of course, be content with it. We should not even miss our vanished novelists. And if life ever became not worth writing fiction about, that, I believe would be the first sign that it wasn't worth living. (151)

In her example, novelists become associated with individuality and freedom of expression: key tenets of American democracy. This contrasts sharply with the Soviet writers, whose visions "must conform, and so must be alike, hence valueless," and diminish the reader's own individuality and freedom in turn. While Welty does not use the word "propaganda," this is the essential function of Soviet art in her imagining. Welty implies that it is precisely because American novels do not have to be political that makes art of the Western democratic order superior; there is the capacity to be political, but why do that if it makes the product no better than Soviet propaganda?

Considering this along with the emphasis on moral convictions, wonder, and representation, "Must the Novelist Crusade?" seems to double down on the late modernist aesthetic. Welty writes that the crusader-novelist cannot address wonder because everything in a crusading novel must have an explanation (152). Writers of this kind do not realize the artistry in what they do, but rather "[use words] as something to brandish, with which to threaten, brag or condemn" (153). Fiction directly engaged in political discourse is not good fiction. Novelists, on the other hand, have moral convictions, but they need not be stated outside the novel because they are at their plainest in their novels (152–53). Most important of all, novelists seek to represent what is true: "The novelist works neither to correct nor to condone, not at all to comfort, but to make what's told alive. He assumes at the start an enlightenment in his reader equal to his own, for they are hopefully on the point of taking off together from that base into the rather different world of the imagination" (152). The novelist is inclusive in his treatment of humanity because "when we write about people, black or white, in the South or anywhere, if our stories are worth the reading, we are writing about everybody" (156). This universalizing statement about the transcendent powers of literature echoes previous notions, such as Faulkner's, that presenting the South can effect change by appealing to the morals of people, who are generally good (we already know what "we ought to be like") (152). Welty's essay makes a direct appeal to New Critical sensibilities, arguing that fiction that moralizes, politicizes, and allegorizes is bad fiction; good fiction creates mystery, wonder, and examines human relationships.

However, at the end of the essay, Welty unambiguously expresses a hope for change: "History will change in Mississippi, and the hope is that it will change in a beneficial direction and with a merciful speed, and above all bring insight, understanding" (157). If we assume that this change is related to what midnight callers have urged Welty to do something about, her statement here suggests that she was of two minds about politics, and scholars have taken note. Many have approached this dichotomy by arguing that Welty trusts art more than politics. Peggy Whitman Prenshaw contends that politics always left a bad taste for Welty because the political discourse of the South maintained the segregated status quo—something Welty associated with "demagogic leaders and racism" ("Welty's Transformations," 20). These are the pitfalls of the novelist-crusader. Jonathan W. Gray recognizes the difficulty of Welty's nuanced argument:

> This cautious valorization of personal understanding was difficult to maintain in the face of racial violence that called for immediate action, but Welty was convinced that the tension in Mississippi would only abate when a plurality of whites attained a humane understanding of the Black Other, one that literature could help produce. This essay seems to endorse the democratic goals of the emancipationist tradition while also preserving southern innocence, an indication of the tightrope that Welty was attempting to negotiate. (90)

One of the cables tensioning this tightrope is the conflict between the writer and reader regarding where the responsibility to effect change resides. This conflict emerges in Welty's evocation of Faulkner at the essay's conclusion. "Once Faulkner had written, we could never unknow what he told us and showed us. And his work will do the same thing tomorrow. We inherit from him, while we can get fresh and firsthand news of ourselves from his work at any time" (Welty, "Must the Novelist Crusade?" 158). Neither Faulkner's work nor the work of all true novelists directly advocates for change but imparts a knowledge of human nature that inspires readers. Ultimately it is the reader's responsibility to act and effect change.

This contradiction makes "Must the Novelist Crusade?" a watershed moment. Welty argues, through her own meditation on her craft and by gesturing toward Faulkner, for late modernist aesthetics; but in the same breath, she acknowledges that even this element is ultimately political. If literature bears witness to history, as she describes it, and readers are the agents of change, then all literature is ultimately political. Her championing of personal interaction supports this position, too. Elsewhere in the essay, she writes, "No matter how fast society around us changes, what remains is that there is a relationship in progress between ourselves and other people. ... There is the relationship between the races. How can one kind of relationship be set apart from the others?" (154–55). Welty does not argue for change through political action, though her canvassing and bumper stickers suggest that while she might not urge others to political action, she might have privately discussed its efficacy. But her vision includes bringing about change in personal interactions with others, especially others of a different race, which are the same kinds of changes that Lillian Smith called for in "Addressed to Intelligent White Southerners." Although pleading for no political literature, Welty creates the space for fiction to be more overtly political again.

The significance of television in shaping how twentieth-century Americans received news, imagined other places, and perceived themselves cannot be overstated. Television news broadcasted beyond the US South Jim Crow's atrocities. Coverage of protests, marches, and riots was intense, including high-profile events in Mississippi in the early 1960s. The broadcasts showed a national audience, for the first time, the extent of the hatred and violence experienced by blacks throughout the South but also had the effect of forcing southerners to confront the realities of their society. No doubt, this caused anger and discomfort, and local affiliates relieved the discomfort by censoring national broadcasts. The historian John Dittmer notes that such censorship occurred frequently in Jackson beginning as early as 1955, when WLBT, the NBC affiliate in Jackson, censored Thurgood Marshall's appearance on *Today* in support of school desegregation; the station manager at the time later told a meeting of a white citizens' council that he had blocked the interview because he viewed the national television networks as outlets of "Negro propaganda" (Dittmer, 65). The practice of blocking national coverage of the civil rights movement and dismissing it as "Yankee propaganda" stifled public knowledge and discussion of the issue and was a common practice in southern local television in the 1960s and into the 1970s for WLBT, when the station nearly lost its broadcast license in a federal court case over racial bias (66, 451n63).

Indeed, television coverage of blacks in the news is a great nuisance to the unnamed narrator of "Where Is the Voice Coming From?," a story that Welty famously wrote immediately following the assassination of Medgar Evers on June 12, 1963, and published three weeks later in the *New Yorker*. Critics have frequently noted Welty's acknowledgment that after the arrest of Byron De La Beckwith for the murder, she had to hastily revise the story over the phone because "the fiction's outward details had to be changed where by chance they had resembled too closely those of actuality, for the story must not be found prejudicial to the case of a person who might be on trial for his life" (*Collected Stories*, xi). Despite significant attention to the historical cognates in the story, critics have devoted little of that attention to the role of television, though some acknowledge that television is integral to how the unnamed assassin in the story constructs his identity. Suzan Harrison notes the extent to which television coverage of marches, bombings, standoffs at the doorways of schools and universities, and assassinations both challenged white middle-class comforts and shaped the way whites constructed their own racial identity in opposition to what they understood as confirmation for their biases against blackness in portrayals of "so-called 'race riots.'" Harrison rightly points to a freedom that the narrator desires from the story's beginning, "the freedom from the black image"; however, his drastic action only increases the visibility of Roland Summers (the story's analogue for Medgar Evers) in television and other media. The narrator finds that in seeking to define himself as separate and above the activist, the two are now forever linked.

Still, the opening of "Where Is the Voice Coming From?" bears an eerie resemblance to reality. The story opens with the narrator saying to his wife, "You can reach and turn it off. You don't have to set and look at a black nigger face no longer than you want to, or listen to what you don't want to hear. It's still a free country" (*Collected Stories*, 603). The narrator, bristling at television coverage of Roland Summers's civil rights activity, suggests to his wife that she turn off the television. He then thinks of how he could turn Summers off permanently. This opening mirrors history. Medgar Evers was leading the local NAACP in boycotts of businesses in Jackson, and the mayor of the city went on WLBT to attack the boycott. Evers petitioned for an opportunity to respond on WLBT, and the Federal Communications Commission issued an order requiring the station to provide Evers with seventeen minutes, the same allotment the mayor had received earlier. The American RadioWorks documentary *State of Siege: Mississippi Whites and the Civil Rights Movement* reports that "Evers appeared on television and told Mississippians in a calm voice that it was time for change in Mississippi," and while there is no extant recording of Evers's broadcast, "WLBT did record phone calls that were made to the station while Evers was on the air." The recordings of these calls, which the documentary provides to listeners, reveal the hatred and disgust of the white viewers.

PHONE SCREENER: WLBT?
WOMAN: Uh, we'd like you to take the tape off of that nigger, please?
SCREENER: Uh, ma'am, we are required to run this under our license commitments with FCC.
WOMAN: What are you people of Mississippi gonna do, just stand by and let the niggers take over?
MAN: You know this black son-of-a-bitch that's on television?
SCREENER: Yes, uh huh.
MAN: He's been on more than goddamn 17 minutes. They'd better get his black ass off or I'm gonna come up there and take it off.
SCREENER: Well, sir, we're required to do this . . .
MAN: Oh, hell no. This is in the South. This is below the Mason-Dixon Line. You don't have to put these black jungle bunnies on TV . . . (quoted in Ellis and Smith)

The complaints are couched ultimately in terms of freedom and liberty. Mississippi is a sovereign, democratic state in the Union and should control its affairs and its airwaves for its citizens, who should be free from seeing and hearing people and perspectives that challenge the tyranny and oppression of Jim Crow society. Three weeks after Evers's television appearance, Byron De La Beckwith shot and killed him outside his home.

The comments from the callers bear remarkable similarity to comments made by the narrator at the opening of "Where Is the Voice Coming From?," especially the caller who threatened to "come up there and take it off." As Jonathan W. Gray suspects, Welty would almost certainly have seen Evers on television that spring. Although she would not have heard the recordings of these angry white viewers complaining to WLBT before writing the story, if ever she heard them, we might infer that she heard some complaints around town. She explains in the preface of her *Collected Stories*:

> That hot August night when Medgar Evers, the local civil rights leader, was shot down from behind in Jackson, I thought, with overwhelming directness: Whoever the murderer is, I know him: not his identity, but his coming about, in this time and place. That is, I ought to have learned by now, from here, what such a man, intent on such a deed, had going on in his mind. (ix)

In light of the transcripts, Welty was more or less right. The only thing that seems to run contrary to the facts of the case in the story is the economic and social status of the narrator. Welty imagines a poor, out-of-work person who is just as jealous of Roland Summers's economic success as he is prejudiced against his race. However, the real killer, De La Beckwith, came from a prominent family and was employed. Welty stated in a 1972 interview with William F. Buckley Jr. that someone had told her, "No, you thought it was a Snopes and it was a Compson" (101). Welty's friend is alluding to Faulkner's famous lineages, the former poor and the latter wealthy. Significantly, Welty is confident she knows the identity of the killer, and yet she is wrong because she cannot imagine that the killer could possibly be affluent. Affluent southerners are guilty only of polite racism, it seems, in Welty's worldview.

"Where Is the Voice Coming From?" is unique in Welty's work for how directly it takes current events as its subject and inspiration, becoming the site for a confluence of tensions. There are the obvious tensions between white and black, which lend the story to an overtly political reading. However, continuing to pull the thread of television reveals the tensions between social and economic classes and southern tradition and liberal progress. The most significant tension, though, is between the apolitically political aesthetics of the vital center, which employed literature to reinforce American democracy during the Cold War, and a literature of social justice, which pointed out the faults in American democracy. With recent diplomatic challenges for the United States, such as the failed Bay of Pigs invasion and the Cuban missile crisis, both of which garnered wide media coverage, the American democratic project could no longer afford troubling accounts of racial oppression in the South tarnishing its image. Given this context, the content of television coverage in the story complicates the narrator's place in both southern and national society. First, for the sight of Roland Summers on television to inspire the deed, the narrator must be a frequent viewer. He, like the callers to WLBT, perceives the appearance of desegregationist ideas and their proponents as unwelcome intrusions into his home. He says, "Even the President so far, he can't walk in my house without being invited, like he's my daddy, just to say whoa. Not yet!" (607).

This rebuke suggests John F. Kennedy's televised address to the nation the day before Evers's murder, June 11, 1963. The speech, in which Kennedy clearly declares all American citizens deserving of equality regardless of race, was delivered to support his actions to quash Alabama governor George Wallace's attempt to keep segregation in place at the University of Alabama. The shooter, whose anonymity implicates any disgruntled white southerner, sees his action as politically motivated. The narrator also seems insecure in his white masculine identity, and terrified of social justice. He borrows a truck from his brother-in-law, and he is ridiculed by his wife, who berates him for leaving their gun at the scene and tells him if he had waited, he might have been able to eliminate a higher-profile target. The murder is a way to restore political order. In this light, the story could be seen in the same vein as Lillian Smith's literary activism and her focus on the local and its connection to national and global problems.

Yet there are several discourses influencing social order that the narrator must navigate, and significantly "Where Is the Voice Coming From?" seems paradoxically to merge television and national politics with literary-historical allusion and appeals to morality. Despite acknowledging how closely her story came to retelling events as they actually happened, Welty hints that reality was not her aim. She told Buckley in the same interview, "I did know the inside and I wrote from the interior, because I felt that I could. That's the only time that kind of thing ever happened to me" (101). In other words, Welty never attempts to write ripped-from-the-headlines stories; rather, as a writer works to create characters who are true to human nature, sometimes lightning strikes. This reveals a second reading of the story: a decontextualization of Evers's assassination through a late modernist appeal to aesthetics and moralistic aims.

The town in which the story takes place is called Thermopylae, a direct allusion to the site of the fabled battle between the Spartans and Persians. Moreover, the name Thermopylae loosely translates to "hot gate" and refers to the number of hot springs in the area. This clever use of a place name with deep historical and mythological associations diverts attention from the story's contemporary parallels, instead directing the reader to attend to the rich implications of its language and word choice—every context needed to understand the story becomes contained therein. In revisions to the story, this name supplanted the use of Welty's hometown and site of the real-life murder, Jackson. Hence the name defamiliarizes Jackson, putting some distance between Welty, the reader, and the killing (in case she did, indeed, "know" the murderer). Of course, Welty made changes to deliberately make the story not match reality, as her description of the editorial process makes clear, but the choice of an ancient Greek site is a fairly ham-fisted allusion. While renaming Jackson helps to disassociate the story from any particular location or event, the story features dissonant clues regarding place to clearly set the story in the US South. Most obvious, the narrator travels down "Nathan B. Forrest Road" and passes the "Kum Back Drive-In and Trailer Camp" to go to Summers's house, passing signs for "Live Bait" and "Peaches" along the way (603).

The narrator's dialect is telling, as well. In the moment of the murder, the narrator tells the dead Roland Summers, "There was one way left, for me to be ahead of you and stay ahead of you, by Dad, and I just taken it. Now I'm alive and you ain't" (604). Also, the narrator repeatedly says that he committed the murder for his own "pure-D satisfaction" (605). While all are explicitly markers for the South, few of the places and the words of the narrator (besides "Nathan B. Forrest Road" and the narrator's and his wife's racial slurs) are by themselves explicit markers for racism. While it is certainly implied, the language in which the narrator provides his reasoning to his victim itself does not explicitly mention race. Moreover, the earliest criticism of the story does not emphasize race and politics, mentioning history in passing. Charles Clerc focuses on the "anatomy" and aesthetics of the story, briefly mentioning that it nonetheless "remains useful as a historical artifact and sociocultural document about life in the United Stated at a crucial point beginning the final third of the twentieth century" (396). To describe the story in this way against its historical backdrop diminishes the role that its contexts play in how the story makes meaning, and leaves only textual details available to the reader.

If one attempts to make this critical move, to set aside the historical correlation between Evers's appearance on WLBT, the callers to the station, President Kennedy's address to the nation, and the opening words of the narrator—all the things that together with the historical and social context of the story make it clear that the narrator acts out of racist convictions—what, then, is the reason that the narrator kills Roland Summers? Critics have identified varied reasons. Ann Romines argues that one reason could be filial responsibility. The narrator, she argues, is a dutiful son if nothing else, pointing to evidence such as his exclamation "by Dad" when he kills Summers (114), and he also speaks to a "white male collective" (113). Romines's reading of the story's final paragraph, in which the narrator plays a ballad, sees the ballad as "implicitly mourning his dead parents and invoking their authority, this bigot and murderer is a pious son" (115). More recently, William Murray argues that the narrator acts under pressure from the power structures that provide access to power and capital, pointing to the bank sign that lights the way (112). Murray further suggests that if the narrator has to explain that he kills for his own "pure-D satisfaction," and not to satisfy the powers that be or to secure his place in the social hierarchy, then he really *is* doing it to cement his place in southern power structures, "part of an old and unacknowledged narrative of southern violence based on conceptions of personal honor and societal duty in the face of a rising minority" (117). But even these readings are informed by some sort of context external to the story (southern emphasis on family values and the stratification of power and capital in society).

One can never escape the specter of racism when writing about southern literature, but one can ignore it. Ignoring the extratextual context of the story's writing, a reader must rely on the richness of Welty's text. The narrator's reason may simply be pride or, indeed, as he repeats throughout the story, his own "pure-D satisfaction," and so he takes pleasure in meanness, similar to Flannery O'Connor's Misfit. Welty leaves her narrator/murderer feeling no remorse. Distant from his wife because she belittles his actions, he is isolated from society and cannot take credit for his deed because "people are dead now" (*Collected Stories*, 607). In the final scene, the narrator is by himself at home playing guitar with only "what I've held on to from way back when, and I never dropped that, never lost or forgot, never hocked it but to get it again" (607). The only thing he has is his malicious pride. If the root of that malicious pride can be sidestepped, then the story becomes a tale of interpersonal alienation due to the moral sins of murder and haughtiness rather than a political allegory for racial violence in the South. Welty nearly admits as much in her preface to her *Collected Stories*: "I wrote his story—my fiction—in the first person: about that character's point of view, I felt, through shock and revolt I could make no mistake" (ix). Her purpose was to capture the character's point of view. The narrator likely sees himself as attempting to preserve his place in society, but he does not understand his act as racism. It is his expression of individual liberty.

Near the beginning of "Must the Novelist Crusade?," Welty writes that one of the problems facing the crusading novelist is "before anything else, speed," indicating how quickly the message must be produced to have the necessary context. "The crusader's message is prompted by crisis; it has to be delivered on time" (148). On the other hand, the novelist's work is timeless. She elaborates on this point at the end of the essay, using Faulkner again as example:

> History will change in Mississippi, and the hope is that it will change in a beneficial direction and with a merciful speed, and above all bring insight, understanding. But when William Faulkner's novels come to be pictures of a society that is no more, they will still be good and still be authentic because of what went into them from the man himself. Mankind still tries the same things and suffers the same falls, climbs up to try again, and novels are as true at one time as at another. Love and hate, hope and despair, justice and injustice, compassion and prejudice, truth-telling and lying work in all men; their story can be told in whatever skin they are wearing and in whatever year the writer can put them down. (157)

Literature written to bring about political and social change has its moment, Welty says, but when that political and social change happens, the moment for that literature has passed, because it does not address the unchanging themes at the core of human experience. The immutable themes of human experience—"love and hate, hope and despair, justice and injustice, compassion and prejudice, truth-telling and lying" (157)—can always be present in the novel because such themes are not temporally constrained by setting. Welty shares this perspective with New Critics, for sure. On the other hand, the racism and poverty of the South, which should change "with merciful speed," are merely parts of a setting against which such themes can be explored; they are always true as part of that discrete setting for fiction, not as a record of social realities. After the racism, segregation, and squalor have been defeated by the New Deal or by the Great Society (if ever), Faulkner's fiction will never have been truly about those things, but about justice, liberty, and individual accountability.

"Where Is the Voice Coming From?," like crusading fiction, was "delivered on time" (148). Welty comments in her preface to her *Collected Stories* and in several published interviews on how quickly she wrote the story as a response to a racially motivated (and therefore politically motivated to keep Mississippi segregated) killing. The *New Yorker* wanted the story ready for publication in an upcoming issue so badly that Welty worked over the telephone with the editor, William Maxwell, to revise portions that were too close to the facts of the murder. In a couple of interviews, she indicates that the revisions were made at the behest of the *New Yorker*'s legal counsel, but in an interview late in her life, Welty tells Joseph Dumas, "Reality was what I had just written, you know. . . . But they could take no chances on any coincidence with reality" (283). The story certainly engages the themes of "love and hate, hope and despair, justice and injustice, compassion and prejudice, truth-telling and lying" ("Crusade," 157). However, the story would have had clear contemporary analogues for readers. Indeed, the narrator seems to see himself as a red-blooded American with a radical commitment to the idea of individual freedom. Near the end of the story, he proclaims, "Ain't it about time us taxpayers starts to calling the moves? Starts to telling the teachers *and* the preachers *and* the judges of our so-called courts how far they can go?" (*Collected Stories*, 607). Readers who know about Medgar Evers's murder know that "Where Is the Voice Coming From?" has factual analogues, but many of the details connecting the story to these factual events have been obscured, whether by an editor concerned about the events of the story being too true or by Welty herself in an attempt to make the story less crusading. Perhaps in a distant future when neither scholars nor students nor casual readers of Welty's work have studied Medgar Evers or read about him, the "crisis" will be lost on readers, and the story will not be "delivered on time" for them. What will remain, however, is a narrative about liberty and freedom, albeit one showing a man who has been oppressed and directs his efforts to maintain his liberty and tradition at the wrong target.

This is just one of a few paradoxes about Welty and her work's relationship to civil rights and the Cold War, paradoxes that seem not to have been thoroughly acknowledged, given the sharp split between "Welty bashers" and "Welty apologists," to again use Banecker's reductive taxonomy. The paradox at hand is the contradiction between late modernist aesthetics and the representation of social and political realities such as racism in "Must the Novelist Crusade?" and "Where Is the Voice Coming From?" Although Welty warns against writing fiction that engages political topics and contemporary events in an effort to effect change, one could argue that she does just that in "Where Is the Voice Coming From?" The story crusades because it presents a shockingly horrific, repulsive worldview that the nation would be better without, and it is precisely a worldview that informs the perpetration of a high-profile murder, bringing the objectives of the civil rights movement to the national consciousness. At the least, the *New Yorker* seemingly wanted the story to crusade, considering the speed with which it was published, despite the heavy revisions to obscure reality. This paradox is even more plausible given Welty's work as a publicity agent for the Works Progress Administration on the front lines of the Great Depression in rural Mississippi. She had an interest and experience in documenting the experiences of people in precarious situations. Those would include the murderer of "Where Is the Voice Coming From?," who is both materially and morally impoverished.

This tension between writing fiction and crusading even appears in the way that Welty talks about the story in interviews. Welty tells a consistent story of the piece's composition, but we can read some nuances in her descriptions of her reasons for writing it and how she thinks about it. In 1973 she told Don Lee Keith, "Right after Medgar Evers got shot, I had this idea about a story told from the viewpoint of the murderer. Of course, it was a man, and I really cannot envision my telling something from the male viewpoint. But somehow, this was more than a man; he was a murderer. Now, does that make me more of a murderer than a man?" (151). The impetus for the story is the imagination: could Welty re-create the voice of a murderer? The same interview goes on to make the point of "Must the Novelist Crusade," that the crucial difference between fiction and journalism is that in the former "there is the possibility that both writer and reader may share an act of imagination" (151). However, in a 1977 interview with Jean Todd Freeman, Welty describes the impetus for the story with some slight differences, which are more compatible with "Must the Novelist Crusade?" After discussing her ire with the "middle-of-the-night, dead-of-the-night telephone calls about the troubles in the sixties" from people who thought she should do something, Welty defends her position, worth quoting at length:

> In 1965 I wrote a piece for the *Atlantic Monthly* called "Must the Novelist Crusade?" in which I tried to express this. Not only on my behalf, but on the behalf of all writers at all times. Some writers may see that as their business, which is their privilege, but I see as my privilege writing about human beings as human beings with all the things that make them up, including bigotry, misunderstanding, injustice, and also love and affection, and whatever else. Whatever makes them up interests me. I try to write as I see real life, which doesn't allow stock characters who get up and illustrate something in the abstract—that was going on a lot at that time.
>
> Well, one thing that I did do, which pertains to this, I guess, was in result of the one really bad thing—one of two really bad things—that happened in Jackson during the 1960s as far as race incidents went. It was the murder of Medgar Evers. I did write a story the night it happened. I was so upset about this and I thought: I live down here where this happened and I believe that I

must know what a person like that felt like—this murderer. There had been so many stories about a character in the stock manner, written by people who didn't know the South, so I wrote about the murderer intimately—in the first person, which was a very daring thing for me to do. (183)

Here the reason Welty gives for why she writes "Where Is the Voice Coming From?" is much more palpable and reactionary; moreover, she does not summarize "Must the Novelist Crusade?" for the interviewer in quite the same way as she did for Keith. The story comes from being angry at Evers's murder and at stock portrayals of southern characters. Welty's anger about the murder surely comes not only from the taking of a human life but from her understanding that it was the racially motivated assassination of a civil rights worker. Yet Welty's anger at the stock portrayals of southerners, which she says were "going on a lot at that time," could be understood as an impetus to portray southerners in a more complex way, and "Where Is the Voice Coming From?" portrays its murderer as complex and no different from the ideal American: concerned with liberty, tradition, and values. Given the speed with which Welty wrote the story and her accounts of the reason why, we should understand "Where Is the Voice Coming From?" as trying both to "see real life" and correct stock portrayals and to reflect the outrage at Evers's death. Of course, both have the capacity to suggest to readers the need for social and political change, that is, the capacity to "crusade."

Other contradictions between "Must the Novelist Crusade?" and "Where Is the Voice Coming From?" involve genre and audience. In the case of the former, Welty argues that the *novelist* must not crusade; "Where Is the Voice Coming From?" is a short story. Welty dispels this contradiction herself by referring interchangeably to "novelists" and "writers of fiction" in her essay. Of more importance is the publication choices she made regarding the two works. Indeed, her first audience for "Must the Novelist Crusade?" was an integrated audience at Millsaps College in Jackson, but when she published the essay two years later, in 1965, she did so in the *Atlantic Monthly*. She published "Where Is the Voice Coming From?" in the *New Yorker* in 1963. Welty made the choices that she did about publication for practical reasons. Welty mentioned over the years in interviews how well the *New Yorker* paid (H. Mitchell, 71; Wheatley, 125), and "Must the Novelist Crusade?" found its way into the *Atlantic Monthly* after *Harper's* requested substantial cuts (Marrs, *Eudora Welty*, 314–15). These publication venues also show who Welty likely sees as readers of her work. Despite the original lecture audience of "Must the Novelist Crusade?," the essay certainly seems to be addressed not to fellow southerners but to northern journalists and literary friends who are concerned that Welty and other writers could contribute their talents to defeating segregation and Jim Crow. As such, the essay reaches precisely that readership in the *Atlantic Monthly*, but probably some southerners as well—but again Compsons, not Snopeses.

This raises the significant issue of white and economic privilege. Welty states in her interview with Freeman that she sees her work as her *privilege*: "Some writers may see that as their business, which is their privilege, but I see as my privilege writing about human beings as human beings with all the things that make them up, including bigotry, misunderstanding, injustice, and also love and affection, and whatever else" (183). But is it the privilege of all writers to not crusade? For the writer of color in the United States, the act of writing itself can be construed as crusading; the assertion of black experience and identity is inherently political, especially during the Cold War and the civil rights movement, despite Robert Penn Warren and Ralph Ellison's conversation in *Who Speaks for the Negro?* Welty's narrative reduces Roland Summers's poor white trash assassin into one of those stock characters upon the realization that in the negative space of that portrait exists the upper- and middle-class whites of Jackson, possibly politically moderate, probably racist.

The material surrounding "Where Is the Voice Coming From?" in the *New Yorker* also reveals something about how the story crusades, whether Welty intends it to or not. At the least, the story's publication in the *New Yorker* shows how the story is situated between the political tensions of the civil rights movement and the Cold War. The July 6, 1963, issue in which Welty published her story was more or less the magazine's Fourth of July issue that year. The cover art depicts a fireworks display over a beach, with crowds gathered to watch. To the left, in the background, an amusement park evokes Coney Island.[4] The issue contains a poem by Theodore Roethke, an essay reporting on a recent professional golf tournament, and a review of a new Russian film. The issue also publishes two stories. One is "In and Out of Never-Never Land," by Maeve Brennan, in which a woman learns a lesson about the surprising maturity of children when a neighborhood six-year-old saves her family home when a brush fire is caused by stray fireworks on the Fourth of July. The other story is "Where Is the Voice Coming From?," which took a prominent place in the issue as the first piece after the opening "Goings On about Town" section. It surely was "shock[ing] and revolt[ing]" (to use Welty's words) to readers to see the cruel logic of how the story's narrator stays ahead of Roland Summers. Welty may argue that her fiction does not crusade, but how does it not subtly crusade when it is the lead piece in the Independence Day issue of a major magazine, calling into question the values being celebrated? As such, we can see a parallel between the *New Yorker* and the northern journalists making dead-of-night calls, pleading with Welty to crusade.

How the story, published on July 6, subtly crusades to readers of the *New Yorker* becomes clearer when we consider the issues published before and after it. The June 22 issue included Richard H. Rovere's "Letter from Washington," reporting and commenting on President Kennedy's June 10 address at American University on nuclear arms and his June 11 televised address to the nation about his actions on civil rights. Rovere leads with the latter, and his commentary emphasizes that getting any civil rights legislation through the southern Democratic filibuster in the Senate might be as difficult as negotiating a nuclear test ban with the Soviet Union. "Enacted and energetically enforced," Rovere argues of Kennedy's legislative goals on civil rights, "they would be a great monument to his administration—perhaps the greatest he could possibly hope for—and a splendid display of a modern democracy's capacity for renewing itself and honoring its best traditions and observance" (92). Rovere decidedly yokes together civil rights and the Cold War as issues near the end of his commentary by quoting President Kennedy and noting recent events:

> "Let us examine our attitude toward peace and freedom here at home. The quality and spirit of our own society must justify and support our efforts abroad. . . . 'When a man's ways please the Lord, he maketh even his enemies to be at peace with him.'" The passage from Scripture isn't susceptible of proof, and it certainly wouldn't be accepted on faith by the family and friends of the late Medgar Evers, of Jackson, Mississippi. (98)

Frequent readers of the *New Yorker* would likely have read this commentary before encountering "Where Is the Voice Coming From?" two issues later. For such readers, the story might have seemed an examination of the "attitude toward peace and freedom here at home" (Rovere, 98). In the next issue, readers would have encountered an excerpt from Calvin Trillin's *An Education in Georgia* (1964), which profiles the experiences of Charlayne Hunter and Hamilton Holmes as the first black students to enroll at the University of Georgia in 1961. In the context of these articles, readers might have perceived Welty's story not as a portrayal of humanity with all its faults in that historical moment, but as an examination that reveals the faults that must be overcome to preserve American democracy in the face of the Cold War.

If we take Welty at her word in "Must the Novelist Crusade?" and set aside the subtle inconsistencies in the manner she discussed the story in her interviews, then "Where Is the Voice Coming From?" does not crusade. This is perhaps more clear because of her choice of publication venue. Readers who encountered "Where Is the Voice Coming From?" in their regular perusal of the *New Yorker* would likely have already been convinced of the ills of segregation and poverty and thus were not the proper target of crusading literature. Publishing the story as quickly in a venue that would have reached more southerners, perhaps specifically Snopeses, would have resulted in a story that more directly crusades. Yet Welty decidedly did not do this: she told one interviewer about a phone call from a northern reporter she received shortly after the story was published, who wanted to know if she had been the target of any violence. When she said no, he said he would call back later to see if things had changed. She told him, "The people who burn crosses on lawns don't read me in *The New Yorker*. Really, don't people know the first thing about the South?" (Clemons, 31). While Welty likely chose the *New Yorker* for practical reasons (she had an interest in protecting herself and her mother, whom she cared for because she was in poor health), her choice shows that she knew the political statement that her story makes. It also divulges a prejudice that Welty may have felt against poor white southerners, as she cannot at that moment imagine middle- and upper-class white southerners being outwardly racist, much less burning crosses or assassinating activists. Even if Compsons likely do not burn crosses and may read the *New Yorker*, they are still racist.

These are difficult, fine distinctions for scholars to draw. As Gray notes, Welty was well versed in New Critical tenets about literary aesthetics, and perhaps her work during the 1960s would have been quite different if she had been educated when theory-based interpretive apparatuses emerged in the 1970s and beyond. Having earlier access to those critical discourses might have enabled Welty to better articulate her paradoxical aesthetic (Gray, 90). In short, Welty likely had difficulty drawing these distinctions and thus became a paradox herself. "Must the Novelist Crusade?" suggests that she holds late modernist aesthetics about fiction in regard, but "Where Is the Voice Coming From?" and her choice to publish it in the *New Yorker* and to revise the story further to prevent it from seeming too much like reality suggest that Welty acknowledges the crusading aspects of that work of fiction. Thus Welty subverts late modernist aesthetics, recognizing in "Where Is the Voice Coming From?" a capacity to effect political change by causing readers to think about their own values in comparison to those of her narrator. The story is apolitically political, but the politics it masks are not those of America's vital center but the political exigency of supporting the civil rights movement because "people are dead now" (*Collected Stories*, 607).

The other side of this paradox is the possibility that Welty does not intend to subvert her late modernist aesthetic in "Where Is the Voice Coming From?" or does not realize how the story is subversive. Her commitment to addressing the truth in fiction and not crusading could have stifled an objectivity about her own work, which prevented her from realizing exactly how such a story would crusade in the climate of the 1960s. Publishing the story in the *New Yorker* reaches an audience who do not need to be crusaded for, but it also places the story among other kinds of writing besides fiction, such as journalism and commentary, that Welty might consider to be crusading.

It is impossible to conclude whether Welty was actively or passively subverting her late modernist aesthetics, but we can have little doubt that such a charged story as "Where Is the Voice Coming From?" does just that. Welty arguably acknowledges this crusading quality when she mentions her friend's comment that she thought the murderer was a Snopes when in fact De La Beckwith was more of a Compson. To miss the truth of the killer's identity in the writing of "Where Is the Voice Coming From?" was at the worst to insert a stock character after all; at best it added a political dimension to the story. The story becomes political because this mistaken identity tacitly acknowledges the material violence associated with the fraught entanglement of Cold War notions of liberty and socioeconomic status with segregation in the Jim Crow South and how the political establishment has manipulated its electoral base to maintain the status quo. The story ultimately leads the way as southern writers explore more overtly the ways that southern values come to be conflated with American ones. The answer to Welty's questioning of whether the novelist must crusade seems itself to depend much on race and agency.

5

Suburbs, Civil Rights, and Southern Identities

Eventually late modernist aesthetics seeped into popular culture via the Cold War mobilization of southern studies. One of the consequences is the growth of a cultural and political identity associated with southernness that supersedes the geographical category of "southern," that is, an identity tied not to earlier received notions of a sense of place but to matching sets of cultural sensibilities formulated by the vital center at the height of the Cold War. Two novels written about the American political climate of 1960s, Alice Walker's *Meridian* (1976) and Walker Percy's *Love in the Ruins* (1971), demonstrate this through Cold War dystopias depicting a post-South in which ideology, socioeconomic realities, and literary and popular-media portrayals of southernness begin to supplant any geographic or cultural understanding of place as the basis for southern identity. In their respective mappings of turbulence in American society through both the perspectives of individuals and collective action at regional and national levels of discourse, these novels suggest a description of regional communities based on how well their values align with a continuum of the vital center that is a precursor to today's political debates in which the United States is not so much classified anymore by southern and northern states as by red states and blue states. Within this model, the values cultivated in literature written by southerners or about the South and identified by intellectuals as American become the guiding principles of a generally conservative political identity; communities are grouped together not necessarily by geography but by correlations in their ideology.

In *Meridian*, the title character's personal life charts a feminist history of the civil rights movement of the 1960s. Meridian Hill's political experiences establish the efficacy of personal identifications with political movements to resist conformist mores. They also address the unique challenges women face when participating in political resistance dominated by men. Unlike

Welty, Meridian does not have the option not to crusade. In *Love in the Ruins*, which can be construed as science fiction in its presentation of an alternate future, Percy's outrageous narrative points toward the emerging red state–blue state model by politicizing nearly every individual and community in the novel, showing a parallel with the spread of conservative politics to the white suburban middle class in the late sixties. The novel's downplaying of racial strife and lampooning of extreme political viewpoints, coupled with the protagonist's supposition that political affiliations are associated with treatable psychological disorders, suggest a diagnosable vital center. However, the book ultimately points toward Percy's own revision of the vital center, making *Love in the Ruins* a resolutely late modernist novel, and a troubling one. In concert, these two novels indicate that personal connections to ideologies play a prominent role in sustaining the vital center's cultural identity once it has been separated from concerns of place.

The sense of place so long associated with southern literature ultimately is proving to have little relevance to geography. It wanes in importance as a growing critical conversation reexamines definitions of "place" and explores the extent to which place defines southern literature. The limitations of the term arise when considering the drastic transformations of landscapes, demographics, and economies throughout the United States in the last quarter of the twentieth century, but especially in the southeastern and Sun Belt states. In his essay "Where Is Southern Literature?" Scott Romine reminds us that "sense of place," in its common usage, "serves as both a description (southern literature has it) and a distinction (southern literature has more of it than other literatures)." The term was originally deployed by southern writers and intellectuals to "prevent 'southern literature' from becoming an arbitrary geographical designation" (23, 24). Romine concludes that, owing to the increasingly global nature of economic and political forces, "The determinants of even the most isolated southern hamlet are increasingly dispersed to other locations: an Indonesian labor force willing to work at low wages, a board of directors' meeting in New York, a Hollywood film set" (41). Place, then, is no longer the concept connecting literary representations to identities of the US South; rather, it is the socioeconomic or political realities tied to that cultural history. Such is the end of late modernism; it is no longer the actual geographic place that has importance but the intellectual, political, and economic forces that codify or define that place, its culture, and conceptions of it. A construct of the "South," or a post-South, as some have termed it, begins at least in media representations to stand in the place of the actual people and material history and culture of the region. Racial and economic privilege determines whether that construct focuses on romanticized fantasies about whiteness or prejudice, poverty, and poor opportunities. Both *Love in the Ruins* and *Meridian* paint portraits of Americans—not necessarily southerners—participating in cultures and practices associated with the US South through such media representations, televised historical events and happenings, real estate developments, and other reproductions of the South.

Meridian and *Love in the Ruins*, as different as they may be, both have significant connections to historical events and the social contexts of the 1960s and early 1970s. The first of these is the work of nonviolent civil rights activists, whose slow march toward equality included demonstrations and voter registration drives and led to the passage of the Civil Rights Act of 1964, finally legally prohibiting discrimination on the basis of race in the electoral process and in public places. The movement proper seems to come to an end (such is the case in *Meridian*) with the assassination of Dr. Martin Luther King Jr. in 1968, leaving a void in the leadership of the movement. This was coupled with Republican president Richard Nixon's victory in the 1968 presidential election, won in part by carrying the traditionally Democratic southern states: a feat he accomplished by targeting his campaigns in the region at middle-class white suburbanites. With the South now vastly different and thoroughly politicized because of the civil rights movement, population shifts to the suburbs, and television coverage of those changes, the late modernist sundering of politics and literature depended more than ever on individuals' commitment to ideology to sustain a vital center so important to the success of American-style democracy. Walker's and Percy's novels both depict individuals deeply devoted to ideologies they perceive as a way to mend a nation fractured by a decade rife with war, political assassinations, and civil unrest.

Each novel has more direct connections with historical circumstances, too. For Walker, they were personal. She participated in many of the same activities as her protagonist, Meridian Hill. As a student at Spelman College in Atlanta, Walker participated locally in the movement and would go on to work in voter registration drives in Mississippi after completing her BA at Sarah Lawrence College. Her novel's eponymous character follows a similar path from rural community to activist in a southern city to experiences in the North, culminating with a return to the South. The parallels are so strong between the historical activities of, and attitudes about, the movement and the fictional events of *Meridian*, the historian Barbara Melosh argues, "In the subjective medium of fiction, we can read the afterimage of history, its imprints on the writer's consciousness and way of seeing the world. In this sense, novels are themselves primary sources, historical evidence of ideology" (65).[1] According to Susan Danielson, *Meridian* is not just a novel in which the civil rights movement is a background or setting; the novel is a record of the reasons individuals got involved, its methods and practices, and how communities changed because of the level of activism within them. In particular, Danielson suggests that the novel chronicles the rise and fall of the Student Nonviolent Coordinating Committee (SNCC), as well as the shortcomings of its philosophy and its activists. Her reading is based on textual details that mark dates, places, and items significant to the SNCC, such as the overalls—the unofficial uniform of the SNCC—that Meridian wears in the novel's opening section (Danielson, 319). Meridian shares her name with the Mississippi town where three SNCC workers disappeared in 1964, and many dates the novel uses are corollary to key dates in the history of the SNCC (318). Danielson reads the novel's first part as covering the rise and fall of the story's SNCC-like organization; the second part covers the disillusionment of each activist (322). As opposed to telling the history of the movement with cold objectivity, Walker's novel offers perspectives from individuals struggling to understand the movement's success and shortcomings through episodes of interpersonal relationships within it and individuals' devotion to (and criticisms of) it.

Percy's *Love in the Ruins*, on the other hand, reveals the complications of American suburban politics at the height of the Cold War and of the civil rights movement by exploring how racial anxieties became disguised as political moderation. Percy had already explored the suburbs as a postsouthern setting in his first novel, *The Moviegoer* (1961), about Binx Bolling, the thirty-year-old scion of a genteel New Orleans family, who is being pressured by his aunt to attend medical school. Part of Binx's initial revolt against his aunt is to move to the suburbs of New Orleans. Of Percy's deployment of the suburbs in the setting of *The Moviegoer*, Martyn Bone argues that Binx's initial rejoicing in his move to the suburbs to escape the oppressive mythos of the Old South allows Percy to "wryly satirize canonical constructions of the southern 'sense of place'" (74). But Bone also notes that the novel provides no escape from capitalist reproduction of a postsouthern sense of place, and this leads Binx to retreat "to his aunt's upper-class enclave" (74). The commodification of the South is inescapable even for the mythical South, Bone concludes. And even in his third novel, Percy is still satirizing the suburbs. Written in the wake of Richard Nixon's successful 1968 run for the presidency, during which his campaign suggested sympathy with white, southern, suburban segregationists to gain popularity in the South (an area where Republican candidates historically performed poorly), *Love in the Ruins* portrays a polarized suburban population in the South of a politically fractured United States: a mishmash of southerners and nonsoutherners, conservatives and liberals, living together united in their racism.

Unlike *The Moviegoer*, *Love in the Ruins* offers no retreat from the suburbs. Because of their ubiquity in American life, the suburbs become all the more associated with the trappings of southern identity detached from geography. The suburbs are universalizing (and dull, which is what Binx likes about them at first). *Love in the Ruins* not only portrays the postsouthern but also forecasts today's red state–blue state political map of the United States in its sheer politicization of nearly every individual and community in the novel, paralleling the spread of conservative politics to the white suburban middle class in the 1960s. This southern identity and politics became suburban identity and politics, uniting communities across the United States not by geography but by ideology, and suburban political moderation morphed into modern conservatism—moral and social conservatism coupled with financial neoliberalism. The novel's emphasis on lampooning extreme political viewpoints and portraying racial strife (long associated with the South but present now in the suburbs) as merely a symptom of such ideological extremes suggests an attempt to divorce geography from sensibilities and values long associated with the South. In depicting suburban politics, the book ultimately points toward Percy's own satirical but telling revision of southern identity, one in which personal connections to ideologies play a prominent role once southern identity has been separated from concerns of place. Ultimately, *Love in the Ruins* paints portraits of Americans—not necessarily southerners—participating in cultures and practices associated with the US South through media representations, televised events, real estate developments, and other reproductions of the South.

Love in the Ruins satirizes the devotion to hyperbolic political views by caricaturing materialistic suburban dwellers, yet throughout the novel, Percy also seems anxious about contemporary social trends, exhibiting a realization that the former foundations of the US South's society were eroding. Michael Kobre argues that Percy really was of two minds and traditions. He was raised in the Old South and with its traditional mores, "yet Percy also recognized that the severe and honorable traditions he had inherited were increasingly outdated in a New South that was, in his own words, 'happy, victorious, Christian, rich, patriotic and Republican'" (4). Indeed, Percy's own vision of this New South is remarkably in line with historical studies that explore the roles that the suburbs played in the turn toward modern Republican conservatism in the US South in the twenty-five years after the end of World War II. During the postwar expansion of industry in the region, Atlanta, Charlotte, and Memphis became centers of commerce, attracting more and more southerners—white and black alike—to their metropolitan regions who decided to give factory and office work a go as opposed to farming in competition with increasingly larger commercial farms. The *Brown v. Board of Education* decision during the migration to cities undoubtedly influenced patterns of suburban growth, as well as white flight from urban centers. Particularly relevant to Percy's imagined suburbs is the historian Kevin Kruse's exploration of white flight in Atlanta and the political identity that developed out of the manner in which whites fought to preserve segregation. Kruse explains that popular notions of civil rights history paint segregationists as a group of folks interested only in depriving others of their equality and rights:

> The conventional wisdom has held that they were only fighting *against* the rights of others. But, in their own minds, segregationists were instead fighting *for* rights of their own—such as the "right" to select their neighbors, their employees, and their children's classmates, the "right" to do as they please with their private property and personal businesses, and, perhaps most important, the "right" to remain free from what they saw as dangerous encroachments by the federal government. (9)

Their insistence on utter freedom from bureaucracies illustrates a concept of the vital center in which American democracy rests on citizens' ability to make their own choices about what will preserve their nation and their livelihood. These sentiments, of course, were not held by all whites in the South during the 1960s. As Jason Sokol writes, "Some white southerners perceived the civil rights movement as a threat to their very notion of freedom. Others saw the civil rights struggles for what they were—attempts to translate American promises of democracy and liberty for all into reality" (17). In the case of Percy's novel, the vehement conservatives and bleeding-heart liberals live peacefully side by side in the suburban development of *Love in the Ruins* because they can agree on one thing: neither wants to have blacks for neighbors.

Along with white flight, Richard Nixon's 1968 presidential campaign is another significant context for the politics portrayed in *Meridian* and *Love in the Ruins*. Matthew Lassiter addresses Nixon's relationship to suburban politics in his study *The Silent Majority: Suburban Politics in the Sunbelt South* (2006), which explores the political mobilization of white southern values among other suburban demographics during Nixon's campaign. Lassiter's argument proposes an alternative to the conventional notion that Nixon managed to win on a "southern strategy," that is, by campaigning on the racially motivated anxieties of poor rural southerners. Instead, Lassiter asserts, "Richard Nixon's triumph in 1968 depended on a de facto suburban strategy that targeted middle-class voters in the metropolitan South and positioned the GOP as the centrist alternative to the racial extremism of George Wallace and the racial liberalism of Hubert Humphrey," Nixon's two opponents in the election (227). To downplay any racial component to his campaign, Nixon focused his attention on suburban, middle-class disgust with protests against the Vietnam War and anxieties about black militants and increasing urban violence; however, he needed to do so without alienating centrists (234). Rick Perlstein, as well, argues that an appeal to the center was part of Nixon's preparation for his second run for the presidency as he calculatingly built a platform for himself that maintained a separation from segregationists such as George Wallace yet remained appealing to reserved racists in the South and elsewhere. In 1966, Nixon said that he did not support segregation, but suggested it would be unwise for Washington Republicans to "dictate" to state parties what positions to hold (quoted in Perlstein, 88). In the position Nixon hammered out for himself as a centrist in 1960s American politics, "He was ventriloquizing to a generation of Southern lost-cause speechifying about Yankees dictating to Dixie" (Perlstein, 88). Publicly, Nixon evoked civil rights in his advertisements in a moderate fashion to further distance himself from his opponents while acknowledging suburban fears: "The first civil right of every American is to be free from domestic violence, so I pledge to you: We shall have order in the United States" (quoted in Lassiter, 236). Nixon's mobilization of these fears dovetails with Percy's suburbanites' distaste for all radicals and nonconformists. Despite the radicals' self-imposed exile in the Honey Island Swamp near Tom More's neighborhood, the residents of Paradise Estates still feel threatened by them, and their homes and bourgeois activities do fall under revolutionary attack, one attempted by reluctant black militants.

These histories and novels show the culmination of American writers' and politicians' attempts to downplay segregation as a major political problem facing the United States. Jim Crow traveled a great distance from being a regional anomaly, to the greatest hurdle facing American democratic ideals both at home and abroad at the beginning of the Cold War, to the motivation of both the civil rights movement and suburban politics. As southern suburban politics disguised racial anxieties as political moderation, the vital center morphed into modern conservatism—moral and social conservatism coupled with financial neoliberalism. Together *Meridian* and *Love in the Ruins* make the literary representation of this new cultural ideology's cleft between the US South and a US post-South: a fracturing of America into red states in political opposition to blue states in all corners of the country.

In "The Black Writer and the Southern Experience," Alice Walker meditates on the importance of her upbringing in a sharecropper family, a situation in which she did not consider herself disadvantaged because of race or poverty, and how her times in college and broader experiences thereafter showed her that others saw her as disadvantaged. As a student of literature, her admiration of William Faulkner ended upon reading *Faulkner in the University*. She discovered that Faulkner found "whites superior morally to blacks" and considered it the duty of whites "to 'bring blacks along' politically"; only under white patronage could they become productive contributors to American democracy (19–20). "For the black person coming of age in the sixties, where Martin Luther King stands against the murderers of Goodman, Chaney, and Schwerner," Walker counters in her essay, "there appears no basis for such assumptions" (20). With its characters' deeply personal yet complex devotion to the work of social and political equality, *Meridian* is Walker's literary counter to Faulkner's provincial and grandfatherly racism. Also countering this view of southern race relations are the book's three principal characters, Meridian Hill, Truman Held, and Lynne Rabinowitz, who all exhibit some degree of personal investment in the movement, though each character has a different kind of commitment to the movement and its ideology. Yet in this book, as Dror Abend-David points out, Walker shows a "firm dislike of mass movements and 'professional' ideologists" (19). This is especially true with regard to the particular perils endured by the novel's women who participate in the movement, and postsouthern suburban populism's depoliticization of segregation only widens the gulf.

Although her background is not an impoverished or uneducated one, indeed, it is the tactics of such suburban politics that cause some of Meridian's early hardships. Countering portrayals of racism as a moral problem that the South would be able to solve on its own time, as Faulkner and the New Critics had suggested in the past, Walker shows how some of the hardships Meridian's family faces are directly related to strategies used by the whites in their Georgia town to maintain segregation. The Hill family farm, inherited from Mr. Hill's grandfather's post–Civil War acquisition, shared land with the Sacred Serpent, an ancient and sacred burial mound built by Native Americans. Meridian's father's respect for the land and the mound are so great that he gives the deed to an Indian, Walter Longknife, who camps on the land for much of the summer before returning the deed to the Hills. Mr. Hill gives Longknife the land for the summer because "the land already belonged to them" (*Meridian*, 47), and also as a duty to a veteran who "killed a lot of people, mainly Italians, in the Second World War. . . . He was looking for reasons, answers, anything to keep his historical vision of himself as a just person from falling apart" (49). Mr. Hill understands how military service, just like Cold War conformity, obscures identities that are neither white nor

American, and he hopes to help Longknife recover his. But in the end, the Hills cannot even keep the farm. Soon after the veteran departs, government workers show up with picnic tables and trash cans and inform Meridian's father that the Sacred Serpent and the Hills' farm are becoming "a tourist attraction, a public park" (49). Upon presenting the deed to county officials to prove his ownership, Mr. Hill learns that the park will not be that public: "[The county] could offer only token payment; that, and the warning to stay away from Sacred Serpent Park which, now that it belonged to the public, was of course not open to Colored" (49). The family's simultaneous loss of their farm and the Sacred Serpent in both private and public ownership demonstrates the length to which white southerners went to exclude blacks from public life. As the majority in power, the white officials in the novel feel they have a right to determine who visits the same park they do. Moreover, they perform a disservice in turning the burial mound into an attraction; doing so is an appropriation of sacred land for the production of a white hegemonic history of the place.

White politics also beset Meridian's father during the years she attends Saxon College (most likely modeled on Spelman College). Meridian takes a typist job for a professor at his off-campus office to earn some money because her father no longer earns much money to send: "He was no longer qualified to teach, now that integration was threatening the school" (*Meridian*, 97). Here Walker satirically adopts the language of the segregationist to highlight the injustice of the situation. The only disqualification that Mr. Hill has for teaching in an integrated school is his race; segregationists in power insisted on their "right" to choose who teaches their children. Yet within the same school system that eventually fired her father, Meridian had to learn a speech "that extolled the virtues of the Constitution and praised the superiority of The American Way of Life"—a speech that Meridian is unable to finish (126). Lauren Berlant argues that the speech's role in this scene, and the predominant role education plays in the novel, is to transmit this American national identity—more or less the ideology of the vital center—to students. However, in the case of Meridian and her peers, this kind of nationalistic education within their social conditions is only a "terrible joke," for the inalienable rights about which black students learn are never actually bestowed (Berlant, 834). It, too, is a fantasy just like the movies that Meridian, after becoming a mother, imagines fills the lives of teenagers just a few years younger than she is: "Blondes against brunettes and cowboys against Indians, good men against bad, darker men. This fantasy world made the other world of school—with its monotony and tedium—bearable" (*Meridian*, 72). Perhaps; yet it is still a fantasy world that underscores their position on the negative side of strict Cold War binaries.

While these personal dealings with Jim Crow could certainly have been reason enough for Meridian to become a civil rights worker, she is spurred into action through a defining feature of Cold War culture: television. A teenage wife and mother, therefore not allowed to finish school, she spends her days watching television, resenting her husband and child for diminishing her agency. She catches a news report at a house where a voter registration drive among blacks in her town and county is being organized, but the next morning she tunes in to see news reports of the same house, this time bombed, with three children dead (*Meridian*, 70–71). Seeing the violence she is used to seeing on television occur in her hometown helps Meridian to realize that the brewing racial conflict locally is connected to a national civil rights struggle and to human rights: "And so it was that one day in the middle of April in 1960 Meridian Hill became aware of the past and present of the larger world" (70).

It is a sense of altruism that sparks Meridian's desire to take back her life that has been weighed down by marriage and motherhood. However, once she decides to divorce her husband and leave her child to attend Saxon, her devotion to the movement is also stirred by her guilt about leaving her child. Before Meridian's departure, her mother tells her, "Everybody else that slips up like you did *bears* it. You're the only one that think you can just outright refuse" (86). Mrs. Hill is upset because what she sees as Meridian's shirking of domestic duties as mother and homemaker disturbs the social order, but the problem runs deeper. The conflict between Meridian and Mrs. Hill and the guilt that Meridian suffers for refusing motherhood open the door to the critique that Walker offers of the movement: often ignored within the issues of race and class that it tackled, the movement did not do well in addressing sexism. Alan Nadel argues that Walker's novel surveys the conflict within African American culture in which women suffer oppression by men parallel to the racial oppression suffered by all blacks:

> This leaves black women at a double remove from power and makes them participants in a double encoding system. If black history forms a repressed, encoded, ruptured alternative to published American history, then maternal history—the chain between generations bound by maternal experience, genetic biases, and empathetic subjugation—is an encoded subtext within the black male cultural history. (Nadel, *Containment Culture*, 255)

Meridian's experiences with Saxon's expectations for its students and her confusion about maternal roles are intertwined with her involvement in the movement. To reconcile Nadel's observation about the double subjugation of black women within *Meridian* means that neither women's issues nor civil rights can be treated as merely a backdrop to the story. The power of women beyond domestic roles is important, a point counter to the limited, domesticated womanhood in the canon of the "Southern Renascence."

Saxon College is doubly complicit in the terrible joke, not only because the school maintains a degree of patriotism and religious hopefulness for those inalienable rights, but also because it oppressively monitors the behavior of its students to ensure they do not break social mores for women. Meridian must hide from her peers that she has a child and was married because Saxon students are assumed to be virgins. The school song declares its women "chaste and pure as the driven snow," a ridiculous lyric cleverly mocked by Meridian's friend Anne-Marion with her own line: "We are as choice and prime as the daily steak" (*Meridian*, 93). The revision vigorously suggests the objectification and consumption of the women who graduate from Saxon, whose education has made them prime candidates for marriage. Because of Saxon College's investment in producing students who conform to the appropriate social role, its administrators attempt to foster an environment that is as apolitical as possible.

> The administration of the college neither condoned Saxon students' participation in the Atlanta Movement nor discouraged it. Once it was understood that the students could not be stopped, their involvement, as much as possible, was ignored. All of Saxon's rules, against smoking, drinking, speaking loudly, going off campus without an escort, remaining off campus after six, talking to boys before visiting hours, remained in effect. It was understood that a student who allowed herself to be arrested did so at her own academic risk. (*Meridian*, 94)

Their apolitically political stance against their students' activity in the Atlanta Movement is a common thread between the Saxon administration and Dr. Bledsoe of *Invisible Man*: like Dr. Bledsoe's college, which has a white benefactor, the northerner Mr. Norton, Saxon College benefits from white wealth. It is built on the land of the old plantation owned by the slaveholding Saxon family. Saxon administrators have white benefactors to keep happy, as well, who would frown on the students' involvement in the movement.

Despite the administration's attitude toward activism, Meridian and others take an interest in the poverty-stricken community surrounding Saxon. While registering voters in the area, Meridian hears about "Wile Chile," an uncouth orphaned girl who had grown up homeless, surviving by rummaging through garbage. Meridian manages to catch the girl and bring her onto campus for a bath. When Wile Chile escapes and is killed when hit by a car, Saxon officials refuse to allow Wile Chile's funeral to take place in the college chapel. This causes a riot on campus that culminates with students chopping down the Sojourner, a magnolia tree surviving from plantation days, despite Meridian's pleas that they aim their rioting at the president's house. The Sojourner holds a special place in the mythology and private culture of the women at Saxon because it is a direct connection to a subversive figure of the past. The tree was planted by a slave woman, Louvinie, when the property was Saxon Plantation, whose family wove elaborate tales to catch murderers in West Africa before she was enslaved. Louvinie planted the tree when she buried her tongue under it: Master Saxon had it clipped out and ground it under his boot because a scary folktale Louvinie told killed his only son by giving him a heart attack at age seven (*Meridian*, 31–39). Rather than tearing down the direct representation of the college's plantation past and oppressive present—the seat of a moderate, vital center on the campus—the students chop down their most tangible link to a subversive figure of the past.

Meridian's interest in the welfare of Wile Chile and the preservation of the Sojourner is certainly propelled by her devotion to the movement and its work for the community surrounding Saxon, but another motivating factor is the guilt that Meridian feels about the life she took away from her mother and the child she abandoned to retain her agency. Brenda O. Daly goes so far as to argue that the most significant dimension of the novel is how "it tells the story of the Civil Rights Movement from the point of view of a mother—or, more accurately, from the point of view of a variety of different mothers, old and young, white and black, violent and nonviolent, self-denying and self-defining" (240). Meridian is the mother at the center of the novel, and her paralytic fits, first encountered by readers in the novel's opening, are physical manifestations of her feelings of inadequacy in her relationship with her mother and her own child. As a child, Meridian felt inexplicable guilt, and when she shared the feeling with her mother, she asked, "Have you stolen anything?" The implied answer is that, through the requirements for her care, Meridian stole her mother's career. With the question, "A stillness fell over Meridian and for seconds she could not move. The question literally stopped her in her tracks" (*Meridian*, 43). Even in her childhood, guilt had a somatic effect on Meridian. She goes on to feel more guilt about the child she gives up to attend Saxon. However, this guilt over refusing socially predetermined roles is evocative of the sexist oppression endured by black women that mirrors racial oppression. After leaving for school, she ponders the condition of mothers in slavery, whose greatest fear was separation by the sale of their children, to torture herself. "And what had Meridian Hill done with her precious child? She had given him away. She thought of her mother as being worthy of this maternal history, and of herself as belonging to an unworthy minority, for which there was no precedent and of which she was, as far as she knew, the only member" (90). Meridian denies herself motherhood a second time after she discovers that Truman Held begins dating Lynne Rabinowitz shortly after ending their affair.

Although it is difficult, Meridian remains a close, supportive friend to Truman and Lynne throughout their marriage, divorce, and the murder of their daughter, Camara. These friendships Meridian forges through her activism are part of her personal connection to the movement, but an even deeper connection is the manner in which her work in the movement compensates for denying herself biological motherhood. Keith Byerman argues that Meridian interprets her work within the movement as maternal, and through that work she heals her own affliction (102). At the least, her maternal vision of her work shines through in her dedication to nonviolent protest, which she sees as a life-sustaining form of resistance. In New York, her inability to declare that she would kill for the cause (maybe, she says) ends with Anne-Marion's cadre of militant revolutionaries literally turning their backs on her. John F. Callahan explains that Meridian certainly sees the crises of American society, but "unlike the others, [Meridian] cannot answer simply as an individual and a contemporary because for her social and political change is bound up with love and with the witnessing, participatory form that belongs to a true community" (156). This only strengthens Meridian's resolve to reject the vital center's individualism and "go back to the people, live among them, like Civil Rights workers used to" (*Meridian*, 19).

Many of her experiences after this return to the South lead her to work as an advocate for children and their parents. The novel's opening episode shows her leading the black children of Chicokema in a peaceful demonstration against a sideshow owner who refuses to admit them to his show until Thursday—the day set aside for "coloreds." In a separate ordeal, she marches into a town meeting and delivers to the mayor the bloated, decomposing body of a five-year-old boy. He drowned because the town closed its public pool rather than integrate it, forcing him and other children to play in a drainage ditch that floods without warning when the town drains its reservoir. The child's family offers to name their next daughter after Meridian to reward her actions: "Instead she made them promise they would learn, as their smallest resistance to the murder of their children, to use the vote" (209). Meridian's activism is always among the community to keep the focus on the movement's objectives instead of its ideology—a fault she sees in Anne-Marion's uncontemplative devotion to revolution. Here Meridian has much in common with Ellison's invisible man, who grows frustrated when he realizes that the Brotherhood wants him to simply deliver its message without thinking much about its content or goals; neither character is a slave to ideology, and both have a sincere desire to take action as opposed to simply advocating for it.

However, it is finally the inconsolable sorrow of a father that makes Meridian believe she could kill for the movement. A "red-eyed man" at a church service where the preacher praises the man's son as a martyr on the anniversary of his death—a young man killed when he merely spoke of armed resistance against discrimination—is so bereaved that he can only say over and over again, "My son died" (*Meridian*, 217). After leaving the church service, "she made a promise to the red-eyed man herself: that yes, indeed she *would* kill, before she allowed anyone to murder his son again" (220). She wavers about whether she could ever make good on the promise, but what is key is that it is parental grief that leads her to even consider it. For her, the movement is not simply about forcing reality to conform to the American fantasy of equality for all; it is also about preserving families. She sees firsthand that community can soothe the pain of families who have lost children, and can take collective action to improve their conditions. This runs counter to the world of Percy's *Love in the Ruins*, in which grown white children become estranged from their parents over ideology. Although she finds her identity in the movement, for Meridian, her work within it is ultimately about the people it sought to help from its inception, not its ideology or militancy.

The other two main characters of *Meridian*, Truman and Lynne, are both northerners who have come to the South to work with the movement, and their personal connection to the region is that they attempt to locate in it an identity for themselves. Their lack of connection to the South, juxtaposed with their participation in a national movement so thoroughly associated with the region, demonstrates a progressive cultural identity splitting off from its regional associations, not unlike the vital center's splitting off of southern values into its new conservative identity. In this light, the pair represents the emerging blue states. One of their personal connections to the movement is also their shortcoming: their objectification of the black folk of the US South as art. Truman is a particularly problematic character because he replicates racial oppression in his mistreatment of women in the movement (namely, Meridian). He abruptly leaves after a sexual encounter with Meridian and almost immediately begins dating Lynne, never realizing that Meridian is pregnant and has an abortion. Yet while taking a break from Lynne, Truman approaches Meridian, calls her beautiful, professes his love for her, and tells her, "*Have* my beautiful black babies" (120). His insensitive pandering, objectification of Meridian's fertility, and reification of cultural prejudices for white beauty in his attraction to Lynne earn him a beating from Meridian. After becoming estranged from Lynne, Truman retires from activism to focus on his art; however, his subjects remain romanticized portraits of black women whom Truman scorns for not caring more about their appearance. "'They are so *fat*,' he would say, even as he sculpted a 'Big Bessie Smith' in solid marble, caressing her monstrous and lovely flanks with an admiring hand" (183).

Rather than replicating oppression, Lynne's artistic objectification of African Americans living in the US South raises concerns about how artistic representations strip the movement of its political aims and become complicit in the production of the post-South. Lynne's notions arise from her disgust with the uniformity of the northern suburbs. The counter she finds to that uniformity lies in the South: "The South—and the people living there—was Art. The songs, the dances, the food, the speech. Oh! She was such a romantic, so in love with the air she breathed, the honeysuckle that grew just beyond the door" (*Meridian*, 136). So Lynne moves south to help with the movement and find the best art. "If Mississippi is the worst place in America for black people, it stood to reason, she thought, that the Art that was their lives would flourish best there" (136–37). Lynne's sentimentalized vision is highly problematic. It participates in a common trope pastoralizing the existence of southern rural blacks as happy workers who are part of the background of the idyllic, relaxing countryside where urbanites can go to escape the hustle and bustle. Like Welty, Lynne has the privilege to not crusade.

Besides being a racist perpetuation, seeing the South as art depoliticizes it by separating the artistic image of the region from the real-life complexities of its social and racial strife. Nadel sees as one of the primary conflicts in the novel the divide between art and politics, in which a balance is difficult to strike. He explains, "When an experience or material condition becomes the subject of art, it is stabilized and is not as subject to change or improvement. But the problem with revolutionary politics . . . is that they are not 'stable or predictable'" (*Containment Culture*, 263). Lynne learns as much through her tenuous status as a white woman involved with the movement. She is also objectified by its black members and seen as a dangerous reminder of, and temptress from, the hegemonic white culture. "To them [the workers] she was a route to Death, pure and simple. . . . They did not even see her as a human being, but as some kind of large, mysterious doll. A thing of movies and television, of billboards and car and soap commercials" (*Meridian*, 146). Lynne endures being raped by Tommy Odds, another civil rights worker, who blames her for his arm being shot off in an attack by white supremacists because they saw Lynne hanging out with black men after dark. She becomes objectified in the attack, and the rape is doubly torturous for Lynne because she feels responsible for the attack that cost Tommy his arm and the pangs of white guilt. She cannot cry rape; doing so would guarantee a lynching. She tells him she forgives him, which only earns her more contempt from Tommy. When Tommy returns the next night with friends and attempts to instigate a gang rape, the friends prevent the second attack when one of them disputes Tommy's calling Lynne "it." "That ain't no *it*," he says, "that's Lynne" (175). The moment provides some hope that artistic and popularized objectifications of people can be overcome. With Lynne, perhaps even more so than with Meridian, Walker surveys the complex relationships and conflicts between genders and races among civil rights workers, especially the personal costs for those workers.

These painful bodily experiences within the movement can combat the post-South tendency to turn geography and material culture into abstraction. After Camara's death, Meridian spends time in New York with the grieving Truman and Lynne, and she has a reconciliation of sorts with Lynne while watching television. The program is "one of those Southern epics" that present stereotypical images of white men and black men, leaving women out. It moves to a scene in which a black man says the movement got him the vote and ended segregation but taught him also that more than that needed changing, and maybe a gun was needed for it. The two women have the same reaction to the man:

> That the country was owned by the rich and that the rich must be relieved of this ownership before "Freedom" meant anything was something so basic to their understanding of America that they felt naïve even discussing it. Still, the face got to them. It was the kind of face they had seen only in the South. A face in which the fever of suffering had left an immense warmth, and the heat of pain had lighted a candle behind the eyes. (*Meridian*, 190)

Their shared response leads them to seek out tangible objects, such as a quilt, that reminds them of their experiences in the South. The moment is significant because their activism is the root of their reconciliation. Despite the waning of the movement after the death of Dr. King, they remain politically aware of the salient economic barriers to equality that persist. Moreover, when they recall the specific individuals whom they set out to help, their shared experiences rebuff depictions of the US South politically diluted in the media. Meridian and Lynne will always find their identities in their particular, tangible participation in the revolution and remembrance of the past.

A similar phenomenon happens in the book's second chapter, which begins with the names of assassinated political leaders and civil rights activists—"MEDGAR EVERS/JOHN F. KENNEDY/MALCOLM X/MARTIN LUTHER KING/ROBERT KENNEDY/CHE GUEVARA/PATRICE LUMUMBA/GEORGE JACKSON/CYNTHIA WESLEY/ADDIE MAE COLLINS/DENISE MCNAIR/CAROLE ROBERTSON/VIOLA LIUZZO" (*Meridian*, 21)—before focusing on John F. Kennedy's televised funeral and Anne-Marion's observation of Meridian's specific response to it. Elliott Butler-Evans notes how the focus remains on "Meridian's specific response to the funeral of John Kennedy, and what is striking here is that, throughout the episode, the horror of Kennedy's death is experienced only through Meridian's reactions to it"; thereby the novel gives an individual perspective on historical events and allows the personal relationship to them to overtake the larger public narrative of history with which the consumer of media can readily identify (117). A second significance of this chapter is how the list of names provides regional, national, and international context to the civil rights movement. The names include national leaders, civil rights workers, the victims of the Sixteenth Street Baptist Church bombing (1963), and, quite tellingly concerning America's ambitions abroad, Patrice Lumumba, the first elected leader of the Congo, who was deposed and executed, most likely with the support of the United States. Lumumba caused problems for US political influence in Africa because he was a socialist and a Soviet sympathizer. He won no points with the Eisenhower administration during his one visit to Washington when he asked his handlers from the State Department to find him a blonde escort for the evening, and within the administration it was accepted that he sought to seize the property of all whites in the Congo. "The oldest and deepest fear of white Americans seemed to be coming true on the international stage in the midst of the Cold War: Patrice Lumumba was Nat Turner" (Borstelmann, 131). In this list of names, Walker takes a page from Lillian Smith's playbook of thirty years earlier: she learns to read her maps, which Smith advises as a way to understand how actions within the local have global implications. Walker reverses the route, however, showing that American political actions abroad to stifle meaningful revolution parallel domestic politics.

Still, Berlant criticizes *Meridian* for not giving up on the utopian dream of American equality as something that all citizens will be able to participate in, for which she favors *The Color Purple* and its rejection of the myth of American national heritage. Perhaps Berlant makes a valid criticism of *Meridian*, but a more important point is that the novel refuses to give up on the value of political action within communities. With her college education,

Meridian could very well have done as Truman did, abandoning the movement to chase an intellectually affluent middle-class existence. However, Truman finds Meridian still living in the rural South, adopting working-class garb, "dressed in dungarees and wearing a light-colored, visored cap, of the sort worn by motormen on trains" (6), as she still pursues activism. Near the end of the novel, Meridian and Truman canvass for voters in a rural area and try to convince a man whose wife is bedridden and close to death (she hopes to die and be buried on Mother's Day) of the power of the vote to bring them better living conditions and health care for his wife. Reluctant to register for fear that doing so will bring him "a lot of trouble," the man would rather devote his energy to caring for his wife and son than to voting (*Meridian*, 225). To lend him their support, Meridian brings the family groceries, making it clear that she does so not to coax him into voting. The Monday after Mother's Day, he comes to Meridian's house to register to vote. The man registers because he sees that Meridian is driven not by any kind of demagoguery or ideology but by her caring for others. To return the kindness of Meridian's charity, he registers to vote in hopes of making a difference in the community. The man and many of the rural characters in *Meridian* "are capable of change and of political action; it is simply that change must be connected to concrete experience" (Byerman, 93). Presenting concrete experiences of the civil rights movement counter to postsouthern imaginings of it is one of the book's merits.

In his reflection on the US South in the fracturing 1960s, Walker Percy looks forward to an even more splintered society in a near future in *Love in the Ruins*: not one aspiring to genuine representation of a region, but one pining for the loss of suburban comforts. The novel departs from *The Moviegoer* (1961) and *The Last Gentleman* (1966) in that it is decidedly satire, but it also begins a trajectory of increasing preachiness for the remainder of Percy's career. Long before beginning work on the novel, however, he had written to his mentor Caroline Gordon, "Actually I do not consider myself a novelist but a moralist or a propagandist. . . . What I really want to do is to tell people *what they must do and what they must believe if they want to live*" (quoted in Tolson, 300). Percy's desire to help people "live" comes on strong in *Love in the Ruins*. The novel depicts an America full of political extremes, and Tom More's objective in his near-apocalyptic adventure is to find not only some kind of middle ground but also a basis for it. Tom explicitly states his anxieties about the disappearance of some sort of middle ground when he paraphrases one of Yeats's most famous lines: "The center did not hold" (*Love in the Ruins*, 18). The middle ground his escapades establish is similar to Nixon's suburban strategy—pandering to complicit racism and fears about unrest. Percy also seems interested in establishing a middle ground. In his own comments to the Publisher's Publicity Association about *Love in the Ruins*, Percy declares the novel is satire, but he also betrays other intentions. "But even to say this [is satire] is misleading," Percy says. "It suggests a political satire which attacks right and left and comes down on the side of moderate Republicans and Democrats. I had a different center in mind" ("Concerning *Love in the Ruins*," 248). If not a political center, then what kind of center? He goes on to declare, "But the novel is not saying: Don't rock the boat, cool it, be moderate, vote moderate Republican or Democrat. No, it rocks the boat" (250). Indeed, *Love in the Ruins* rocks the boat by *emphasizing* polarizing political, social, racial, and economic differences as opposed to mediating them. This approach suggests that both within the novel's world and at the height of the Cold War, to *not* be ideologically extreme—to be moderate, even in suburban Middle America—is to be un-American.

Tom's world is certainly full of hyperbole, schism, and fluctuations between insightful hilarity and shortsightedness. The setting is the early 1980s (in his comments on the novel, Percy said he imagined around 1983), and the Catholic Church in America has split into three different sects. The sect faithful to Rome, of which Tom considers himself a member, is "scattered and demoralized" and has let its church go to ruin (*Love in the Ruins*, 6). The United States has wasted away into deserted urban areas and increasingly independent states:

> Americans have turned against each other; race against race, right against left, believer against heathens, San Francisco against Los Angeles, Chicago against Cicero. Vines sprout in sections of New York where not even Negroes will live. Wolves have been seen in downtown Cleveland, like Rome during the Black Plague. Some Southern states have established diplomatic ties with Rhodesia. Minnesota and Oregon have their own consulates in Sweden (where so many deserters from their states dwell). (17)

Such a shattered country would have been the cold warrior's worst nightmare, and the passage hints at the international implications of such problems in the states' commencement of foreign relations, a power constitutionally reserved for the federal government. Quite telling is the southern states' diplomatic exchange with Rhodesia, a British colony in Africa whose white colonial government declared independence in 1970. The morass of political discourse is further complicated in the two major parties' becoming caricatures of themselves. The Republicans become the Knothead Party, an epithet they embraced after it was proposed they change their name to "the Christian Conservative

Constitutional Party, and campaign buttons were even printed with the letters CCCP on them" before pundits recognized the abbreviation was shared with the Soviets, and "called it the most knotheaded political bungle of the century" (17–18). The Democrats emerge as the Left Party, a shortening of "a derisive acronym that the Right made up and the Left accepted ... LEFTPAPASANE, which stood for what, according to the Right, the Left believed in: Liberty, Equality, Fraternity, The Pill, Atheism, Pot, Anti-Pollution, Sex, Abortion Now, Euthanasia" (18). Tom is either unable or does not think it important to name any individuals associated with the parties; therefore readers must assume that these parties are more easily identified now by their talking points than their leadership, ideals, or platforms for practical, responsible policy.

Even more jarring and relevant for the events of the novel is how these deep political divides manifest in media, demographic, and geographical lines of the country and Tom More's community. "There are Left states and Knothead states, Left towns and Knothead towns, but no center towns ... Left networks and Knothead networks, Left movies and Knothead movies" (18). In this manner, *Love in the Ruins* prefigures the red state–blue state model of American politics that emerges near the end of the twentieth century and continues today. While Tom still addresses a South and a North within the United States, the greatest indicators of cultural difference are no longer tied to such a distinction. Every aspect of cultural identity within the United States' various populations depends thoroughly on a political identification that has no middle ground. Preference for neighborhood is dictated by a desire to live near politically like-minded people—the "right" to choose one's neighbors asserted by suburban politics. Yet neighborhoods are separated along more than just partisan lines. The setting appears to be Louisiana—the setting of most of Percy's novels—and Tom identifies at least four distinct areas. The first is the unnamed town where Tom's office is located, populated by Knotheads. Fedville is a federal complex comprising a hospital, medical school, NASA facilities, and a research center for behavior, geriatrics, and sex where Lefts work. Tom's own neighborhood is called Paradise Estates, where Knotheads and Lefts live peacefully side by side, united in their relief that no blacks live in the neighborhood; it is also home to northerners who have moved south and taken up southern customs. Finally, the Honey Island Swamp is the domain of "dropouts from and castoffs of and rebels against our society" (15), including college dropouts, militant guerrillas, deserters from foreign armies, "ex–Ayn Randers, Choctaw Zionists ... and even a few old graybeard Kerouac beats" (16). Essentially Honey Island is home to anyone who refuses either of the two accepted political persuasions; in other words, its inhabitants have similarities with the characters in Walker's *Meridian*.

We learn about the features of this imaginary 1983 in a lengthy exposition, though there is much else to be learned. The structure of the book introduces Tom, his country, and his neighborhood on the Fourth of July, with Tom sitting in a pine forest near the interstate, waiting for the world to end. He nods off to sleep at the end of the book's first part, and the book returns to July 1, catching the reader up to speed on the events that led to Tom's current situation. Tom wakes from his catnap to commence the book's resolution, which is followed by an epilogue. Two key forces drive the plot: the repercussions of Tom's use and development of his invention, the ontological lapsometer, and a planned armed revolution by the Bantus, a black paramilitary organization whose name Percy sourced from a factual student group with a similar name in the 1960s. The plans for their revolution end up becoming secondary to the plot. This subordinating of the revolution to the main narrative mirrors society's, and perhaps even Percy's own, unwillingness to confront racial discrimination in the South and elsewhere as a continued political problem after the end of segregation. This leaves the problems Tom both identifies and causes with the lapsometer sharing the limelight.

Tom describes his lapsometer and its potential in the lengthy exposition. It is a device able to measure the electrical activity in specific places within a patient's brain, and Tom conjectures, "Could the readings then be correlated with the manifold woes of the Western world, its terrors and rages and murderous impulses? And if so, could the latter be treated by treating the former?" (*Love in the Ruins*, 28–29). He sees his invention as diagnosing the "deep perturbations of the soul" (29), and it is from this idea that Tom derives the machine's name: a device for measuring a "lapse." Tom elaborates in some scientific jargon that only with measurements taken of the brains of humans—not animals—can he detect a sense of self. He sees his discovery as a major advance in understanding the human condition: "Only in man does the self miss itself, *fall* from itself (hence *laps*ometer!). Suppose—! Suppose I could hit on the right dosage and weld the broken self whole! What if man could reenter paradise, so to speak, and live there both as man and spirit, whole and intact man-spirit, as solid flesh as a speckled trout, a dappled thing, yet aware of itself as a self!" (36).

If we examine Percy's work strictly through his devout Catholicism, the etymology of the device suggests the lapse that was the fall of man in Genesis (or that of the lapsed, or secular, Christian); therefore the lapsometer also measures how far the individual has fallen from God. Kieran Quinlan, on the other hand, develops the argument further, advancing the idea that the device is part of a larger comment the novel makes on the *cogito ergo sum*. Thus part of what the lapsometer measures is the span of the Cartesian split between mind and body (131). Martin Luschei pushes beyond the Cartesian split to construe Tom's tool as measuring an existentialist separation from the body in which a "socially conditioned self-consciousness" is alienated enough from material existence to cause the great wars of the twentieth century (188). At its most basic level, the lapsometer is a tool that leads Tom to believe he can repair the fragmented United States.

What these readings do not fully account for is that the lapsometer is just as much a political gauge as it is a spiritual one, connecting psychiatric symptoms with ideology. Tom uses his first subject's measurements to draw correlations between the subject's righteous, conservative rage and his headaches. Through the data collected on his second subject, a graduate student, Tom connects the student's terrors and self-abstraction to his liberalism; and in his third patient, Tom links the man's deep depression and ire against his son—who has joined the hippies in Honey Island Swamp—to his near dependence on television news to provide him something to be angry about. The invention may as well be a political continuum that can be used to adjust a patient's particular sentiments as needed and, in the climate of the Cold War, determine exactly how American or un-American a subject may be. Coupled with Tom More's desire to develop his invention in a "crash program," the lapsometer is a tool for preserving American-style democracy, and even its global ambitions. "It's not even the U.S.A.," Tom explains to his friend, doctor, and colleague at Fedville, Max Gottlieb. "It's the soul of Western man that is in the very act of flying apart HERE and NOW" (*Love in the Ruins*, 115). Max criticizes such notions as being metaphysical and abstract, but Tom insists on the realities of the situation: "There is nothing metaphysical about the tenfold increase in atrocities in this area. There's nothing metaphysical about the vines sprouting. There's nothing metaphysical about the Bantu guerrillas and this country falling about between the Knotheads and the Leftpapas" (115). Through Tom, Percy insists that some semblance of ideological or cultural middle ground must be maintained for the American way of life to survive.

Yet in a novel so conspicuously critical of the ways that political ideology informs individual identity, neither women nor blacks participate meaningfully in its political discourse or even its plot. Fully developed, strong, or admirable female characters are lacking in Percy's body of fiction, and *Love in the Ruins* is no exception. Tom's daughter, Samantha, dies before the events of the book, and her death causes his marriage to his wife, Doris, to disintegrate. She becomes bookish and leaves him for an Englishman (also before the events of the novel). In his reminiscing, Tom pokes fun at her favorite books: *Siddhartha*, *Atlas Shrugged*, and *ESP and the New Spirituality*. "My poor wife, Doris, was ruined by books," Tom laments, "by books and a heathen Englishman, not by dirty books but by clean books, not by depraved books but by spiritual books" (64). As many times as he repeats the point, Tom seems ultimately more upset about his wife having cuckolded him—sexually and intellectually—than mournful about her death.

In the time since he became a widower, Tom has been a womanizer, and there are three women—Moira Schaeffer, Lola Rhodes, and Ellen Oglethorpe—to whom he is attracted, though they have little agency in the novel's plot or discourse. At Tom's behest, all three are holed up in the abandoned Howard Johnson Inn for their safety during the novel's climax. (Meanwhile Tom sits in the pines, waiting for the end of the world, catnapping, and amusing himself with the thought of having three beautiful women with him to endure the apocalypse.) Tom's compulsion to protect the three women in the face of a revolution by a group predominately made up of blacks is all too similar to southern obsessions with the taboo of miscegenation and irrational fears regarding the protection of white femininity from violation by nonwhites. It is a sentiment held by Tom's neighbors in Paradise Estates. Colonel Ringo tells him, while crouched behind a guardhouse and under fire from Bantus who have occupied the Paradise Estates Country Club, that he cherishes "the Southern womanhood right here in Paradise!" (*Love in the Ruins*, 283). Additionally, descriptions and behavior portray Moira and Lola as extremely one-dimensional. Moira is quite simple, even childlike, in her sensibilities, preferring the poems of the singer-songwriter Rod McKuen to the collection of Great Books Tom has stashed in the Howard Johnson. Lola is an accomplished cellist but also has an air of simplicity, referring to herself frequently in the third person. Ellen, Tom's nurse and sidekick (as opposed to partner), is the woman Tom eventually marries in the interval between the end of the novel proper and the epilogue, a role that contributes to the novel's problematic resolution.

Conversely, at least some of the black characters in the novel are involved in a revolution, the same way that Meridian is committed to activism to improve conditions for working-class blacks. But the revolution in *Love in the Ruins* gets belittled by Percy's satire. Percy himself was opposed to segregation from his college days but was not a vocal proponent of civil rights. The extent to which the novel—even as satire—downplays racial inequality as the principal problem of the novel and for the United States is difficult to ignore. During his musings under the pines, Tom articulates a mythology that explains how the United States got into its current mess:

> Was it always the nigger business from the beginning? What a bad joke: God saying, here it is, the new Eden, and it is yours because you're the apple of

my eye; because you the lordly Westerners, the fierce Caucasian-Gentile-Visigoths, believed in me and in the outlandish Jewish Event even though you were nowhere near it and had to hear the news of it from strangers. But you believed and so I gave it all to you, gave you Israel and Greece and science and art and the lordship of the earth, and finally even gave you the new world that I blessed for you. And all you had to do was pass one little test, which was surely child's play for you because you had already passed the big one. One little test: here's a helpless man in Africa, all you have to do is not violate him. That's all.

One little test: you flunk! (*Love in the Ruins*, 57)

Satire this may be, but the story told in the passage has some serious complications, the least of which is reducing African American history into "nigger business." First, it trivializes the long and sordid history of the slave trade and chattel slavery in the founding and development of the United States into merely an exam that whites were required to pass to maintain stability for their new nation. Second, the story recapitulates a white nationalist myth that God favors Caucasians and that the United States is the result of that favor. In its telling, Tom abstracts centuries of racism and brutality into one simple little allegory that explains away contemporary political strife. One purpose of myths is to provide a basis for the collective identity of a group of people, and being a nationalist narrative that does not question the validity of American democracy and expansion, it falls well within the purview of Cold War sensibilities. But Tom has also upped the ante on Faulkner, whose Ike McCaslin in *Go Down, Moses* declares the region, the South, cursed because of the *sin* of slavery. Tom More declares the entire nation cursed for failing this test.

William Rodney Allen, John Edward Hardy, and John F. Desmond all draw the comparison between Tom More and Ike McCaslin. However, my assertion breaks a pattern in their criticism, a pattern in which critics typically diminish the import of Percy's depictions of race and race relations by arguing, as Desmond does, that "Percy suggests through More that the racism splintering America (the novel was written during the racial turmoil of the 1960s) is a manifestation of deeper spiritual ills" (127). Episodes such as Tom's articulation of racial discrimination against blacks as a flunked test, these critics argue, are merely symptoms of a basic human problem that Percy diagnoses. Allen uses the comparison between Tom More and Ike McCaslin in a book that has the larger purpose of "reclaim[ing] Percy as an American and, more specifically, a southern writer" well within its traditions and values as opposed to just another existentialist writer (xiv, 88).

Hardy goes a step further in his analysis of this passage, saying, "The 'nigger business' is simply the most conspicuous example of our failure as a nation to keep Christ's commandments—first and foremost, as the title again suggests, those *two* commandments (Matt. 22:39–40) upon which 'hang all the law and the prophets': (1) that we love God, (2) that we love our neighbors 'as ourselves'" (114). Hardy goes on to argue that Percy simply uses relations between whites and blacks in America as an allegory for all varieties of hatred between groups and individuals.

The exception I take to all these readings of Percy's work is that they trivialize what racism and discrimination have done to shape the course of American history and culture, and especially the manner in which intellectuals' manipulations of the problem altered policy in the mid-twentieth century. On the contrary, the true import of race relations in the novel is quite clear, as Kobre, who also breaks the pattern, points out: "The real issue that corrupts and rends society is race. As a result, conservatives and liberals can live side by side happily in the segregated utopia of Paradise Estates *as long as everyone tacitly agrees to forget or abridge the real history of America's racial troubles*" (129; italics mine).

Tom gets his own chance to directly diminish the revolution when he is taken prisoner by Uru, the leader of the revolution, and Victor Charles. Victor has moved back to the South after several years in the North and is frustrated because his efforts to buy a house in Paradise Estates have repeatedly been blocked by its segregationist residents. But Tom's encounter with the revolution reveals conflicts within it and disrupts its order. Victor has a deep respect for Tom for visiting and staying with his dying "auntee" all night, and he affords his prisoner more courtesy than Uru advises. Tom asks them if their plan is to take over Paradise Estates, and Victor volunteers, "Not in the beginning" (*Love in the Ruins*, 298), but says that scaring Tom away from his home was the first step because it sat under the television transmitter. The revolution required access to it to communicate its platform across a larger area. Uru tells Tom, "We're going to build a new society right here" (300). However, Tom does what he can to disparage the revolution. He tells Uru in response to the declaration of building a new society, "You haven't done very well so far," mentioning Liberia and Haiti (300). His pandering is magnified by Victor's insistence on treating him with respect—he even moves to make a drink for the doctor before Uru stops him. Their relationship undermines the revolution because it reinforces not only southern mores about interaction between races but also honor: Victor trusts Tom and wishes to indicate his gratitude for kind work he does, not just for his auntee but for many more blacks who depended on him for house calls.

On the other hand, Tom recognizes Uru as Elijah Washington, a former professional football player and holder of a PhD in political science—a product of the American academy turned revolutionary. Kobre infers that Tom sees Uru as assuming the identity of a revolutionary in the same way that his northern neighbors in Paradise Estates have assumed the identity of southerners: "Uru refuses to see the past clearly and, therefore, is caught up in violence and discord. Just as the whites of Paradise Estates cannot redress past injustices because they insist on obscuring them with a sentimentalized vision of southern history, so too, Percy seems to argue, will blacks like Uru fail to overcome those injustices . . . because the injustices are all they see of the past" (131). In this reading, revolution is not praxis or effective political activism. Rather, it is simply another cultural identity informed by politics, just like the postsouthern, suburban conservatism espoused by Paradise Estates homeowners. This exchange is the last that readers see of the revolution; the remainder of the novel focuses on the chaos created by Tom's lapsometers, which have been distributed without his consent.

The final undermining of the revolution and marginalization of racial conflict comes in the novel's epilogue, which reveals Percy's revised South-as-center. It takes place five years after the events of the novel proper, and while the fissures still exist on a national level, to our protagonist they seem mostly cured in the area surrounding Paradise Estates. Readers find Tom married to Ellen, with two children, living in poverty in the abandoned "Quarters"— row houses that originally housed slaves on the sugar plantation that were renovated but then abandoned by the developers after they failed to attract as residents the domestic workers employed in Paradise Estates—and attending church again. Tom reveals that the "revolution was a flop" (*Love in the Ruins*, 385), but the Bantus did manage to take over Paradise Estates and now own 99 percent of the homes there. In a turn of fortune, they had been living in the Honey Island Swamp for so long that they claimed squatters' rights to own it. Soon thereafter, they struck oil. With their new wealth, the Bantus bought up the houses in Paradise Estates and took up golf and the other pastimes of the white former owners. What desegregates Paradise is not the vote or even armed revolution but good old-fashioned capitalism. The only cultural practice the Bantus bring with them is their religion; otherwise they adopt wholesale the lives of the whites they displace. The drive to conformity is alive and well, and consumerism has an important place in the novel's established middle ground. This resolution of the conflict in *Love in the Ruins* reflects an attitude toward the civil rights movement that sees it as a revolution that could be placated by the emergence of a black middle class. The vital center can be preserved, even as its suburban neighborhoods are segregated.

Of this reversal between the Mores and the Bantus in living spaces and wealth, Hardy writes that nothing has really changed: "Whether whites are up and blacks down, or vice versa, social inequity is social inequity, racial discrimination is racial discrimination" (116). Whether this is Percy's intention or merely Hardy's own perspective, the statement is shortsighted. Like the whole of *Love in the Ruins*, it demeans the material struggles of African Americans and other minorities suffering in poverty as a result of Jim Crow and other societal disadvantages. To compare the prior living condition of the Bantus with More, who is now happy to be living a simpler life in the Quarters with his family, is unfair, especially given More's *choice* to live there. Additionally, it displaces the detriments caused by specifically white-on-black racism in American history with a general, vague moral imperative for equality with which any red-blooded American would agree. Besides, to place the Bantus in the subdivision by virtue of property rights is a literary preservation of suburban, middle-class politics that divorces it from its racial component in the US South.

In its portrayal of a post-South, *Love in the Ruins* strips the segregationist sentiments from the emerging conservatism of the suburban middle-class identity. Such is Percy's revision of the South within Cold War sensibilities, and it is all too similar to Nixon's suburban strategy and furtive campaigning to southern segregationists. It is a unifying gesture of American identity that only further drives the stake in the cleft between races and classes. The novel also goes a step further to reinforce a religious angle. Through the licentious protagonist's settling down with Ellen and recommencing his religious life, the novel continues to reinforce a couple of Cold War staples in American culture: the nuclear family and the faith in God in the face of atheistic communism. Today, however, these social values have become tied to modern conservatism in the decades since *Love in the Ruins* was published. With all its abstractions and mythologizing of America's political, regional, and cultural realities, *Love in the Ruins* is among the last late modernist novels and a satire that attempts to unify, but only by exploiting fractures in society.

EPILOGUE

White Working-Class Identity and US Nationalism in Twenty-First-Century Popular Texts

My primary aims for this project have been historical, examining how Cold War authors and intellectuals presented southern identity and values as congruent with American democracy in an effort to package racism and poverty as moral problems that would not affect the United States' foreign policy ambitions. Although the Cold War was notionally won in the early 1990s, its politics persist. The consequences of Cold War ideology are real and manifest in the present, especially in diminished connections between southern identity and its values and a specific geographic region. Since the late 1960s, "southern" has increasingly become a cultural identity associated not just with a set of cultural practices but with US nationalism, conservative politics, and working-class populism. This divides the country no longer between North and South but between red states and blue states, and the lines are not always as sharply drawn as intellectuals imagine. The 2016 election made this perfectly clear when the electoral map showed a breach in Hillary Clinton's "blue wall," with many midwestern industrial states gravitating toward Donald Trump's "America first" brand of nationalism and helping to elect him president—along with every former Confederate state, save Virginia. Although the drama of the election unfolded on cable and broadcast news beginning in 2015, the portrayal of the US South's popular notions of its cultural practices and values were appearing on the television screens of a national audience long before.

Increasingly prolific, television is enjoying a renaissance in the second decade of the twenty-first century, and scholars have noticed its impact. At the 2014 meeting of the Society for the Study of Southern Literature in Arlington, Virginia, Erich Nunn implored those of us attending a session called "Future Souths" to "watch more television." The gist of his plea was that when more and more consumption of narrative, news, and documentary in the United States is television (and internet streaming) based, it is scholars of literature, who have been pioneers of cultural studies and have long practiced the analysis of narrative, who are in the best position to describe, interrogate, and analyze the productions that shape viewers' understanding of the world and their place in it. Indeed, notions of the "South" continue to be a deep well for TV in the twenty-first century, and scholars in southern studies are capitalizing on its use. In the introduction to their recent collection of essays focusing on portrayals of the South in television, Lisa Hinrichsen, Gina Caison, and Stephanie Roundtree describe how television continues to frequently uses regionalist tropes, especially in the South, to establish authenticity, collective identity, and citizenship; given its dynamism, the medium serves in the role well (3–4). Several high-quality scripted productions use the South as their setting. Examples are *Treme, True Blood, True Detective* (all HBO productions), and *The Walking Dead* (AMC). The protagonist of *House of Cards* (Netflix) is a southerner. More problematic, though, are the socioeconomic trappings of southern-themed reality TV, in which purportedly authentic southerners perform their southern identities. Many of these programs, such as *My Big Redneck Wedding, Here Comes Honey Boo Boo, Southern Justice,* and *Party Down South* can be painfully obvious to a wide range of viewers and critics, making programs easy critical pickings for the scholar looking for romantic metanarratives about place, race, and class with populist appeal. As the definition of television changes with the progression from broadcast to narrowcast to streaming TV and providers now owning the means of production (e.g., Comcast/Universal, Netflix, Amazon Prime), these metanarratives persist. With so many more outlets for television content, all that airtime needs to be filled somehow. Reality TV is cheap to produce, and the power of relatable celebrity personalities makes the genre appealing to TV executives and viewers alike. Of course, these so-called reality programs are blocked, heavily edited, and produced in such a way as to merely seem "real" to viewers. Although they may lack screenwriters, they often have crafted narrative and dialogue that present to the viewer a carefully crafted identity for their stars that viewers can identify with, as well. In short, reality TV creates extremely powerful screen surrogates.

Some of the most striking examples of this genre are reality TV programs set in the US South. Given the long intellectual project of leveraging southern values in support of US nationalism, it follows that such associations would find their way into popular portrayals of the region. This association on television between savory politics, national identity, and rural southern folksiness has a longer history than contemporary reality television, of course. *The Andy Griffith Show* (1960–68) offers perhaps the most important example. In the thick of the civil rights movement, the Cold War, and the federal government's legislative and executive interventions in southern states to stymie Jim Crow, CBS's long-running sitcom presented to a national audience the rural South as a bucolic paradise of the vital center. Rather than the local political turmoil of protests and racism, or international political threats, such as war between nuclear superpowers, the show gave viewers church on Sundays, problems solved without government intervention (the sheriff, Andy Taylor, solves problems more often through his personal connection with the citizens of Mayberry than through his governmental authority), and deep respect for the nation's history. Also contributing to the lack of racial unrest in Mayberry was the absence of black people. *The Andy Griffith Show* and other programs set in the South or rural places frequently portray white southern values, identity, and culture as part of national identity in the United States, though as time has gone on, and especially with the advent of reality TV, the most notable southern identity is "redneck" or otherwise working-class. This identity does not have the same wholesomeness as sheriff Andy Taylor's antics, but portrayals of the redneck on reality television show this population of individuals as holding strongly to an identity that is perceived as being regionally southern, but also identifying strongly with US nationalism and working-class mentality. Moreover, a large swath of viewers see themselves in a similar light, and the marketing and licensing deals of late capitalism make it ever easier to adopt any identity, severing any fetters that make such an identity regionally bound. Southern individualism and tradition do not just represent centrist national political values in the twenty-first century but are also highly marketable, coupling this identity with the trappings of class more clearly than ever.

One of the clearest indicators of this is A&E's popular reality series *Duck Dynasty* (2012–17). The show emphasizes southernness, ruralness, and down-home-ness in a way that cloaks its ideology about class and material culture. This is significant in two key ways: in the way the show theorizes the relationship between what is labor and what is recreation for the Robertsons, the show's protagonists; and in the Robertsons' own adoption of the "redneck" identity. The show packages this portrayal of seemingly working-class folks with their outdoors product line for consumption by an engaged viewing public. Coupled with the Robertsons' conservative values both on and off screen, *Duck Dynasty* presents a nationalistic white southern identity that transcends geographical boundaries in the United States and is available to any viewers who choose to adopt it.

The program presents the wealthy Robertson family, who live and work in and around West Monroe, Louisiana, as the quintessential self-made

American family with strong values and simple pleasures. Shannon E. M. O'Sullivan notes that the show "perfectly captures the inherent tension of social class operating simultaneously as both a socioeconomic category and a lifestyle orientation in mainstream US discourse" (369). Contrived as the show's presentation is, it suggests to a large swath of its viewers that the Robertsons are just like them: working-class in values, interests, accents, and material status. Indeed, David McKillop, A&E's general manager, said in 2013 that "the Robertsons represent a lot things we as Americans cherish ... self-made wealth, independence, three generations living together" (quoted in Cohen). The key device by which the show accomplishes this is by creating tension about labor between the CEO in the family, Willie, and his interest in keeping Duck Commander running efficiently with the family's/friends'/employees' interest more in having fun than in working. This group includes much of the Robertson family tree, which is headed by the patriarch and founder of the business, Phil (who did, indeed, grow up poor in Louisiana), and his wife, Kay. Willie's brothers Jase and Jep, and their wives, Korie, Missy, and Jessica respectively, along with their children, play prominent roles. Uncle Si, Phil's brother and a Vietnam veteran, is also a central figure. Children and employees appear as characters, too. The boss is family, and the employees are family; just as in any family, there is tension, but they can all work together to make the company profitable because they have the same interests at heart.

This bait and switch with regard to class interests is common to many reality television programs. To use a prominent example, the ubiquitous Kardashians of *Keeping Up with the Kardashians* provide the vicarious consumption of excessive wealth while also showing family spats, lovers' quarrels, and the pains of growing up. The gesture made to viewers is that members of the economic upper class have the same problems as everyone else, which fosters viewers' investment in the lives of celebrities and the notion that they have the same social, political, and economic interests. *Duck Dynasty* makes this move, too, but with an emphasis on southern folksiness and patriotism. No problem is too big for the Robertsons' faith and redneck sensibilities to solve, and while the money helps, it has not changed them or their values, either. As Jase declares when he and Si stop to pick up a dead nutria, "In the South roadkill is a redneck's paycheck. The state of Louisiana has a $5 bounty on all nutra rats because they are destroying the marsh. That's five bucks a tail. Just cause I got money in my pocket doesn't mean I'm too good to pick up a five-dollar bill that's laying in the middle of the road" ("Too Close for Comfort").

Furthermore, in its portrayal of the Robertsons' hunting goods business and their relationship with property, animals, and natural resources, *Duck Dynasty* produces for viewers even a construct of nature that becomes key to their identity, labor, and leisure. The family's land is portrayed as a wilderness to which they turn for some subsistence, such as fishing and hunting. But hunting on the family land is also their most basic simple pleasure—that and ridiculing Willie the CEO's more "refined" interests in golf and gadgets, reinforcing the idea that their pleasures are simple. Ultimately for the TV Robertsons, their work *is* their play, and their work is based on the notion of nature as a product accessible via their program as well as the Duck Commander brand. The show demonstrates an ideology about not just class but also rural southern identity and notions of nature and wilderness, which are associated with rural imagery. These become products packaged and sold under the Duck Commander name.

The basis for this analysis of *Duck Dynasty* is Neil Smith's theorization of the production of nature. Smith argues in *Uneven Development* that the activity of human civilization begins with the perceived human separation from nature—moving from a nature that humans inhabit to a nature that humans investigate, romanticize, and use. But it is industrial capitalism that perfects the production of nature: on a global scale, capitalism produces nature through its harvesting of natural resources (timber, fish, and oil are all said to be produced), but it also produces the conceptions and apparatus through which humans experience nature. While the laboring class spends its labor adding surplus value to raw materials, the leisure class devotes the labor it does not have to sell to producing its experiences of nature. "Material nature," Smith argues, "is produced as a unity in the labour process, which is in turn guided by the needs, the logic, the quirks of the second nature" (56). Smith turns to Yosemite and Yellowstone, the United States' premier national parks, for one of the most compelling examples of this process:

> These are produced environments in every conceivable sense. From the management of wildlife to the alteration of the landscape by human occupancy, the material environment bears the stamp of human labour; from the beauty salons to the restaurants, and from the camper parks to the Yogi Bear postcards, Yosemite and Yellowstone are neatly packaged cultural experiences of environment on which substantial profits are recorded each year. (57)

With their duck call and hunting DVD business preceding their reality TV success with *Duck Dynasty*, the Robertsons' family business and land, to be sure, produce nature to the same, if not greater, degree as these national parks. Furthermore, in the *Duck Dynasty* series, these contrived portrayals of nature are morphed into portrayals of self-reliance, blurring the lines between the work and the leisure of the Robertson family. The blurring provides the conduit for southern values and identity to pass as nationalism. At other times, this occurs through Willie's American flag do-rag, church suppers, and the before-meal blessing that ends each episode.

Many elements of *Duck Dynasty* emphasize its produced southernness and produced nature; the two go hand in hand in the Robertsons' self-identification as "rednecks." What gets portrayed as wilderness is really just rural northern Louisiana. The program's use of these tropes is a false construction, especially the use of outdoor activities to emphasize the Robertsons' southernness. Of course, the geographic region of the US South is heterogeneous, comprising both rural areas and large urban centers, such as Atlanta, Charlotte, and Miami. *Duck Dynasty*'s conflation of southern with rural/wilderness also shows the mobility of southern identity; its values become just as rural as southern, and the rural exists all over the United States. These elements appear from the first episode, and my reading of the show will focus on the first three seasons, which aired between March 2012 and April 2013. In particular, the use of activities and items associated with rural life as status symbols, and the Robertsons' relationship with their land and the outdoors framed within their "work," are important tropes tied up with portrayals of (white) southernness through the transmission of tradition, values, and culture perceived as southern, readily adopted by viewers.

Most episodes of *Duck Dynasty* adapt the sitcom formula of A and B plot into the reality television genre. The narrative advances through scenes of the cast working, hunting, fishing, and attending family gatherings, punctuated with commentary on these actions in direct addresses to the camera—typically Willie complaining about the family and employees not doing their job, Phil and Jase ribbing Willie for going soft and becoming a "yuppie" (an insult with urban connotations, not far off from "city slicker"), and Si telling tall tales. These direct addresses to the camera allow the cast to state directly to the audience their perceived relationship to the land. Phil carries this forward himself in the pilot through his discussion of his appreciation for frogging and eating frogs, relating this experience of nature as important education for his grandchildren. The action scene portrays Phil at a makeshift butcher's block under a shelter at his home. Phil is showing one of his grandsons how to kill and clean frogs: chop off the head, skin the frog, and harvest the legs. In Phil's commentary on the scene, he says, "My task is to teach them [my grandchildren] to live off the land. It's a good thing. Clean and honorable. Frog killing.... There are a lot of fine things that grow in this swamp. I would consider [frogs] a delicacy of the highest order" ("Family Funny Business"). Here Phil espouses a moral imperative to provide his grandchildren with both the experience and the consumable bounty of the family's land. It is a clear gesture toward individual responsibility and self-reliance left over from Cold War values. But teaching others how to live off the land is just as much family values as the family business in multiple ways: it is Phil's personal business to teach these things to his progeny, but the Robertsons' family business is to provide and teach customers how to consume the outdoors with duck calls and instructional hunting DVDs. Indeed, in the pilot's B plot, Kay is working with her sons and daughters-in-law to film an instructional cooking DVD that Duck Commander will sell on its website, purportedly to meet demand from their customers who want to know how to prepare game, particularly frog legs, in the same way as Kay.

This is the first of many instances in the series in which the Robertsons depict an identity that consumers can purchase, through an audiovisual presentation or through a fetishized object. In the third episode, "High Tech Redneck," the A plot involves Willie negotiating and then needing to fulfill an order by a client who wishes to increase his purchase of Duck Commander merchandise tenfold. "This is where the swamp meets corporate America," Willie says in his direct-to-camera commentary about his meeting with the client, and the swamp really is his product. Duck Commander sells access to the swamp through duck calls, hunting and cooking DVDs, novelties, and apparel, a lot of it camouflage. Mary Ann Wilson asserts that this emphasis on the swamp should be perceived as a construct, too, for the area around West Monroe has a "piney-woods Protestant ethos" that is "more like East Texas, Arkansas, or Mississippi, resolutely not the New Orleans of *Treme*, the southern Louisiana swamps of *Swamp People*, or the oil-rig-blighted wastelands of Erath and Lake Charles from HBO's *True Detective*" (152).

Given the show's privileging of simple pleasures and its conflation of the working class and redneck within the Robertsons, the hunting camouflage pattern used on much of their merchandise and on the clothing the Robertsons frequently wear on the show becomes a status symbol that viewers can purchase to show off their own commitment to *Duck Dynasty*'s fabricated southern or redneck identity. Willie even wears a camouflage tuxedo jacket for the show's opening sequence, and the other men wear other pieces of hunting attire mix-matched with formal wear. Because the camouflage is designed to replicate the patterns of foliage, brush, and timber in order for the hunter to blend into the wilderness, to wear camo outside that context is to produce the wilderness (or the idea of it), as well as to produce the working-class, southern, redneck identity—an identity the Robertsons explicitly cling to even in their wealth. The woods become literally bought and sold as status symbols showing one's commitment to a set of values and an identity, one that the Robertsons demonstrate can be big business. Commercializing and marketing their lifestyle make them seem like regular folks to viewers.

The Robertsons also perform a working-class identity via the scenes that show the family and their employees/friends working at the Duck Commander facilities. Nearly all the work that the Robertsons and the extended cast of employees/friends do is actually play: though plenty of scenes show them making duck calls, arguably no *real* labor is happening there. These scenes feature goofing off—not legitimate manufacturing—such as building an improvised conveyor belt, running fool's errands as busywork, and initiating slam dunk and ping-pong tournaments in the warehouse. The work the characters do outside the Duck Commander factory and warehouse is work cultivating their southern-rural identities via their relationship to the wilderness: maintaining their land and their hunting blinds, hunting and cleaning animals, and on one occasion harvesting wild honey. This emphasizes again their self-reliant southern resourcefulness by suggesting that they gain subsistence from the wilderness. Yet all this work is truly leisure. This is emphasized best in the season 3 episode "Duck Season Eve."

In this episode, the A plot focuses on the Robertson family tradition of camping out in the woods on the night before the opening of duck season so that at first light they can head to the blind and begin what they describe as the most wonderful time of the year. Jase, again, states the Robertson position best when he explains, "The night before duck season we rough it. We are going to wake up and show nature who's still in charge." He arrives at the campsite with Jep, Si, and Godwin and Martin (two Duck Commander employees who are regulars on the show and seemingly may as well be members of the Robertson family) to set up camp, every movement and action demonstrating that they are going to "rough it." The mosquitoes become nearly unbearable. The fire is difficult to start. They forgot the hot dogs and get hungry. Everyone but Jase begins to seem annoyed at the lack of creature comforts. The conflict begins when Willie arrives at the campsite in the Duck Commander RV, complete with comfy cots, video games, climate control, and food far above campsite fare. Jase makes much fun of Willie for this. According to Jase, Willie yields any claim to outdoor acumen and status by refusing to participate in Jase's experience of the wilderness as a precursor to the new duck season. "That's parking," Jase says of bringing the RV out, and he insists that he will rough it: "This is a declaration that we are lords of the wilderness," he proclaims. For Jase, roughing it is not just about experiencing the wilderness; it is about conquering it and asserting one's agency—one's identity. But as the night wears on, everyone in the party heads for the comfort of the RV, except Si, who has headed for the comfort of Phil and Kay's house (where he had walked back to retrieve deer sausage to replace the forgotten hot dogs).

The dichotomy that Jase presents between his roughing it and Willie's more comfortable RV seems intended to focus viewers' attention on a stark contrast between the authentic and inauthentic camping experiences. This is an easy trick to fall for. It is easy to agree with the assertion that RV camping is "parking." But there again, just how authentic is Jase's experience of roughing it? He is wearing modern outdoor clothing, camouflage in color. He pitches a modern tent. The planned meal is hot dogs and roasting marshmallows. What is primitive about that, really? How does that exactly make him a "lord of the wilderness"? And would it even be possible to rough it on the family land, territory that is very familiar, in fact, so familiar that he has formed it into an ideal habitat by creating wetlands to attract ducks and blinds from which to hunt them? Not to mention that none of this is really *required* for the Robertsons to enjoy duck season. Camping, RV or no, is not a necessary precursor. Rather, Jase's idea of roughing it is really recreational labor that produces for the viewer a vicarious experience. The notion that "roughing it" results in a more authentic, primitive, and superior experience of the outdoors turns out to be much like Si taking point-blank shots into the hollow of a log that he claims a snake poked its head out of. No one else sees the snake, yet Si repeatedly fires. Jase asks him, "Si, have you ever heard of the term 'ricochet'?" To which Si replies, "Hey, that's superstition." As he frequently does in his tall tales, Si rejects one reality in favor of one that serves his pleasure: firing a gun haphazardly at possibly imagined wildlife that may or may not be a threat. Just as the reality of a ricochet is relegated to superstition, so fulfilling the notion of truly roughing it outside the human sphere of influence becomes more and more obscure through Jase's own claims about camping and Willie's arrival in the RV.

The other facet of *Duck Dynasty*'s portrayal of labor and leisure associated with "nature" is the production of a variety of southern identity. Many of the Robertsons self-identify as "rednecks." This further complicates the fraught history of the epithet: when used pejoratively, the term typically refers to poor, uneducated, racist whites in rural areas, mostly farmers; but there have been many attempts to reclaim the term to describe "honest, hard-working common folks" (Huber, 146).[1] Although Phil may have grown up poor, the twenty-first-century Robertsons are neither poor nor truly working-class but claim the mantle of redneck. O'Sullivan describes what the Robertsons do in *Duck Dynasty* as performing in "redneck drag" because most are college educated and grew their beards for the show (368, 372). Yet Willie is the only one prominently identified as such, and this is often a source of tension in the show. For example, Willie, who frequently wears a sport coat or blazer with his American flag do-rag and beard, wishes his family would not be such "rednecks" who get in trouble at the golf course for gigging frogs in the water hazards at night or get fined by the homeowner's association for burning leaves. But the other Robertsons, Jase, Phil, and Si, romanticize the redneck identity and associate it with certain values. For one, true rednecks, according to Jase, would not camp in an RV. Reliance on the land, laboring for subsistence rather than wages, and resourcefulness are also qualities of rednecks. Distributed to a national audience, this recovered redneck identity can be claimed by anyone who, like the Robertsons, believes in hard work, self-reliance, and family values. No doubt, such an identity appeals to the working class in all parts of the country, not just the rural South where the redneck stereotype was born. But thanks to Duck Commander brand duck calls, apparel, and accessories, the idea of the rugged wilderness of the rural South is available everywhere in the country.

In part, *Duck Dynasty* illustrates how easily capitalism can provide a political platform by camouflaging ideology: the program presents an easily digestible southern redneck identity developed through attention to rural self-reliance and wholesome values. And with less fanfare but at times in more overt gestures, *Duck Dynasty* endorses socially conservative values to evoke southern redneck identity, as well. O'Sullivan notes that most episodes predictably show the Robertson men in the woods or at work and the women at home cooking or in the community at church fund-raisers and ladies' organizations. The show reveals politics and prejudices deliberately rooted in ideas of nature and identity. These come most obviously at the end of every episode when Phil asks the blessing when the family sits down together for supper. However, we can observe more subtle instances. The fourth season begins with the episode "Till Duck Do Us Part." In this episode, the Robertson children plan a ceremony for Phil and Kay to renew their wedding vows on their anniversary, giving them the gift of the ceremony they never had. This episode is the first time viewers meet Alan, the oldest Robertson boy and a pastor. The ceremony occurs outdoors on the Robertsons' land, reinforcing heteronormative marriage as perfectly natural in the Duck Commander packaging of nature and implicitly suggesting that other kinds of unions may not be so natural. The episode aired in August 2013, about two months after the Supreme Court struck down the Defense of Marriage Act in *United States v. Windsor* and held that spouses in same-sex unions were guaranteed the same rights under federal law as all other spouses. The season 4 premiere was the highest-rated show among adults that evening, drawing "11.8 million viewers . . . the largest audience ever for a nonfiction telecast on cable television" (Cohen). Later in 2013, *GQ* would publish Phil Robertson's infamous offensive remarks about homosexuality. Phil's words confirm that Phil and Kay's vow renewal to replace the wedding they never had is a performance of what the Robertsons find to be a religiously and politically appropriate marriage, confirming certain biases and beliefs among their viewers.

Phil's comments calling homosexuality a sin would earn him a brief suspension from the show that was reversed after public outcry and the rest of the Robertsons threatening to quit the show (Jonsson). However, the elder Robertson also made comments about working alongside blacks in the Jim Crow South:

> I never, with my eyes, saw the mistreatment of any black person. Not once. Where we lived was all farmers. The blacks worked for the farmers. I hoed cotton with them. I'm with the blacks, because we're white trash. We're going across the field.... They're singing and happy. I never heard one of them, one black person, say, I tell you what: These doggone white people—not a word! ... Pre-entitlement, pre-welfare, you say: Were they happy? They were godly; they were happy; no one was singing the blues. (Quoted in Magary)

Phil's description of his childhood in segregated Louisiana sounds remarkably harmonious with the claim of Cold War intellectuals that race problems in the South were moral problems best left to the people. In Phil's telling of history, one compatible with Faulkner's or Warren's moderation on race, no racial strife existed before the federal government got involved with entitlements and welfare; poverty and faith united him with the blacks he worked alongside in one social bloc, and glad they all were to work. However, in the twenty-first century, the show depicts few interactions of the Robertson family with blacks in and around West Monroe.[2]

This fantasy of past racial harmony in the US South has been enabled and proliferated through divisive conservative politics in the backlash against President Barack Obama's election in 2008 and was further exacerbated in the populism of the Trump era. A group of researchers confirmed with survey data that race played an outsized role in voter choice in the 2008 presidential election, finding that racial prejudice not only led voters to vote for McCain but led individuals who would not have voted at all or for a third-party candidate to vote for McCain instead (Pasek et al., 981–82). In analyzing predictors for affiliation with the Tea Party, a conservative movement that spearheaded the Republican takeover of the House of Representatives in the 2010 elections, Angie Maxwell and T. Wayne Parent determined that disapproval of Obama was a stronger predictor for an individual's membership with the movement than the espousal of "conservative economic policy" (1388). Maxwell and Parent conclude, "Absent a polarizing figure with Obama's unique characteristics, the Tea Party will have trouble maintaining its internal cohesion . . . and creating stable coalitions over time" (1398). Of course, part of Obama's unique characteristics is his race, which even gave rise to "birtherism," the conspiracy theory that Obama was not born in the United States and therefore ineligible to be president. President Trump capitalized on birtherism's popularity among white conservatives during the 2016 campaign. Also during the campaign and since his inauguration, Trump has borrowed a page from Nixon's Cold War–era playbook by dressing racist ideology with a thin veneer of policy discussion, especially regarding appeals to law-and-order and immigration policy. Furthermore, Phil Robertson's narrative about pre-civil-rights Louisiana may as well be the same narrative that conservative commentators used to dispel concern about the backlash: that is, to blame Obama and the Democratic Party for sowing racial and class discord by pandering to "identity politics" (akin to how Trump ultimately blamed Hillary Clinton for starting the birtherism conspiracy theory). For example, in a March 2018 print editorial, Matthew Continetti, the editor in chief of the conservative news website the *Washington Free Beacon*, claims that Obama was able to win the 2008 and 2012 elections by appealing to racial differences and notions of white privilege. Continetti claims that this was how the Democratic Party lost "the voters of the rural Midwest" in the 2016 presidential election, and that the whole country can "combat identity politics" by recommitting to "a history and culture of individual freedom and religious pluralism, resistant to centralized authority and ever expanding into new frontiers and possibilities" (12). Continetti's perspective resonates with both Schlesinger's Cold War vital center and Phil Robertson's romanticized southern past.

If Phil's comments about race had produced as much of a public outcry as his comments about homosexuality, it would have served as a stark reminder for the public that some facets of the redneck identity might be irrecoverable. On the other hand, his recounting of a fantasy of racial harmony and moral accord in the Jim Crow South serves as a harbinger of the post-truth era: in 2016 Phil Robertson endorsed Donald Trump for president (Stone); so did Willie (Parks). As contrived as the presentation of themselves on television may be, there is truth to the Robertsons' brand of conservatism, and they act on it in real life. Arguably, it makes them all the more appealing to a broad swath of working-class people who have accepted the Robertsons to be rednecks rejecting the values of wealthy liberal elites, as well as more affluent conservatives enticed into performing a more rugged, hypermasculinized redneck drag. The bait-and-switch reality represented by *Duck Dynasty*, in which all viewers are persuaded they have a common interest, should be seen as a twenty-first-century vital center. O'Sullivan argues that *Duck Dynasty* "promotes the dominant myth that the United States is a classless society" through its depiction of redneck as an identity that can be adopted and performed (381). Indeed, the construct that the Robertsons present may appeal to political moderates and liberals and maybe even urban elites. Patrik Jonsson claims, "Self-admittedly liberal and urban writers . . . have romanticized the rural Christian lifestyle, suggesting that Phil Robertson and his clan may have gotten the American idea right."

The bait-and-switch strategy of twenty-first-century reality television is so powerful that it has leaped to nonfiction writing, as well. One of the best-selling books of 2016 was J. D. Vance's *Hillbilly Elegy: A Memoir of a Family and Culture in Crisis*, a classic bootstraps narrative in which Vance recounts his unstable upbringing, living with his grandparents in Ohio but frequently visiting Appalachian Kentucky, the region from where his family hails. The book has frequently been discussed as an important barometer for understanding the populist sentiments among Midwestern and Appalachian white working-class voters who helped Trump win the 2016 election.[3] In his current situation, Vance seems to have little in common with the hillbilly he describes himself and his family and friends to be when he was growing up. Via a stint in the Marines, he achieved social mobility, eventually graduating from the Ohio State University and Yale Law School and starting a career in the financial sector. However, his memoir makes clear that even though he is well educated, successful, and living in San Francisco (a town he refers to as "ultra-liberal" [93]), he still considers himself a hillbilly. He describes his Mamaw and Papaw as rough, violent people, but he loves them and cherishes the values they taught him. These values include rugged individualism and a love of country: "Mamaw and Papaw taught me that we live in the best and greatest country on earth. This fact gave meaning to my childhood" (190). Focusing so intently on his grandparents may be required of Vance's narrative, since they did effectively raise him. However, praising ancestors two generations earlier can be read as a kind of nostalgia. In the context of my project, this nostalgia turns out to be for a Cold War vital center: love of country, love of freedom, love of individual responsibility.

From the beginning of the book, Vance argues that "too many young men [are] immune to hard work," and he feels that when young people in the region squander opportunities, "There is a lack of agency here—a feeling that you have little control over your life and a willingness to blame everyone but yourself. This is distinct from the larger economic landscape of modern America" (7). Yet Vance ultimately concludes that the crisis of poverty and drug abuse in hillbilly culture, which affected him and his mother, cannot be solved by government intervention. In the course of his narrative, he describes his observation, while working in a grocery store as a teenager, of what he characterizes as abuse of the welfare system. He recalls seeing welfare recipients use their benefits to purchase goods while having a cell phone conversation; others would exchange benefits for cash or purchase items to sell at a discount (139). In passages such as this, Vance evokes the figure of the welfare queen, first formulated by President Ronald Reagan in the 1980s. Vance himself foresees this comparison, writing in his introduction:

> I do hope that readers of this book will be able to take from it an appreciation of how class and family affect the poor without filtering their views through a racial prism. To many analysts, terms like "welfare queen" conjure unfair images of the lazy black mom living on the dole. Readers of this book will realize quickly that there is little relationship between that specter and my argument: I have known many welfare queens; some were my neighbors, and all were white. (7–8)

There is no reason to dispute what Vance reports seeing in the grocery store. Nonetheless the welfare queen is a familiar racist image that suggests government assistance is part of the problem, not the solution. His appeal to that ethos here is extremely similar to Phil Robertson's narrative about racial harmony before the civil rights movement: everything was fine, but then the region had some problems that it could have solved on its own, but were exacerbated by outside influence. Vance admits that he does not have a solution for the social decay of the culture that he grew up in, but he nonetheless concludes, "I know it starts when we stop blaming Obama or Bush or faceless companies and ask ourselves what we can do to make things better" (256). For all the differences between Appalachian whites and whites in other parts of the US South, Vance's comment here is roughly congruent with something Welty's narrator in "Where Is the Voice Coming From?" says: "Even the President so far, he can't walk in my house without being invited, like he's my daddy, just to say whoa. Not yet!" (Welty, *Collected Stories*, 607). (However, Vance's social mobility has turned him into a Compson, unlike Welty's narrator.) Similarly to the Robertsons, can Vance's interest truly be the same as that of the people he elegizes? Certainly Vance's conclusion echoes even farther back to writers such as Faulkner, who recognized the social and political ills in the US South but insisted that they must be solved without government intervention. This ideology has endured, still encouraging individuals to vote against their own interests.

Both *Duck Dynasty* and *Hillbilly Elegy* are narratives capable of convincing more and more people in the United States to identify with rednecks and white southerners because they see political values that have endured from the Cold War attached to the morals, individualism, and patriotism they cherish. Indeed, the Confederate flag now flies all over the United States, hoisted by people who feel a kinship with nineteenth-century southerners because they, too, have fallen for the myth that the Confederate states were fighting for states' rights, preserving a nation truer to the vision of the men who wrote the Constitution. An Iowan explained in 2017 that he developed a significant interest in the Civil War during President Barack Obama's administration and what he thought was its habit of executive overreach into the business of states. This made him feel a "resonance" with Confederates: "Those people were fighting for states' rights, and the freedom to make their own way and to choose their own way against a tyrannical federal government" (McCammon). This is why Erich Nunn's advice to watch more TV is significant. Reality television, sound-bite journalism, and fabricated narratives spreading via social media frequently confirm the comforting worldview of their audience or convince them that their ways of life are under siege from government, elites, and others who do not look like them. Some of these fictions have evolved from the notions of southern identity deployed in the culture industry since the Cold War. Scholars of literature, especially those studying the US South, have the knowledge to see when myths of the Lost Cause and romanticized tales of the Confederacy, racism, and southern poverty are evoked and how they are used to manipulate viewers by activating their perceptions of identity, history, community, progress, and fear. *Duck Dynasty* and *Hillbilly Elegy* are purveyors of myth, and literary scholars and other expert close readers can readily see and explain this.

The redneck and hillbilly identities and politics ultimately presented by the Robertsons in *Duck Dynasty* and Vance in *Hillbilly Elegy* are twenty-first-century southern political identities. When performed, they also perform certain prejudices: lack of support for social safety nets, civil rights protections, women's rights, and LGBT rights are the most significant. These prejudices found popular validation in the election of Donald Trump. Furthermore, the Cold War may never have ended, given tense relations between the United States and Russia after the latter's interference in the 2016 presidential election. Similar conflicts are emerging in tense diplomatic standoffs with North Korea and even with American allies over the sharing of defense resources, intelligence, and humanitarian aid in the war on terror. The crisis facing the

American democratic system in 2019 is the result of nearly a century of a lack of political will to combat overt racism in American culture.[4] Instead American culture continues to borrow portrayals of white southern values and tradition to bolster a seemingly moderate patriotism. This vital center has been supplanted by, as *Love in the Ruins* and the appearance of rebel flags all over the country show, the modern conservative identity. The faults in literature and reality television that were so painfully obvious have now evolved into a reality that is too painful to watch. More than at any other time in recent history, scholars of American and southern literature must be critical of notions of southern identity, lest the myth supplant reality altogether.

NOTES

Introduction

1. The term "postsouthern" was coined by Lewis P. Simpson in his essay "The Closure of History in a Postsouthern America," in *The Brazen Face of History: Studies in the Literary Consciousness of America* (Baton Rouge: Louisiana State University Press, 1980).

2. Later that year, Moore was suspended from the bench for his defiance and resigned to run for Senate in the special election to replace Alabama senator Jeff Sessions, who vacated the seat after he was appointed attorney general by President Donald Trump (Cason). After beating Luther Strange in a runoff in the Republican primary, Moore went on to lose the special election to Doug Jones (Burns and Martin).

1. Reviewing the South

1. For a recent history of periodical culture and the literary economy during this period that focuses on critics and book reviewers rather than authors, see Sarah E. Gardner, *Reviewing the South: The Literary Marketplace and the Southern Renaissance, 1920–1941* (Cambridge: Cambridge University Press, 2017).

2. The Lillian Smith Papers at the Smathers Libraries, University of Florida, contain issues from the entire run of Smith and Snelling's magazine. Letters and additional items from the Smith Papers are quoted extensively with the permission of Smith's literary estate.

3. This included a rather ambivalent review of Faulkner's *Absalom, Absalom!*—the other notable publication in southern fiction in 1936—which Snelling criticized for its violence but deemed "well worth anyone's reading" ("Mr. Faulkner Adds a Cubit," 16).

4. This letter and Mitchell's letter to Smith of May 21, 1936, are quoted with the permission of GWTW Partners, LLC.

5. Comparing the dates of these letters from the separate Smith and Mitchell collections, one finds that Smith's reply to Mitchell's letter of May 19 is dated May 18, and envelopes are not saved in the archive to examine postmarks. Based on the logic of the dialogue, Smith's May 18 letter is obviously a reply to Mitchell's May 19 correspondence.

6. Will Brantley documents this in "The Surveillance of Georgia Writer and Civil Rights Activist Lillian Smith: Another Story from the Federal Bureau of Investigation," *Georgia Historical Quarterly* 85, no. 1 (2001): 59–82.

7. The quotation comes from an incomplete draft, and it remains unclear whether a final draft of the letter was sent to Winn. The letter lacks a signature, but based on the letter's style, the author seems to be Snelling. The letter draft goes on to ask Winn to shorten and edit her

submitted piece along the parameters quoted for possible later publication, though no articles by Winn were ever published in the magazine. Despite uncertainty regarding the letter's final disposition, its draft retains significance in making such a blatant statement regarding race and the magazine's strict editorial policy.

2. Southern Studies as Area Studies

1. See also John T. Matthews, "The Rhetoric of Containment in Faulkner," in *Faulkner's Discourse: An International Symposium*, ed. Lothar Hönnighausen (Tübingen: M. Niemeyer, 1989), 55–67. Matthews argues that while representations of the social and history appear in Faulkner's work, his modernist techniques, particularly in *The Sound and the Fury*, "conceal history's conditioning of [the novel's] apparent free play" and create work in which "history and its representation abide in a dissonant relation" (59).

2. See Deborah Cohn, "'In between Propaganda and Escapism': William Faulkner as Cold War Cultural Ambassador," *Diplomatic History* 40, no. 1 (2016): 392–420, for an extensive account and analysis of how Faulkner's work as a cultural ambassador in South America and Asia coincided with the escalation of Cold War tensions and the growing battles over segregation in the United States.

3. Borstelmann notes that southern politicians generally believed that links existed between integration and communism, especially in terms of foreign policy, where the United States was having the most difficulty comporting its domestic and international policy on race. Governor Herman Talmadge and Senator Richard B. Russell, both of Georgia, "believed liberals were being suckered by Moscow's Cold War rhetoric. Rather than try to satisfy Soviet demands, the United States should stand up proudly for its own traditions. If Communists supported racial integration, could there be any clearer sign of its immorality?" Borstelmann, *The Cold War and the Color Line*, 108.

4. It is worth noting that Faulkner continues to dominate southern literary studies. He features prominently even in *Look Away! The U.S. South and New World Studies*, ed. Jon Smith and Deborah Cohn (Durham: Duke University Press, 2004), a collection that seeks to destabilize the US South's firm place at the center of discussions on the South more generally. Moreover, Taylor Hagood's *Faulkner, Writer of Disability* (Baton Rouge: Louisiana State University Press, 2015) won the Society for the Study of Southern Literature's C. Hugh Holman Award for the best book of literary scholarship in the field of southern literature when it was published. The same is true anecdotally. Here is a story that circulated at one of the programs I attended for graduate school: When the southern literature specialist in the department retired, it was asked among faculty at a department meeting if anyone could teach Faulkner. After two faculty members said they could, it was decided that there was no need to hire a new southern literature specialist.

5. See Valencia Eloris Matthews, "Irene Olivia Colbert Edmonds: Her Historic Tenure at Florida Agricultural and Mechanical University, 1947–1968" (PhD diss., Florida State University, 1995), electronic dissertation, UMI, 9608883. Edmonds, a longtime professor at Florida Agricultural and Mechanical University, wrote the essay for one of Rubin's seminars while a master's student at Johns Hopkins. According to Matthews, Rubin faced "objections from some corners of academia" for putting Edmonds's essay in his collection. Matthews also states that "Faulkner and the Black Shadow" "was perhaps the first perspective published from an African-American in a general study discourse examining the

representation of African-Americans in the works of an acknowledged leader in modern American literature" (93).

3. American Canons, Southern Fiction, and the Institution of Literary Prizes

1. In *Proud Flesh*, the protagonist and pseudo–Huey Long is named Willie Talos, an allusion to the "brutal, blank-eyed 'iron groom' of Spenser's *Faerie Queene*, the pitiless servant of the knight of justice" (Warren, introduction, vi). The initial drafts of *All the King's Men* retained the name. Noel Polk restores the name Willie Talos, along with other alterations insisted on by Warren's editors, in his 2001 restored edition of the novel.

2. W. J. Stuckey has gone so far as to say that the wholesomeness criterion became "irrelevant to second- and third-rate American novels" well before 1930 (8).

3. Perhaps the most famous example of this is the advisory board's refusal to accede to the jurors' selection of Thomas Pynchon's *Gravity's Rainbow* for the 1973 prize; consequently the board presented no award for fiction that year. A similar situation occurred for the 1954 award because the eligibility period "had produced no novel by an American author that merited such distinction" (Hohenberg, 166).

4. No critical, exhaustive, or authorized history of the National Book Awards has been published. What resources do exist are a pamphlet published in 1974 by the Committee for the Twenty-Fifth Anniversary of the National Book Awards—cited earlier in this chapter, but more a commemorative booklet than history of the awards—and works listing the award winners, such as Joseph F. Trimmer's *The National Book Awards for Fiction: An Index to the First Twenty-Five Years* (1978).

5. Although Augspurger assists in elucidating the democratic parable of *All the King's Men*, his article primarily addresses discrepancies between the novel and the 1949 film adaptation by director Robert Rossen. Augspurger argues that the film adaptation's portrayal of idealism such as Adam Stanton's as the best defense against fascism departs dramatically from the novel's lesson centering on the individual's guarding of democracy and is therefore a much more pointed and direct film about how easily totalitarianism could take root in America. Relevant to my discussion here, Augspurger begins by reminding us that Rossen narrowly avoided becoming one of the "Hollywood Ten" at the center of the House Un-American Activities Committee's scrutiny. In the aftermath, he renounced his membership in the Communist Party and gave up on progressive politics, thereby de-Marxifying himself. His film version of *All the King's Men* won three Academy Awards, including Best Picture, ensuring its Cold War cultural capital.

6. Lawrence R. Rodgers's *Canaan Bound: The African-American Great Migration Novel* (1997) deals explicitly with *Invisible Man* as a migration novel.

4. Eudora Welty and the Problem of Crusading

1. According to the rules governing the Nobel prizes, lists of nominees, reports, and minutes of deliberations are kept secret for fifty years. A search of the nominee database reveals no nominations of Eudora Welty up to 1966 ("Nomination Database").

2. See Harriet Pollack and Suzanne Marrs, eds., *Eudora Welty and Politics: Did the Writer Crusade?* (Baton Rouge: Louisiana State University Press, 2001); and Harriet Pollack, ed., *Eudora Welty, Whiteness, and Race* (Athens: University of Georgia Press, 2013).

3. Pollack dismisses as "facetious" ("Reading Welty on Whiteness and Race," 4) Flower's pithy comment "Why, Eudora is hardly guilty of racism at all" (330), which critiques Marrs's evidence that the word *nigger* appears only four times in all of Welty's correspondence; and to defend Welty's record on race, Marrs herself devotes an entire essay in *Eudora Welty, Whiteness, and Race* to examining the use of the word in Welty's correspondence with John Robinson.

4. The illustration is signed "Kovarsky." Nowhere in the issue is more complete credit provided for the cover art.

5. Suburbs, Civil Rights, and Southern Identities

1. Melosh's article additionally considers *Civil Wars* (1984), by Rosellen Brown; and *Only Great Changes* (1985), by Meredith Sue Willis.

Epilogue

1. Huber's "A Short History of *Redneck*: The Fashioning of a Southern White Masculine Identity" further provides the origins and history of the term's use throughout the twentieth century.

2. Jep and Jessica Robertson, however, did adopt a black infant in early 2016, a story line in a spin-off series featuring them (Clarke). Also, Willie and Korie have two adopted children who have appeared on *Duck Dynasty*: a son, Will, who is biracial; and a daughter, Rebecca, who is Taiwanese.

3. For examples of such discussions, see Mona Charen, "What *Hillbilly Elegy* Reveals about Trump and America," *National Review*, July 28, 2016; Sarah Jones, "J. D. Vance, the False Prophet of Blue America," *New Republic*, November 17, 2016; and Jared Yates Sexton, "Hillbilly Sellout: The Politics of J. D. Vance's 'Hillbilly Elegy' Are Already Being Used to Gut the Working Poor," *Salon*, March 11, 2017.

4. Brandon Terry even goes so far as to argue that Obama's appeal to a moderation in his politics of "racial uplift" and respectability is "largely pernicious and a distraction from fighting white supremacy" and can hamstring the Black Lives Matter movement and other progressive activists (52). Rather, Obama aimed his appeals toward a vital center.

BIBLIOGRAPHY

Abend-David, Dror. "The Occupational Hazard: The Loss of Historical Context in Twentieth Century Feminist Readings, and a New Reading of the Heroine's Story in Alice Walker's *The Color Purple*." In *Critical Essays on Alice Walker*, ed. Ikenna Dieke, 13–20. Westport, CT: Greenwood, 1999. Print.
Allen, Danielle. "Ralph Ellison on the Tragicomedy of Citizenship." *Raritan* 23, no. 3 (2004): 56–74.
Allen, John D. "Southern Agrarianism: Revised Version." *Pseudopodia* 1, no. 2 (Summer 1936): 1–3, 14.
Allen, William Rodney. *Walker Percy: A Southern Wayfarer*. Jackson: University Press of Mississippi, 1986.
Anderson, Quentin. "Notes on the Theatre." *Kenyon Review* 8, no. 3 (1946): 477–83. Print.
Archibold, Randal C. "Arizona Enacts Stringent Law on Immigration." *New York Times*, April 23, 2010. Web.
Augspurger, Mike. "Heading West: *All the King's Men* and Robert Rossen's Search for the Ideal." *Southern Quarterly* 39, no. 3 (2001): 51–64. Print.
Bacon, Jon Lance. *Flannery O'Connor and Cold War Culture*. Cambridge: Cambridge University Press, 1993. Print.
Baker, Houston A., Jr., and Dana D. Nelson. "Preface: Violence, the Body, and 'The South.'" *American Literature* 73, no. 2 (2001): 231–43. Print.
Banecker, Andrew. "'No Cause Was Cited for the Fracas': Ambivalent Racism in Eudora Welty's 'Where Is the Voice Coming From?' and 'The Demonstrators.'" In *Turning Points and Transformations: Essays on Language, Literature and Culture*, ed. Christine DeVine and Marie Hendry, 125–40. Newcastle-upon-Tyne, England: Cambridge Scholars, 2011.
Barnhisel, Greg. *Cold War Modernists: Art, Literature, and American Cultural Diplomacy*. New York: Columbia University Press, 2013. Print.
Bates, J. Douglas. *The Pulitzer Prize: The Inside Story of America's Most Prestigious Award*. New York: Birch Lane, 1991. Print.
Belletto, Steven, and Daniel Grausam, eds. *American Literature and Culture in an Age of Cold War: A Critical Reassessment*. Iowa City: University of Iowa Press, 2012. Print.
Bentley, Eric. "The Meaning of Robert Penn Warren's Novels." *Kenyon Review* 10, no. 3 (1948): 407–24. Print.
Berlant, Lauren. "Race, Gender, and Nation in *The Color Purple*." *Critical Inquiry* 14, no. 4 (1988): 831–59. Print.
Bishop, John Peale. "The Arts." *Kenyon Review* 3, no. 2 (1941): 179–90. Print.
Bishop, John Peale. "The Sorrows of Thomas Wolfe." *Kenyon Review* 1, no. 1 (1939): 1–17. Print.
Bishop, John Peale. "World's Fair Notes." *Kenyon Review* 1, no. 3 (1939): 239–50. Print.

Blackwell, Louise, and Frances Clay. *Lillian Smith*. New York: Twayne, 1971.
Blair, John. "'The Lie We Must Learn to Live By': Honor and Tradition in *All the King's Men*." *Studies in the Novel* 25, no. 4 (1993): 457–72. Print.
Blinder, Alan. "Alabama Judge Defies Gay Marriage Law." *New York Times*, February 8, 2015. Web.
Blotner, Joseph. *Faulkner: A Biography*. 2 vols. New York: Random House, 1974. Print.
Blotner, Joseph. *Robert Penn Warren: A Biography*. New York: Random House, 1997. Print.
Bone, Martyn. *The Postsouthern Sense of Place in Contemporary Fiction*. Baton Rouge: Louisiana State University Press, 2005. Print.
Borstelmann, Thomas. *The Cold War and the Color Line: American Race Relations in the Global Arena*. Cambridge, MA: Harvard University Press, 2001. Print.
Brantley, Will. "The Surveillance of Georgia Writer and Civil Rights Activist Lillian Smith: Another Story from the Federal Bureau of Investigation." *Georgia Historical Quarterly* 85, no. 1 (2001): 59–82. Print.
Brinkmeyer, Robert. *The Fourth Ghost: White Southern Writers and European Fascism, 1930–1950*. Baton Rouge: Louisiana State University Press, 2009. Print.
Brooks, Cleanth. *William Faulkner: The Yoknapatawpha Country*. New Haven: Yale University Press, 1963. Print.
Brown, Robbie. "Georgia Gives Police Added Power to Seek Out Illegal Immigrants." *New York Times*, May 13, 2011. Web.
Buckley, William F. "The Southern Imagination: An Interview with Eudora Welty and Walker Percy." In *Conversations with Eudora Welty*, ed. Peggy Whitman Prenshaw, 92–114. Jackson: University Press of Mississippi, 1984.
Burns, Alexander, and Jonathan Martin. "Once a Long Shot, Democrat Doug Jones Wins Alabama Senate Race." *New York Times*, December 12, 2017. Web.
Butler-Evans, Elliott. "History and Genealogy in Walker's *The Third Life of Grange Copeland* and *Meridian*." In *Alice Walker: Critical Perspectives Past and Present*, ed. Henry Louis Gates Jr. and K. A. Appiah, 105–25. New York: Amistad, 1993. Print.
Byerman, Keith. "Gender and Justice: Alice Walker and the Sexual Politics of Civil Rights." In *The World Is Our Home: Society and Culture in Contemporary Southern Writing*, ed. Jeffrey J. Folks and Nancy Summers Folks, 93–106. Lexington: University Press of Kentucky, 2000. Print.
Callahan, John F. "The Hoop of Language." In *Alice Walker: Modern Critical Views*, ed. Harold Bloom, 153–84. New York: Chelsea, 1989. Print.
Callahan, John F., ed. *The Collected Essays of Ralph Ellison*. New York: Modern Library, 1995. Print.
Cash, W. J. Letter to Lillian Smith. February 26, 1941. MS. Lillian Smith Papers, Department of Special and Area Studies Collections, George A. Smathers Libraries, University of Florida.
Cason, Mike. "Roy Moore Running for Senate, Resigns from Supreme Court to Challenge Luther Strange." *AL.com*. Advance Local Media, April 26, 2017. Web.
Charen, Mona. "What *Hillbilly Elegy* Reveals about Trump and America." *National Review*, July 28, 2016. Web.
Chase, Richard. "A Novel Is a Novel." Review of *Invisible Man*, by Ralph Ellison, and *Let It Come Down*, by Paul Bowles. *Kenyon Review* 14, no. 4 (1952): 678–84. Print.
Clarke, Suzan. "'Duck Dynasty' Stars Jep and Jessica Robertson Speak Out on Newly-Adopted Son, Jules Augustus." *ABC News*, January 20, 2016. Web. Accessed May 3, 2017.
Clemons, Walter. "Meeting Miss Welty." In *Conversations with Eudora Welty*, ed. Peggy Whitman Prenshaw, 30–34. Jackson: University Press of Mississippi, 1984.

Clerc, Charles. "Anatomy of Welty's 'Where Is the Voice Coming From?'" *Studies in Short Fiction* 23, no. 4 (1986): 389–400.
Cohen, Noam. "A&E's 'Duck Dynasty' Hits New Milestone." *New York Times*, August 16, 2013. Late Edition. Final. LexisNexis Academic. C2. Accessed May 1, 2017.
Cohn, Deborah. "'In between Propaganda and Escapism': William Faulkner as Cold War Cultural Ambassador." *Diplomatic History* 40, no. 3 (2016): 392–420. Print.
Colladay, Morrison. "Apologia of a Dictator." *North Georgia Review* 2, no. 2 (Summer 1937): 3–4, 21–22.
Committee for the Twenty-Fifth Anniversary of the National Book Awards. *A Celebration of Letters: The Twenty-Fifth Anniversary of the National Book Awards*. New York: Committee for the Twenty-Fifth Anniversary of the National Book Awards, 1974. Print.
Continetti, Matthew. "The Left's Reliance on Identity Politics." *USA Today* [magazine], March 2018, 10–12.
Core, George. "The Literary Quarterly in the South." In *The Southern Review and Modern Literature, 1935–1985*, ed. Lewis P. Simpson, James Olney, and Jo Gulledge, 186–93. Baton Rouge: Louisiana State University Press, 1988.
Cowley, Malcolm. "'Not Men': A Natural History of Naturalism." *Kenyon Review* 9, no. 3 (1947): 414–35. Print.
Cowley, Malcolm. *The Faulkner-Cowley File: Letters and Memories, 1944–1962*. New York: Viking, 1966. Print.
Cox, Karen L. *Dreaming of Dixie: How the South Was Created in American Popular Culture*. Chapel Hill: University of North Carolina Press, 2011. Print.
Daly, Brenda O. "Teaching Alice Walker's *Meridian*." In *Narrating Mothers: Theorizing Maternal Subjectivities*, ed. Brenda O. Daly and Maureen T. Reddy, 239–57. Knoxville: University of Tennessee Press, 1991. Print.
Danielson, Susan. "Alice Walker's *Meridian*, Feminism, and the 'Movement.'" *Women's Studies* 16, nos. 3–4 (1989): 317–30. Print.
Denning, Michael. *The Cultural Front: The Laboring of American Culture in the Twentieth Century*. New York: Verso, 1997. Print.
Desmond, John F. *Walker Percy's Search for Community*. Athens: University of Georgia Press, 2004.
Dittmer, John. *Local People: The Struggle for Civil Rights in Mississippi*. Urbana: University of Illinois Press, 1995. Print.
Douglas, Christopher. *Reciting America: Culture and Cliché in Contemporary U.S. Fiction*. Urbana: University of Illinois Press, 2001. Print.
Duck, Leigh Anne. *The Nation's Region: Southern Modernism, Segregation, and U.S. Nationalism*. Athens: University of Georgia Press, 2006. Print.
"Duck Season Eve." *Duck Dynasty: Season Three*. A&E, 2013. DVD.
Dudziak, Mary L. *Cold War Civil Rights: Race and the Image of American Democracy*. Princeton: Princeton University Press, 2000. Print.
Dumas, Joseph. "An Afternoon with Miss Welty." In *More Conversations with Eudora Welty*, ed. Peggy Whitman Prenshaw, 281–88. Jackson: University Press of Mississippi, 1996.
"Editor's Note." *North Georgia Review* 2, no. 2 (Summer 1937): 3.
Edmonds, Irene C. "Faulkner and the Black Shadow." In *Southern Renascence: The Literature of the Modern South*, ed. Louis D. Rubin Jr. and Robert D. Jacobs, 192–206. Baltimore: Johns Hopkins University Press, 1953.

Ellis, Kate, and Stephen Smith, producers and narrators. *State of Siege: Mississippi Whites and the Civil Rights Movement*. American RadioWorks. American Public Media. Online Transcript. 2011. Accessed March 6, 2017.

Ellison, Ralph. "Brave Words for a Startling Occasion." 1953. In *The Collected Essays of Ralph Ellison*, ed. John F. Callahan, 151–54. New York: Modern Library, 1995.

Ellison, Ralph. *Invisible Man*. 1952. New York: Vintage, 1995. Print.

Ellison, Ralph. "Twentieth-Century Fiction and the Black Mask of Humanity." 1953. In *The Collected Essays of Ralph Ellison*, ed. John F. Callahan, 81–99. New York: Modern Library, 1995.

English, James F. *The Economy of Prestige: Prizes, Awards, and the Circulation of Cultural Value*. Cambridge, MA: Harvard University Press, 2005. Print.

"Family Funny Business." *Duck Dynasty: Season One*. A&E, 2012. DVD.

Faulkner, William. *Absalom, Absalom!* 1936. New York: Vintage, 1990. Print.

Faulkner, William. "Address upon Receiving the Nobel Prize for Literature [Stockholm, December 10, 1950]." In *Essays, Speeches, and Public Letters*, ed. James B. Meriwether, 119–21. New York: Random House, 1965. Print.

Faulkner, William. *Go Down, Moses*. 1942. New York: Vintage, 1990. Print.

Faulkner, William. *Intruder in the Dust*. 1948. New York: Vintage, 1991. Print.

Faulkner, William. *Light in August*. 1932. New York: Vintage, 1990. Print.

Faulkner, William. "On Fear: Deep South in Labor; Mississippi. [*Harper's*, June 1956]." In *Essays, Speeches, and Public Letters*, ed. James B. Meriwether, 92–106. New York: Random House, 1965. Print.

Faulkner, William. *Selected Letters of William Faulkner*. Ed. Joseph Blotner. New York: Random House, 1977. Print.

Faulkner, William. *The Sound and the Fury*. 1929. New York: Vintage, 1990. Print.

Fausset, Richard. "Alabama Enacts Anti-Illegal-Immigration Law Described as Nation's Strictest." *Los Angeles Times*, June 10, 2011. Web.

Fiedler, Leslie A. "The Fate of the Novel." *Kenyon Review* 10, no. 3 (1948): 519–27. Print.

Flower, Dean. "Eudora Welty and Racism." *Hudson Review* 60, no. 2 (2007): 325–32. Print.

Foley, Barbara. "From Communism to Brotherhood: The Drafts of *Invisible Man*." In *Left of the Color Line: Race, Radicalism, and Twentieth-Century Literature of the United States*, ed. Bill V. Mullen and James Smethurst, 163–82. Chapel Hill: University of North Carolina Press, 2003. Print.

Freeman, Jean Todd. "An Interview with Eudora Welty." In *Conversations with Eudora Welty*, ed. Peggy Whitman Prenshaw, 172–99. Jackson: University Press of Mississippi, 1984.

"From Lack of Understanding." Editorial. *Pseudopodia* 1, no. 3 (Fall 1936): 8–9.

Gardner, Sara E. *Reviewing the South: The Literary Marketplace and the Southern Renaissance, 1920–1941*. Cambridge: Cambridge University Press, 2017. Print.

Graham, Jean E. "Gavin Stevens in *Intruder in the Dust*: Only Too Rhetorical Rhetoric?" *Southern Literary Journal* 22, no. 3 (1990): 78–89. Print.

Gray, Jonathan W. *Civil Rights in the White Literary Imagination: Innocence by Association*. Jackson: University Press of Mississippi, 2013. Print.

Greenberg, Clement. "Avant-Garde and Kitsch." *Partisan Review* 6, no. 5 (1939): 34–49. Print.

Gregory, James N. *The Southern Diaspora: How the Great Migrations of Black and White Southerners Transformed America*. Chapel Hill: University of North Carolina Press, 2005. Print.

Gresset, Michel, and Patrick Samway, eds. *A Gathering of Evidence: Essays on William Faulkner's "Intruder in the Dust."* Philadelphia: Saint Joseph's University Press, 2004. Print.

Guilbaut, Serge. *How New York Stole the Idea of Modern Art*. Trans. Arthur Goldhammer. Chicago: University of Chicago Press, 1983. Print.

Hardwick, Elizabeth. "Faulkner and the South Today." *Partisan Review* 15, no. 4 (1948): 1130–35. Print.

Hardy, John Edward. *The Fiction of Walker Percy*. Urbana: University of Illinois Press, 1987.

Harrison, Suzan. "'It's Still a Free Country': Constructing Race, Identity, and History in Eudora Welty's 'Where Is the Voice Coming From?'" *Mississippi Quarterly* 50, no. 4 (1997): 631–46. MLA International Bibliography. Web.

Hegeman, Susan. *Patterns for America: Modernism and the Concept of Culture*. Princeton: Princeton University Press, 1999. Print.

Hinrichsen, Lisa, Gina Caison, and Stephanie Roundtree. Introduction. In *Small-Screen Souths: Region, Identity, and the Cultural Politics of Television*, 1–23. Baton Rouge: Louisiana State University Press, 2017. Print.

"High Tech Redneck." *Duck Dynasty: Season One*. A&E, 2012. DVD.

Hobson, Fred. "Surveyors and Boundaries: Southern Literature and Southern Literary Scholarship after Mid-Century." *Southern Review* 27, no. 4 (1991): 739–55. Print.

Hohenberg, John. *The Pulitzer Prizes: A History of the Awards in Books, Drama, Music, and Journalism, Based on the Private Files over Six Decades*. New York: Columbia University Press, 1974. Print.

Huber, Patrick. "A Short History of *Redneck*: The Fashioning of a Southern White Masculine Identity." *Southern Cultures* 1, no. 2 (1995): 144–66.

Hutner, Gordon. "Reviewing America: John Crowe Ransom's *Kenyon Review*." *American Quarterly* 44, no. 1 (1992): 101–14. Print.

Hyman, Stanley Edgar. "Some Bankrupt Treasuries." *Kenyon Review* 10, no. 3 (1948): 484–500. Print.

Jameson, Fredric. *A Singular Modernity: Essay on the Ontology of the Present*. New York: Verso, 2002. Print.

Janssen, Marian. *The Kenyon Review, 1939–1970: A Critical History*. Baton Rouge: Louisiana State University Press, 1990. Print.

Jones, Sarah. "J. D. Vance, the False Prophet of Blue America." *New Republic*, November 17, 2016. Web.

Jonsson, Patrik. "Phil Robertson reinstated: How Christmas saved 'Duck Dynasty'; After a stand-off with the 'Duck Dynasty' family over patriarch Phil Robertson's comments about gay people, which many found offensive, the A&E cable network backed down in return for the family's pledge to promote tolerance." *Christian Science Monitor*, December 28, 2013. LexisNexis Academic. Accessed May 3, 2017.

Karaganis, Joe. "Negotiating the National Voice in Faulkner's Late Work." In *A Gathering of Evidence: Essays on William Faulkner's "Intruder in the Dust*," ed. Michel Gresset and Patrick Samway, 97–129. Philadelphia: Saint Joseph's University Press, 2004.

Keith, Don Lee. "Eudora Welty: I Worry over My Stories." In *Conversations with Eudora Welty*, ed. Peggy Whitman Prenshaw, 141–54. Jackson: University Press of Mississippi, 1984.

Kelley, Robin D. G. *Hammer and Hoe: Alabama Communists during the Great Depression*. Chapel Hill: University of North Carolina Press, 1990. Print.

Klein, Christina. *Cold War Orientalism: Asia in the Middlebrow Imagination, 1945–1961*. Berkeley: University of California Press, 2003. Print.

Kluckhohn, Clyde. "The Way of Life." *Kenyon Review* 3, no. 2 (1941): 160–79. Print.

Kobre, Michael. *Walker Percy's Voices*. Athens: University of Georgia Press, 2000.

Kreyling, Michael. *Inventing Southern Literature*. Jackson: University Press of Mississippi, 1998. Print.

Kreyling, Michael. *The South That Wasn't There: Postsouthern Memory and History*. Baton Rouge: Louisiana State University Press, 2010. Print.

Kruse, Kevin M. *White Flight: Atlanta and the Making of Modern Conservatism*. Princeton: Princeton University Press, 2007.

Larkin, Lesley. "Postwar Liberalism, Close Reading, and 'You': Ralph Ellison's *Invisible Man*." *Literature Interpretation Theory* 19, no. 3 (2008): 268–304. Print.

Lassiter, Matthew D. *The Silent Majority: Suburban Politics in the Sunbelt South*. Princeton: Princeton University Press, 2006.

Lassiter, Matthew D., and Joseph Crespino. *The Myth of Southern Exceptionalism*. New York: Oxford University Press, 2010. Print.

Lillian Smith Papers. Department of Special and Area Studies Collections. George A. Smathers Libraries, University of Florida.

Loveland, Anne C. *Lillian Smith: A Southerner Confronting the South*. Baton Rouge: Louisiana State University Press, 1986.

Luschei, Martin. *The Sovereign Wayfarer: Walker Percy's Diagnosis of the Malaise*. Baton Rouge: Louisiana State University Press, 1972.

MacLachlan, John. "No Faulkner in Metropolis." In *Southern Renascence: The Literature of the Modern South*, ed. Louis D. Rubin Jr. and Robert D. Jacobs, 101–12. Baltimore: Johns Hopkins University Press, 1953.

Magary, Drew. "What the Duck?" *GQ*, December 17, 2013. Web. Accessed May 1, 2017.

Marrs, Suzanne. *Eudora Welty: A Biography*. New York: Harcourt, 2005. Print.

Marrs, Suzanne. "'The Huge Fateful Stage of the Outside World': Eudora Welty's Life in Politics." In *Eudora Welty and Politics: Did the Writer Crusade?* ed. Harriet Pollack and Suzanne Marrs, 69–87. Baton Rouge: Louisiana State University Press, 2001.

Matthews, John T. "The Rhetoric of Containment in Faulkner." In *Faulkner's Discourse: An International Symposium*, ed. Lothar Hönnighausen, 55–67. Tübingen: M. Niemeyer, 1989.

Matthews, Kristin L. *Reading America: Citizenship, Democracy, and Cold War Literature*. Amherst: University of Massachusetts Press, 2016. Print.

Matthews, Valencia Eloris. "Irene Olivia Colbert Edmonds: Her Historic Tenure at Florida Agricultural and Mechanical University, 1947–1968." PhD diss., Florida State University, 1995. Ann Arbor: UMI, 1996. 9608883. Electronic.

Maxwell, Angie, and T. Wayne Parent. "The Obama Trigger: Presidential Approval and Tea Party Membership." *Social Science Quarterly* 93, no. 5 (2012): 1384–1401. Print.

McCammon, Sarah. "Feeling Kinship with the South, Northerners Let Their Confederate Flags Fly." *NPR*, May 4, 2017. Web.

McPherson, Tara. *Reconstructing Dixie: Race, Gender, and Nostalgia in the Imagined South*. Durham: Duke University Press, 2003. Print.

Medovoi, Leerom. *Rebels: Youth and the Cold War Origins of Identity*. Durham: Duke University Press, 2005. Print.

Melosh, Barbara. "Historical Memory in Fiction: The Civil Rights Movement in Three Novels." *Radical History Review* 40 (1988): 64–76. Print.

Millichap, Joseph R. "Robert Penn Warren and Regionalism." *Mississippi Quarterly* 48, no. 1 (1994–95): 29–38. Print.

Minter, David. *William Faulkner: His Life and Work*. Baltimore: Johns Hopkins University Press, 1980. Print.

Mitchell, Henry. "Eudora Welty: Rose-Garden Realist, Storyteller of the South." In *Conversations with Eudora Welty*, ed. Peggy Whitman Prenshaw, 64–73. Jackson: University Press of Mississippi, 1984.

Mitchell, Margaret. Letter to Lillian Smith. May 4, 1936. MS. Lillian Smith Papers, Department of Special and Area Studies Collections, George A. Smathers Libraries, University of Florida.

Mitchell, Margaret. Letter to Lillian Smith. May 19, 1936. MS. Lillian Smith Papers, Department of Special and Area Studies Collections, George A. Smathers Libraries, University of Florida.

Mitchell, Margaret. Letter to Lillian Smith. May 21, 1936. TS. Lillian Smith Papers, Department of Special and Area Studies Collections, George A. Smathers Libraries, University of Florida.

Murray, William. "Learning to Listen: The Way a Society Speaks in Eudora Welty's 'Where Is the Voice Coming From?' and 'The Demonstrators.'" *Eudora Welty Review* 8 (2016): 109–22. MLA International Bibliography. Web.

Nadel, Alan. *Containment Culture: American Narratives, Postmodernism, and the Atomic Age.* Durham: Duke University Press, 1995. Print.

Nadel, Alan. *Invisible Criticism: Ralph Ellison and the American Canon.* Iowa City: University of Iowa Press, 1988. Print.

Nashville. Dir. Robert Altman. Perf. Ned Beatty, Ronee Blakley, and Keith Carradine. Paramount, 1975. Film.

"Nomination Database." Nobelprize.org. Nobel Media AB 2014. http://www.nobelprize.org/nomination/archive/search_people.php. Accessed February 12, 2017.

Nunn, Erich. "Future Souths: A Roundtable of Emerging Voices." Paper presented at the conference "Other Souths: Approaches, Alliances, Antagonisms." Society for the Study of Southern Literature, March 28, 2014, George Mason University, Arlington, VA.

O'Brien, Michael. *Rethinking the South: Essays in Intellectual History.* Baltimore: Johns Hopkins University Press, 1988. Print.

Odum, Howard W. "On Southern Literature and Southern Culture." In *Southern Renascence: The Literature of the Modern South*, ed. Louis D. Rubin Jr. and Robert D. Jacobs, 84–100. Baltimore: Johns Hopkins University Press, 1953.

O'Sullivan, Shannon E. M. "Playing 'Redneck': White Masculinity and Working-Class Performance on *Duck Dynasty.*" *Journal of Popular Culture* 49, no. 2 (2016): 367–84.

Parks, Maryalice. "'Duck Dynasty' Star Willie Robertson Backs Trump, Saying 'I Do Like Me Some Trump.'" *ABC News*, September 25, 2015. Web. Accessed May 3, 2017.

Pasek, Josh, Alexander Tahk, Yphtach Lelkes, Jon A. Krosnak, B. Keith Payne, Omair Akhtar, and Trevor Thompson. "Determinants of Turnout and Candidate Choice in the 2008 Presidential Election: Illuminating the Impact of Racial Prejudice and Other Considerations." *Public Opinion Quarterly* 73, no. 5 (2009): 943–94. Print.

Percy, Walker. "Concerning *Love in the Ruins.*" In *Signposts in a Strange Land*, ed. Patrick Samway, 247–50. 1991. New York: Picador, 2000.

Percy, Walker. *Love in the Ruins: The Adventures of a Bad Catholic at a Time Near the End of the World.* 1971. New York: Picador, 1999.

Perlstein, Rick. *Nixonland: The Rise of a President and the Fracturing of America.* New York: Scribner, 2008.

Pletsch, Carl E. "The Three Worlds, or the Division of Social Scientific Labor, circa 1950–1975." *Comparative Studies in Society and History* 23, no. 4 (1981): 565–90. Print.

Polk, Noel. "Man in the Middle: Faulkner and the Southern White Moderate." In *A Gathering of Evidence: Essays on William Faulkner's "Intruder in the Dust,"* ed. Michel Gresset and Patrick Samway, 167–88. Philadelphia: Saint Joseph's University Press, 2004.
Pollack, Harriet, ed. *Eudora Welty, Whiteness, and Race.* Athens: University of Georgia Press, 2013. Print.
Pollack, Harriet. "Reading Welty on Whiteness and Race." In *Eudora Welty, Whiteness, and Race,* ed. Harriet Pollack, 1–22. Athens: University of Georgia Press, 2013.
Pollack, Harriet, and Suzanne Marrs, eds. *Eudora Welty and Politics: Did the Writer Crusade?* Baton Rouge: Louisiana State University Press, 2001. Print.
Porter, Katherine Anne. "The Days Before." *Kenyon Review* 5, no. 4 (1943): 481–94. Print.
Powdermaker, Hortense. "Disunion in Dixie." *North Georgia Review* 3, no. 1 (Spring 1938): 6.
Prenshaw, Peggy Whitman, ed. *Conversations with Eudora Welty.* Jackson: University Press of Mississippi, 1984. Print.
Prenshaw, Peggy Whitman., ed. *More Conversations with Eudora Welty.* Jackson: University Press of Mississippi, 1996. Print.
Prenshaw, Peggy Whitman. "Welty's Transformations of the Public, the Private, and the Political." In *Eudora Welty and Politics: Did the Writer Crusade?* ed. Harriet Pollack and Suzanne Marrs, 19–46. Baton Rouge: Louisiana State University Press, 2001.
"Prize Contest Announcement." *Pseudopodia* 1, no. 4 (Winter 1937): 10–11.
Pyron, Darden Asbury. *Southern Daughter: The Life of Margaret Mitchell.* New York: Oxford University Press, 1991.
Quinlan, Kieran. *Walker Percy: The Last Catholic Novelist.* Baton Rouge: Louisiana State University Press, 1996.
Rampersad, Arnold. *Ralph Ellison: A Biography.* New York: Knopf, 2007. Print.
Ransom, John Crowe. *Selected Letters of John Crowe Ransom.* Ed. Thomas Daniel Young and George Gore. Baton Rouge: Louisiana State University Press, 1985. Print.
Ransom, John Crowe. "The Teaching of Poetry." *Kenyon Review* 1, no. 1 (1939): 81–83. Print.
Redding, Arthur. *Turncoats, Traitors, and Fellow Travelers: Culture and Politics of the Early Cold War.* Jackson: University Press of Mississippi, 2008. Print.
Rice, Philip Blair. "Existentialism and the Self." *Kenyon Review* 12, no. 2 (1950): 304–30. Print.
Robinson, Forrest G. "A Combat with the Past: Robert Penn Warren on Race and Slavery." *American Literature* 67 (1995): 511–30. Print.
Rodger, Lawrence. *Canaan Bound: The African-American Great Migration Novel.* Urbana: University of Illinois Press, 1997. Print.
Romine, Scott. *The Real South: Southern Narrative in the Age of Cultural Reproduction.* Baton Rouge: Louisiana State University Press, 2008. Print.
Romine, Scott. "Where Is Southern Literature? The Practice of Place in a Postsouthern Age." In *South to a New Place: Region, Literature, Culture,* ed. Suzanne W. Jones and Sharon Monteith. Baton Rouge: Louisiana State University Press, 2002.
Romines, Ann. "A Voice from a Jackson Interior: Eudora Welty and the Politics of Filial Piety." In *Eudora Welty and Politics: Did the Writer Crusade?* ed. Harriet Pollack and Suzanne Marrs, 109–22. Baton Rouge: Louisiana State University Press, 2001.
Rovere, Richard H. "Letter from Washington, June 13." *New Yorker,* June 22, 1963, 90–98. Print.
Rubin, Louis D., Jr., and Robert D. Jacobs. Editors' note. "Literature in the South: An Exchange of Views." In *Southern Renascence: The Literature of the Modern South,* ed. Louis D. Rubin Jr. and Robert D. Jacobs, 83. Baltimore: Johns Hopkins University Press, 1953.

Rubin, Louis D., Jr., and Robert D. Jacobs, eds. *Southern Renascence: The Literature of the Modern South*. Baltimore: Johns Hopkins University Press, 1953. Print.

Saunders, Frances Stonor. *The Cultural Cold War: The CIA and the World of Arts and Letters*. New York: New Press, 1999. Print.

Schaub, Thomas Hill. *American Fiction in the Cold War*. Madison: University of Wisconsin Press, 1991. Print.

Schlesinger, Arthur, Jr. "Not Left, not Right, but a Vital Center." *New York Times Magazine*, April 4, 1948, 7, 44–47. Microfilm. UMI Microfilms.

Schlesinger, Arthur, Jr. *The Vital Center: The Politics of Freedom*. Boston: Houghton, 1949. Print.

Schmidt, Tyler T. *Desegregating Desire: Race and Sexuality in Cold War American Literature*. Jackson: University Press of Mississippi, 2013. Print.

Schwartz, Lawrence H. *Creating Faulkner's Reputation: The Politics of Modern Literary Criticism*. Knoxville: University of Tennessee Press, 1988. Print.

Sexton, Jared Yates. "Hillbilly Sellout: The Politics of J. D. Vance's 'Hillbilly Elegy' Are Already Being Used to Gut the Working Poor." *Salon*, March 11, 2017. Web.

Shapiro, Meyer. "French Reaction in Exile." *Kenyon Review* 7, no. 1 (1945): 29–42. Print.

Simpson, Lewis. "The Closure of History in a Postsouthern America." In *The Brazen Face of History: Studies in the Literary Consciousness of America*. Baton Rouge: Louisiana State University Press, 1980. Print.

Singal, Daniel Joseph. *The War Within: From Victorian to Modernist Thought in the South, 1919–1945*. Chapel Hill: University of North Carolina Press, 1982. Print.

Smith, Jon. *Finding Purple America: The South and the Future of American Cultural Studies*. Athens: University of Georgia Press, 2013. Print.

Smith, Lillian. "Addressed to Intelligent White Southerners." *South Today* 7, no. 2 (Autumn–Winter 1942–43): 34–43.

Smith, Lillian. "Along Their Way." *North Georgia Review* 2, no. 1 (Spring 1937): 3–4, 20–22.

Smith, Lillian. "Buying a New World with Old Confederate Bills." *South Today* 7, no. 2 (Autumn–Winter 1942–43): 7–30.

Smith, Lillian. "Dope with Lime." *North Georgia Review* 2, no. 2 (Summer 1937): 2, 23–24.

Smith, Lillian. "Dope with Lime." *North Georgia Review* 2, no. 4 (Winter 1937–38): 2, 32.

Smith, Lillian. "Dope with Lime." *North Georgia Review* 5, nos. 3–4 (Winter 1940–41): 4–8.

Smith, Lillian. "Dope with Lime." *Pseudopodia* 1, no. 1 (Spring 1936): 7, 12.

Smith, Lillian. "Dope with Lime." *Pseudopodia* 1, no. 2 (Summer 1936): 11–12.

Smith, Lillian. Letter to Dr. [H. C.] Nixon. February 3, 1943. Lillian Smith Papers, Department of Special and Area Studies Collections, George A. Smathers Libraries, University of Florida.

Smith, Lillian. Letter to Margaret Mitchell. May 16, 1936. TS. Margaret Mitchell Family Papers, MS 905. Hargrett Rare Book and Manuscript Library, University of Georgia Libraries.

Smith, Lillian. Letter to Margaret Mitchell. May 18, 1936. TS. Margaret Mitchell Family Papers, MS 905. Hargrett Rare Book and Manuscript Library, University of Georgia Libraries.

Smith, Lillian. "Mr. Lafayette, Heah We Is—." *North Georgia Review* 4, no. 1 (Spring 1939): 14–17.

Smith, Lillian. "One More Sigh for the Good Old South." Review of *Gone with the Wind*, by Margaret Mitchell. *Pseudopodia* 1, no. 3 (Fall 1936): 6, 15.

Smith, Neil. *Uneven Development: Nature, Capital, and the Production of Space*. New York: Blackwell, 1984. Print.

Snelling, Paula. "Ground Itch, Art and Erskine Caldwell." *Pseudopodia* 1, no. 2 (Summer 1936): 6, 10, 13.

Snelling, Paula. Letter to Lucy Winn. May 19, 1937. TS. Lillian Smith Papers, Department of Special and Area Studies Collections, George A. Smathers Libraries, University of Florida.

Snelling, Paula. "Mr. Faulkner Adds a Cubit." Review of *Absalom, Absalom!* by William Faulkner. *Pseudopodia* 1, no. 3 (Fall 1936): 4, 16.

Snelling, Paula. "Southern Fiction and Chronic Suicide." *North Georgia Review* 3, no. 2 (Summer 1938): 3–6, 25–28.

Snelling, Paula, and Lillian Smith, eds. Editorial statement. *Pseudopodia* 1, no. 1 (Spring 1936): 6.

Sokol, Jason. *There Goes My Everything: White Southerners in the Age of Civil Rights, 1945–1975*. New York: Knopf, 2006.

Sosna, Morton. *In Search of the Silent South: Southern Liberals and the Race Issue*. New York: Columbia University Press, 1977.

Stone, Natalie. "'Duck Dynasty's' Phil Robertson Discusses Donald Trump, A&E Firing." *Hollywood Reporter*, July 21, 2016. LexisNexis Academic. Accessed May 1, 2017.

Stuckey, W. J. *The Pulitzer Prize Novels: A Critical Backward Look*. 2nd ed. Norman: University of Oklahoma Press, 1981. Print.

Sullivan, Walter. "Southern Novelists and the Civil War." In *Southern Renascence: The Literature of the Modern South*, ed. Louis D. Rubin Jr. and Robert D. Jacobs, 112–25. Baltimore: Johns Hopkins University Press, 1953.

Terry, Brandon. "Racial Politics after Obama." *Dissent* 63, no. 3 (2016): 47–54. Print.

Tolson, Jay. *Pilgrim in the Ruins: A Life of Walker Percy*. New York: Simon, 1992.

"Too Close for Comfort." *Duck Dynasty: Season One*. A&E, 2012. DVD.

Trillin, Calvin. "An Education in Georgia." *New Yorker*, July 13, 1963, 30–67. Print.

Trillin, Calvin. *An Education in Georgia: The Integration of Charlayne Hunter and Hamilton Holmes*. New York: Viking, 1964.

Trilling, Lionel. "Greatness with One Fault in It." Review of *Let Us Now Praise Famous Men*, by James Agee and Walker Evans. *Kenyon Review* 4, no. 1 (1942): 99–102. Print.

Trimmer, Joseph F. *The National Book Awards for Fiction: An Index to the First Twenty-Five Years*. Boston: Hall, 1978. Print.

Urgo, Joseph. *Novel Frames: Literature as Guide to Race, Sex, and History in American Culture*. Jackson: University Press of Mississippi, 1991. Print.

Vance, J. D. *Hillbilly Elegy: A Memoir of a Family and Culture in Crisis*. New York: Harper, 2016. Print.

Walker, Alice. "The Black Writer and the Southern Experience." In *In Search of Our Mother's Gardens*, 51–21. New York: Harcourt, 1983. Print.

Walker, Alice. *Meridian*. 1976. New York: Harvest, 2003. Print.

Warren, Robert Penn. *All the King's Men*. 1946. New York: Harcourt, 1996. Print.

Warren, Robert Penn. Introduction to *All the King's Men*, by Robert Penn Warren. 1946. New York: Modern Library, 1953. Print.

Warren, Robert Penn. "Irony with a Center." *Kenyon Review* 4, no. 1 (1942): 29–42. Print.

Warren, Robert Penn. "Love and the Separateness in Miss Welty." *Kenyon Review* 6, no. 2 (1944): 246–59. Print.

Warren, Robert Penn. *Who Speaks for the Negro?* New York: Random House, 1965. Print.

Welty, Eudora. *The Collected Stories of Eudora Welty*. New York: Harcourt, 1980. Print.

Welty, Eudora. "Must the Novelist Crusade?" In *The Eye of the Story: Selected Essays and Reviews*, 146–58. New York: Random House, 1979. Print.

Wheatley, Patricia. "Eudora Welty: A Writer's Beginnings." In *More Conversations with Eudora Welty*, ed. Peggy Whitman Prenshaw, 120–45. Jackson: University Press of Mississippi, 1996.

Wilson, Edmund. "William Faulkner's Reply to the Civil-Rights Program." *New Yorker*, October 23, 1948, 120–28. Microfilm. UMI Microfilms.

Wilson, Mary Ann. "'Redneck Feng-Shui': *Duck Dynasty*, Paula Deen, and the Other Louisiana." In *Small-Screen Souths: Region, Identity, and the Cultural Politics of Television*, eds. Lisa Hinrichsen, Gina Caison, and Stephanie Roundtree, 150–65. Baton Rouge: Louisiana State University Press, 2017. Print.

Woodward, C. Vann. "The Irony of Southern History." In *Southern Renascence: The Literature of the Modern South*, ed. Louis D. Rubin Jr. and Robert D. Jacobs, 63–79. Baltimore: Johns Hopkins University Press, 1953.

Young, Thomas Daniel. *Gentleman in a Dustcoat: A Biography of John Crowe Ransom*. Baton Rouge: Louisiana State University Press, 1976. Print.

Zack Brown Band. "Chicken Fried—Full Video Version." YouTube. November 6, 2008. Online video.

INDEX

Absalom, Absalom!, 37, 39, 56, 139n3
abstract expressionism, xii, xv, xx, 30
activism: literary, 17, 21, 23, 25, 26, 83; political, xxv, 13, 17, 26, 55, 83, 98; portrayals of political activism, 105, 107, 109, 111, 112, 118, 120
"Addressed to Intelligent White Southerners," 23, 25–26, 79
Agee, James, 12–13, 15
All the King's Men, xxv, 49–50, 54, 57, 59–66, 70–71, 141n1, 141n5; film adaptation, 141n5
American cultural hegemony, xi–xii, 22, 31
Andy Griffith Show, The, 124–25
anticommunism, xii, xvi, xvii, 11, 24, 32, 44, 54, 55
Appalachia, 135–36
area studies, xxiv, xxv, 29–38, 43, 44, 45, 46, 50
Atlanta, Georgia, 7–8, 97, 99, 100, 105, 128
Atlantic, The, 76, 88, 89, 90
"Avant-Garde and Kitsch," xiii

Bellow, Saul, 58
Bishop, John Peale, 12, 22
blue states, 95, 101
Bone, Martyn, xxi, 98
Brazil, 46
Brinkmeyer, Robert H., Jr., 18, 20–21, 26, 54–55
Brooks, Cleanth, 6, 40–41
Brown v. Board of Education, 42, 46, 100
Buckley, William F., 82–83
Bush, George W., 136
Butler, Nicholas Murray, 56
"Buying a New World with Old Confederate Bills," 23–25

Caldwell, Erskine, 7
Calverton, V. F., 10
Capote, Truman, 27
Cash, W. J., 11, 27
Central High School (Little Rock, Arkansas), xv
Chalmers, Gordon Keith, 11
Chaney, James, 102
Chase, Richard, 15–16, 59, 66
Christianity, 115–16, 118–19
CIA (Central Intelligence Agency), xiii, xiv
Civil Rights Act of 1964, 97
civil rights, xiv, 39, 89, 90, 95, 97, 98, 105, 107, 109–11, 117, 120; authors' positions on, 16–17, 32, 70–72, 75–76, 82, 83, 117; civil rights movement, xxvi, 27, 46, 49, 70–72, 76, 87, 104, 106, 112, 124–25; erosion of, 137; hostility towards, xv, 54, 80–82, 100, 134; paramilitary organizations, 115; portrayed as moral issue, 43–44, 53, 70–72, 77, 134, 136; relationship to foreign and domestic policy, xiv, xv, 23, 91, 92, 98, 100–101, 104, 120
Clayton, Georgia, 3, 11, 23
Cohn, Deborah, 32–33, 46, 140n2, 140n4
Cold War, the: art and literature of, xii, 22, 55; civil rights movement during, xv, 53, 76, 90; the cultural Cold War as part of, xiii, 28, 30–31, 33, 38, 42, 57, 59, 72; culture of, xviii–xx, xxii, xxvii, 36, 46, 77, 83, 90, 125, 129, 137; ideology of, xvi, 44, 51, 86, 91, 93, 123; and US nationalism, xi, 22
collectivism, 25, 44
Collins, Addie Mae, 111

colonialism, xiv, 20, 31, 46, 113
Color Purple, The, 59, 111
Columbia University, 55–56
Communism, xi, xii, xiii, xv, xvii, xxiv, 4, 5, 10, 11, 16, 27, 32, 33, 34, 40, 42, 44, 46, 50, 53, 54, 55, 62, 72, 121, 140n3
Communist Party, xvi, xvii, 51, 52, 55, 69, 141n5
Confederate flags, 137–38
conservatism, xi, xxvi, 57, 99, 101, 120, 121, 134
containment, xviii–xix
Cowley, Malcolm, xiv, 15, 30, 41, 47

Davidson, Donald, 18, 36, 37, 45
De La Beckwith, Byron, 80, 82, 93
departments of English, xviii, 3, 45, 140n4
Dixiecrats. *See* Wallace, George
Du Bois, W. E. B., 16, 70
Duck Dynasty, xxvi, 125–32, 135, 137, 145n2
Duck, Leigh Anne, xvi, 13
Dunbar, Paul Lawrence, 16

economic classes, 17, 29, 82, 90, 110, 112, 120, 124–26, 130, 135–36, 142n3 (epilogue). *See also* working class
economic inequality, xv, xvii, xx, 5, 26, 29, 36, 42, 43, 60, 63, 71, 72, 95, 96, 110, 113, 120
economic policy, xii, 6, 10, 11, 26, 29, 35, 53, 63, 72, 95–96, 134
editorial policy, 4, 5, 12, 17, 19, 23, 26, 84, 140n7
Edmonds, Irene C., 37–38, 140n5
Eisenhower, Dwight D., xiv, xv, 46, 111
Eliot, T. S., 4, 30
Ellison, Ralph, xxiv–xxv, xxvi, 16, 49–50, 51–55, 58–60, 66–67, 69–72, 90, 108
Encounter, xiii
Erskine, Albert, 49
Evans, Walker, 12–13, 15
Evers, Medgar, xxv, 76, 80–84, 87, 91, 111

fascism, xi–xii, 5, 16, 19–20, 54, 61–64, 72, 141n5
Faulkner, William, xiii, xviii, xxiv–xxv, 10, 27, 29–34, 36–47, 49, 52, 56, 58, 60, 64, 78, 79, 82, 86, 102, 118, 133, 136, 139n2 (chap. 1), 140nn1–2, 140nn4–5
Federal Bureau of Investigation (FBI), 14, 139n6
Federal Communications Commission (FCC), 81

Federal Writer's Project, 5
feminism, 95, 110
Fiedler, Leslie, 27
Frost, Robert, 60

gender stereotypes, 7–8, 61, 84–85, 95, 104–5, 106–7, 108–10, 117, 119, 132
geography, xxvi, 63, 95–96, 99, 110
Georgia Bureau of Investigation (GBI), 23
Go Down Moses, 37, 39, 118
Gold, Michael, 10
Gone with the Wind, 7–11, 17, 56–57, 60
Goodman, Andrew, 102
Gordon, Caroline, 112
Gravity's Rainbow, 141n3
Great Migration, 66
Greenberg, Clement, xiii
Guevara, Che, 111
Guilbaut, Serge, xii–xiii, xv, xix, 22, 30

Hemingway, Ernest, 52, 56, 58
Hicks, Granville, 10
hillbilly, xxvii, 135–37
Holmes, Hamilton, 91
Holocaust, xiv
House Un-American Activities Committee, 141n5
Howe, Irving, 58
Humphrey, Hubert, 101
Hunter, Charlayne, 91
Hurston, Zora Neale, 15–17
Hyman, Stanley Edgar, 15

individualism, xv, xxiv, xxv, 24–25, 29–30, 34, 40–42, 45, 52, 57–58, 66, 69–70, 77–78, 86–87, 107, 125, 129, 135, 137
intellectuals in the United States, xxiii, xxiv, xxv, 4, 11, 13, 25, 30–31, 37–38, 42, 44–45, 50, 53–54, 72, 76, 95–96, 119, 123, 133
Intruder in the Dust, xxv, 29, 37–45
Invisible Man, xxv, xxvi, 15, 49–51, 54–55, 58–60, 66–71, 105, 141n6

Jackson, George, 111
Jackson, Mississippi, xxv, 75, 76, 80, 81, 82, 84, 88–91
Jacobs, Robert D., xxv, 29, 33–34, 35–36, 38, 41

Index

Jameson, Fredric, xvii–xviii, xx, 4
Japan, xiv, 46, 57
Jefferson, Thomas, 26
Jim Crow, xiv–xv, 15, 20, 31, 51, 65, 80, 82, 90, 93, 101, 104, 121, 125, 133–34
Johnson, James Weldon, 16
Johnson, Lyndon B., 72
Jones, Doug, 139n2 (introduction)
Joyce, James, 4

Kazin, Alfred, 58
Kennedy, John F., 83–84, 91, 111
Kenyon College, 11
Kenyon Review, xiii–xiv, 3–6, 11–15, 21–22, 27–28, 61
Killers of the Dream (Smith memoir), 26
King, Martin Luther, Jr., 97, 102, 110, 111
Kirk, David, 32
Kluckhohn, Clyde, 15, 22
Kreyling, Michael, xv–xvi, 33, 37–38, 45
Kruse, Kevin M., 100
Ku Klux Klan (KKK), 13, 23

labor unions, 4, 14, 24–25, 52
Last Gentleman, The, 112
late modernism, xvii–xviii, xx–xxi, xxii, xxiv, 4–5, 28, 61, 70, 76, 96
Lauren Falls Camp, 26
Lee, Robert E., 26
leftism, 4, 12, 16–17, 30
Light in August, 39, 41
literary canons, xx, xxiv, 28, 30–31, 38, 47, 49
literary criticism, xxiv, 5, 7, 9–10, 29, 34
Liuzzo, Viola, 111
Long, Huey, 19, 54, 61, 141n1 (chap. 3)
Lost Cause, xxiii, 6, 17–18, 101
Louisiana, 19, 54, 64, 114, 125, 126, 128, 129, 133–34
Lumumba, Patrice, 111

MacLachlan, John, 36–37
Malcolm X, 72, 111
Marshall, Thurgood, 80
Marxism, 10, 30
Mason, Lucy Randolph, 11
Maxwell, William, 87
McCullers, Carson, 14, 27
McKay, Claude, 16

McNair, Denise, 111
media, 76, 81, 83, 95, 96, 97, 99, 110–11, 114; newspapers, xiv
Mencken, H. L., 36
Mitchell, Margaret, 7–10, 56–57, 139nn3–4
moderates (political), 90, 101, 106, 113, 133, 135, 138
modernism, xvii, xx, 4, 7
Moore, Roy, xxiii, 139n2 (introduction)
Moviegoer, The, 98, 112
Mumford, Lewis, 15
"Must the Novelist Crusade?," xxv, 76–79, 86–89, 91–93

Nashville Agrarians, xxi, 6–7, 11–12, 18, 33, 50–51
National Association for the Advancement of Colored People (NAACP), 81
National Book Award, xxiv, xxvi, 49, 50, 55, 58–59, 75, 141n4
National Broadcasting Company (NBC), 80
nationalism (United States), xi, xvii, xxii, xxiii, xxvii, 30–31, 42, 123–25, 128
Native Americans: portrayal of, 102–3, 114
Nazism, xi, xiv, xvi, 18, 26
New Criticism, xviii, 3, 5–6, 10, 21, 70
New Deal, 30, 86
New Masses, 4, 10, 51–52
new Southern studies, xxvii
New York, New York, 10, 12, 14, 22, 23, 51, 66, 75, 110, 113
New Yorker, 39, 80, 86–87, 89–93
Nixon, H. C., 23
Nixon, Richard M., xxvi, 97–98, 100–101, 112, 121, 134
Nobel Prize, 31–32, 44, 45, 59, 75, 141n1 (chap. 4)
North Georgia Review. See *South Today*
North Korea, 137

Obama, Barack H., 133–34, 136, 137, 142n4
Obergefell v. Hodges, xxiii
O'Connor, Flannery, xxii, 85
Odum, Howard W., 11, 16, 36–37, 45
Old South. See Lost Cause

Partisan Review, 4
patriotism, xv, xx–xxi, xxii, 54, 59, 76, 99, 105, 126, 137–38

People's Voice, 52
Percy, Walker, xxvi, 95–101, 112–21
periodical culture, 4, 10, 139n1 (chap. 1)
place, xvi, xxi, 24, 35, 36–38, 50, 63–64, 80, 82, 84, 95–96, 98–99, 103, 109, 124–25, 128–29; fictional place names, 84
politics in literature, 52–54
Polk, Noel, 41, 44, 141n1 (chap. 3)
Pollock, Jackson, 30
popular culture, xxi, xxvi, 95, 96, 97, 99, 110, 111, 137
populism, xxvi, 102, 123, 133
postsouthern, xxi, 95–96, 98–99, 101–2, 112, 120, 139n1 (introduction)
Pound, Ezra, 4
propaganda, xviii, 14, 22, 39, 52, 55, 62, 76, 78, 80
Proud Flesh, 54–55, 141n1 (chap. 3)
Pseudopodia. See *South Today*
Pulitzer Prize, xxiv, 49, 50, 55–59, 75
Pynchon, Thomas, 141n3

racism: as a moral problem, xv–xvi, 12, 15, 32, 33, 39, 65–66, 82, 86, 112–13, 117–18, 121, 123; as a political problem, xiv, xxii, 5, 25, 41, 46, 68, 81–82, 101; portrayals of racism and racist stereotypes, 17–18, 38–40, 64–66, 84, 87, 98, 102, 109–10, 118, 125, 133; treatments in criticism, 85–86, 118–19, 137–38
Random House, 49
Ransom, John Crowe, xiv, xviii, xxiv, 3, 5–6, 11–15, 21, 28, 50
Reagan, Ronald W., 136
red states, 95, 101
redneck, 125–26, 128–29, 131–32, 134–35, 137, 142n1 (epilogue)
Report of Committee on Civil Rights (1948), 53–54
Republican Party, 98–99, 101, 113, 133
Rhodesia, 113
Rice, Philip Blair, 11–12, 15
Robertson family and friends (*Duck Dynasty*), 125–33, 134–35, 136–37
Robertson, Carole, 111
Robertson, Jep and Jessica, 142n2
Robertson, Phil, 126, 132–35, 136
Romine, Scott, xxi, 96
Roosevelt, Franklin D., xx, 18

Rovere, Richard H., 91
Rubin, Louis D., Jr., xxv, 29, 33–34, 35–36, 37–38, 41, 44, 140n5
rural areas, xxi, xxii, xxvi, 37, 88, 97, 100, 109, 112, 124–35
Russell, Richard B., xv, 140n3
Russia, xiii, 22, 32, 90, 137. *See also* Soviet Union

Sarah Lawrence College, 97
Schaub, Thomas Hill, xii, xviii, 53, 70
Schlesinger, Arthur M., Jr., xii–xiii, 31, 50, 53–54, 59, 70, 134
Schwartz, Lawrence H., 30–31
Schwerner, Michael, 102
segregation, xv, 14, 23–25, 27, 50–51, 83, 86, 90, 92–93, 100–102, 110, 115, 117, 140n2; desegregation, xix, 5, 11, 17, 26, 54, 80, 83; federal actions to end segregation in southern states, xv, xxiii, 24, 42, 81, 100–101, 125, 132–33; as a foreign policy issue, 31–32; as a moral problem, 53
sense of place. *See* place
Shapiro, Meyer, 15
Sixteenth Street Baptist Church, 111
Smith, Lillian, xv, xvi, xxiv, 3, 5, 6–11, 13–21, 23–27, 79, 83, 111, 139n2 (chap. 1), 139n5 (chap. 1)
Snelling, Paula, xxiv, 3, 5–8, 10–11, 13, 16–21, 23–24, 26–27, 139nn2–3 (chap. 1), 139n7
Sound and the Fury, The, 37, 40, 140n1
South Today, xxiv, 3–6, 7, 8, 9, 10, 11, 13–16, 17, 18, 20–21, 23–24, 26–27
Southern Review, 4
Southern studies, xvi, 46
Soviet Union, xiii, xv, xvi, 22, 29, 31, 39, 77–78, 91, 111, 114, 140n3. *See also* Russia
Spelman College, 97, 103
states' rights, xxiii, 20, 137
Steinbeck, John, 30, 58
Strange Fruit (Lillian Smith novel), 14, 26
Strange, Luther, 139n2 (introduction)
Student Nonviolent Coordinating Committee (SNCC), 98
suburban areas, xxvi, 96–102, 109, 112–14, 119, 120–21
Sullivan, Walter, 34

Sun Belt states, xxiii
Supreme Court of the United States, xxiii

Talmadge, Herman, 140n3
Tate, Allen, 5, 7, 11, 12, 50
television, xxiv, xxvi, 49, 57, 76, 80–83, 97, 104, 109–10, 116, 123; reality television, 124–28, 135, 137–38
Today, 80
Toomer, Jean, 16
Trillin, Calvin, 91
Trilling, Lionel, 12–13, 15, 70
Truman, Harry S., xiii, xv, 46, 53
Trump, Donald J., xxvi, 123, 133–35, 137, 139n2 (introduction), 142n3 (epilogue)
TV. *See* television
Twain, Mark, 52, 58

United States, the: Civil War, 34; exceptionalism, 46; foreign policy, xiv, xvi, xx, xvi, 43, 51, 53, 66, 123, 140n3; State Department, 31, 46, 111
United States South, the, xiii, 26–27, 78; honor in the, 61, 84–85, 119; provincialism and, 42; stereotypes of, 89, 92, 110, 124–25
United States v. Windsor, xxiii, 132
universities and colleges, xi, xviii, xxiv, 3–4, 6, 29, 102, 103, 105–7; outside the United States, 46
urban areas, xxvii, 37, 66, 100–101, 113, 128
US Elections, Presidential, xi, xv, xxvi, 97, 101, 123, 133–35, 137; Senatorial, 139n2 (introduction)

Vance, J. D., xxvi, 135–37
Vietnam War, 101
vital center, xii, xiv–xvi, 10, 15, 31, 50, 53–55, 57–59, 64, 70, 76, 82–83, 92, 95–97, 100–101, 107–8, 120, 125, 134–35, 138, 142n4 (epilogue)

Walker, Alice, xv, xxvi, 59, 95, 97–98, 101–4, 110–11
Wallace, George, 83, 101
war on terror, 137
Warren, Robert Penn, xiii, xviii, xxiv, xxv, 6, 13, 36, 49–51, 53–58, 60–65, 70–72, 90, 133, 141n1 (chap. 3)

Welty, Eudora, xviii, xxv, 13, 27, 49, 75–80, 82–93, 96, 109, 136, 141n1 (chap. 4), 142n3 (chap. 4)
Wesley, Cynthia, 111
"Where Is the Voice Coming From?," xxv, 76, 80–93, 136
white nationalism, 24, 118, 125, 142n4 (epilogue)
Who Speaks for the Negro, 49–50, 70–72, 90
Williams, Claude, 11
Williams, William Carlos, 49
WLBT, 80–84
Wolfe, Thomas, 6, 9, 12
Woodward, C. Vann, 35
working class, xxi, xxvi, 5, 112, 117, 123, 125–26, 129–31, 134–35. *See also* economic classes
World War I, 66
World War II, xi, xiv, xviii, xx, xxiv, 3, 6, 19, 21–22, 27, 31, 38, 44, 59, 63, 66, 99
Wright, Richard, 15

Yeats, William Butler, 4, 112

ABOUT THE AUTHOR

Photograph by Amber Mills, JAmber Photography

Jordan J. Dominy is associate professor of English at Savannah State University. He teaches and studies American and US southern literature and popular culture. His work has appeared in *Mississippi Quarterly, American Studies (AMSJ), Southern Literary Journal,* and the *Cormac McCarthy Journal.*

www.ingramcontent.com/pod-product-compliance
Lightning Source LLC
Chambersburg PA
CBHW030625230426
43661CB00053B/2140